Praise for *The Awakened Family*

"[Dr. Shefali is] absolutely revolutionary."   —Oprah Winfrey

"Stop struggling, parents. Here is the key to relaxing into your family and into your parenting. . . . [Tsabary] has a new book releasing us all from the stresses of 'making' the perfect child."
                                                            —*The Washington Post*

"I want to give this book to everyone I know who is a parent, a grand-parent, a child, a grown-up child . . . everyone. It's not only a primer for the kind of family life we all long for, it's also a guide to being human—to living with more ease, more love, more joy."
            —Elizabeth Lesser, cofounder of Omega Institute and author of *Broken Open* and *Marrow*

"Shefali Tsabary shines the light of wisdom on the most enlightened aspect of parenting: discovering a child's individual personhood and purpose, and nurturing the path to its fulfillment."
            —Michael Bernard Beckwith, author of *Life Visioning*

"Bestselling author and speaker Tsabary combines the spirit of Thich Nhat Hanh's 1975 classic, *The Miracle of Mindfulness*, with an intensive family therapy session—and the result is a transforming read for any parent."   —*Booklist* (starred review)

"Useful and encouraging . . . Tsabary's message is an antidote to recent trends such as 'helicopter parenting,' teaching respect for children as people in their own right and urging parents to let them thrive."   —*Publishers Weekly* (starred review)

"I loved *The Awakened Family*. . . . [Tsabary] explains why we need to trust in our children's potential and argues that the best parenting lies in being quiet and open."   —*Bookpage*

PENGUIN BOOKS

THE AWAKENED FAMILY

Shefali Tsabary, Ph.D., received her doctorate in clinical psychology from Columbia University. Specializing in the integration of Western psychology and Eastern philosophy, Dr. Shefali brings together the best of both worlds for her clients. She is an expert in family dynamics and personal development and runs a private practice in New York City. Dr. Shefali has written three books, including the award-winning *New York Times* bestselling book *The Conscious Parent*. Dr. Shefali is also a keynote speaker who has presented at TEDx, Kellogg Business School, the Dalai Lama Center for Peace and Education, and other conferences and workshops around the world. She's been featured on Oprah Winfrey's *SuperSoul Sunday* and *Oprah's Lifeclass*.

www.drshefali.com

 DrShefaliTsabary

 @DrShefali

@drshefalitsabary

The Awakened Family

How to Raise Empowered,
Resilient, and Conscious Children

Shefali Tsabary, Ph.D.

PENGUIN BOOKS

PENGUIN BOOKS
An imprint of Penguin Random House LLC
375 Hudson Street
New York, New York 10014
penguin.com

First published in the United States of America by Viking Penguin,
an imprint of Penguin Random House LLC, 2016
Published in Penguin Books 2017

ISBN 9780399563973 (paperback)

THE LIBRARY OF CONGRESS HAS CATALOGED THE
HARDCOVER EDITION AS FOLLOWS:
Names: Tsabary, Shefali, 1972- author.
Title: The awakened family : a revolution in parenting / Shefali Tsabary, Ph.D.
Description: New York : Viking, [2016]
Identifiers: LCCN 2016003716 (print) | LCCN 2016009019 (ebook) | ISBN
9780399563966 (hardcover) | ISBN 9780399563980 (ebook)
Subjects: LCSH: Parenting. | Parent and child. | Families.
Classification: LCC HQ755.8 .T8165 2016 (print) | LCC HQ755.8 (ebook) |
DDC 306.874—dc23
LC record available at http://lccn.loc.gov/2016003716

Printed in the United States of America
9   10

Set in Mercury and Sentinel
Designed by Amy Hill

About the Examples in This Book
Although the examples in this book reflect real-life situations, they aren't necessarily
descriptions of actual people. In some cases, they are composites created from my
years of working with countless different parents in many varied contexts. The names
and identities of my clients have been changed to protect their privacy. Any
resemblance to actual persons is entirely coincidental.

This book is dedicated to the
children we are blessed to call our own.

Inspired by our love for them,
we are offered the invaluable opportunity to
awaken ourselves, and thereby liberate humanity.

This book holds the vision that every child
will stay planted in their true self,
for this is their birthright.

Contents

The Awakened Family

The Mandate of
the Awakened Family

The time for a new beginning has arrived,
Where family is no longer the chain that binds us
But is the earth from which we blossom
And the sky we learn to fly.

No matter how the family unit looks,
It begins with a parent and child.
A relationship that holds the energy of the sun,
With power to break patterns and resurrect the spirit.

The awakened family waits for no one,
It begins to heal right here, right now.
It recognizes that these sacred bonds
Can revolutionize the planet.

We awaken when we become aware of who we *truly* are. This awareness brings a realization of how liberating it is to be authentic—to be *real*, instead of who we think we are supposed to be or who others want us to be. Once we have connected with our sovereign spirit, creating the space for our children to get in touch with their own spirit becomes the critical objective of parenthood. Committed to the manifestation of the true self in each member of the family, the awakened family paves the way for children to own, discover, and express their inner voice, through which they foster connectivity with both their own being and that of others. Cognizant that this *right to express their own spirit* is the key ingredient for their present and future resilience and empowerment, they become a part of the global evolution of a world built on compassion, nonviolence, and prosperity.

An awakened parent is one who is aware that the traditional paradigms of parenting, where the parent is seen as *greater than* the child, are obsolete in the modern world, producing dysfunction and disconnection in families. Instead, they are willing to be the architects of a new model of parenthood where parent and child are seen as equal, serving as mutual partners on a path of growth founded on increasing consciousness.

In an awakened family, parents are aware that every relationship in their family exists to help each person grow. Parents view their children as mirrors through which they are able to see how they themselves need to mature and develop. Instead of fixing what they see as faults in their children, these parents seek to work on themselves, raising their own levels of maturity and presence. The focus is always on the parent's awareness rather than the child's behavior. This is the core insight of the book.

When parents are aware in the present moment, learning and growing alongside their children, the entire family thrives. Free to actualize their individual destiny, each family member lives unencumbered and unafraid. Empowered with self-awareness, boundless in self-belief, liberated in self-expression, each feels free to explore, discover, and manifest their authentic being. This is the mandate of the awakened family.

Part One

A New Awakening

CHAPTER ONE

Learning a New Way

N o, Mom, I just don't want to!" my independent daughter argued. "I shouldn't have to go to your friend's boring event."
I knew Maia had no interest in what I had planned for our afternoon, but I wanted her to come anyway to keep me company. Besides, I reasoned, attending such events was "good for her."

She reacted as only preteens can, with just the right mix of indignation, insistence, and cheekiness. She turned her back on me, walked into her room, and shut her door.

I stood there with my mouth wide open. Having raised her to be independent, a part of me had to admire her assertiveness. But then there was that other part of me that felt upset that she would talk to me in such a way. "She should, just once in a while, do as she was told," I could hear a voice in my head say.

You can guess which side of this argument won out, and before I knew it, I stormed into her room. "You will not speak to me in that tone of voice," I announced loudly. "You will not disrespect me. You will apologize and you will attend the event." With this, I turned my back on her, in much the way she had done to me only moments before, slamming the door behind me as I hurried out of her room.

"Ha," I told myself proudly, "that will show her! No way am I going to have a disrespectful brat growing up in my house. She needs to do as I say, no matter what."

It wasn't the first verbal scuffle my daughter and I had gotten into lately. When she turned twelve, she found herself experiencing a maelstrom of emotions that were difficult for her to understand. Like most mothers of girls this age, I frequently forgot to relate to her in a calm and caring manner, which is what preteens need, and became caught up in a tidal wave of emotion myself.

On this occasion, the cause of our squabble clearly lay not with Maia but with me. Later that day, after I had calmed down, I snuggled with her for a postmortem of this blowup. As we discussed how we tended to trigger each other, I confessed apologetically, "I should have known better than to push you in such a way, since I'm your mom and the adult."

With an uncanny clarity, her eyes looked directly into my own, and she responded, "Why, Mom? I shouldn't have argued in that rude way. I should've known better too! I'm twelve!"

It's hard to admit, but a part of me was actually relieved to hear that she felt just as bad as I did. This part of me even took secret pleasure that I wasn't the only one who had lost it, but that she too was guilty.

It was then that I became acutely aware of how there are two contradictory sides of myself—the one side that was in touch with Maia's inherent power and was deeply connected to her, and the other side that reacted to her in such a blind and unthinking way, creating antipathy and disconnection. One of these, I realized, was how I really felt, whereas the other was my irrational side—or what I often refer to as my "ego."

Once I realized that the voice in my head telling me that Maia should "do as she was told" was my ego, not my real self, I stopped listening to it. "You've had enough time telling me what to do today," I whispered.

As I quieted down and found myself back in my right mind, I was at last able to admit that the whole ugly episode had been caused by my ego. When I'm being true to myself as a caring parent, I would never compel my daughter to attend an event of the kind I had tried to force on her if she didn't wish to. I was doing it purely for selfish reasons and to exert control over my daughter.

Over the years, I have come to understand that my ego, which often takes the form of a controlling, demanding, angry voice in my head, isn't who I really am. It isn't who any of us actually is. Rather, it's just a habit of reacting that leaps to life when triggered—an emotionally charged aspect of us that we can tame once we become aware of it.

The better we learn to tame our ego—to quiet its often contradictory and negative self-talk that stirs up so many irrational emotions—the more capable we become of relating to each other from our authentic self. This self is our essence, and who we really are. It is always present deep within us, though much of the time it is drowned out by the ego's constant chatter and emotional reactions. A client of mine once asked, "Are you saying that the ego, our blindly reactive side, this voice in the head, isn't actually who we are?" Yes, that's exactly what I'm saying. As I explained in my first book, *The Conscious Parent*:

> I see the ego as more like a picture of ourselves we carry around in our head—a picture we hold of ourselves that may be far from who we are in our essential being. All of us grow up with such an image of ourselves. This self-image begins to form when we are young, based largely on our interactions with others.
>
> "Ego" as I'm using the term is an artificial sense of ourselves. It's an idea we have about ourselves based mostly on other people's opinions. It's the person we have come to believe we are and think of ourselves as. This self-image is layered over who we truly are in our essence. Once our self-image has formed in childhood, we tend to hold on to it for dear life.

The key to conscious parenting is to become aware of our ego, this persistent voice in our head, and its false ways. To parent well, it is imperative that we realize the ego isn't who we *are*. Then, as we learn to identify its voice and its antics, we won't blindly react to our children, which is what the ego wants us to do.

The reason this voice in our head causes us to be reactive is that it is rooted in fear. If you listen to the countless things that voice in your head tells you about your children, you'll discover that they mostly spring from fear. Whether you have inflated, grandiose ideas of your children and what they will accomplish in life, or whether you are frightened for them or disappointed in them, all of this ultimately is rooted in fear.

For instance, you want your children to be successful in life. But why is this so important to you? If you look closely enough, you'll see that it's because you see the world as a rather frightening, dog-eat-dog place and you're concerned for your children's future. Or you want your children to be admired and gifted in one or more ways. But what's behind this desire? Is it simply an appreciation of your children's gifts? Or is it the fear that they might not fit in, perhaps even turning out to be quite ordinary and, in society's eyes, not amounting to much?

I propose throughout this book that most of the problems we experience in raising children stem from fear, which is a characteristic of the ego. Our fearfulness is extremely detrimental to our children and ultimately the cause of much of their undesirable behavior. At the same time, I will show that this fear is baseless, and that far from needing to be afraid, we ought to realize that we have every reason to believe in our children and trust in their future because we live in a universe that is intelligent in its purpose, co-creating life's circumstances with us, each circumstance designed for our growth and expansion. Of course, you might argue that some circumstances and people are just pure evil. Instead of having this unidimensional perspective that breeds only fear and distrust, I prefer to understand these human forces in more psychological nuances, so that instead of just being against another, we are brought to a greater understanding of their true nature and, through this, of our own.

Good and evil have existed through the eons, pushing us to find the strength within ourselves to overcome tragedy. There is no logical explanation for why violence exists, except that it emerges from a childhood brutally brainwashed out of its connection to the heart. Such blind ignorance has existed throughout time, which is all the more reason why we need to parent consciously. Children learn about blind reactivity in their homes, which causes them to unleash this in society. It is therefore the task of a parent to tame the reactive elements in a home, paving the path for a more conscious relationship with oneself and the world.

Only when we divorce the blind reactivity of our parental ego can we teach our children to create harmony wherever they are. The path to a peaceful world begins with a childhood that's resplendent with a sense of worth and the freedom to be true to ourselves.

How did our ego develop? Although it often represents itself violently—against either the self or others—it really develops out of a quiet desperation of spirit. It develops out of a need to protect ourselves from the unconscious elements in our upbringing. We were all raised with a plethora of "shoulds," and a host of dogmatic impositions on how to be that we began to mistake for our authentic self. So, for example, if we were teased by our parents or siblings for crying easily when we were young, it's quite possible that we developed the persona of a stoic, unemotional person. While our feeling self was true to our authentic nature, our stoicism is the ego's veneer, which we created when still young in order to protect ourselves from the jabs and jeers of our loved ones. Or perhaps we were raised by parents who were simply unable to be there for us as we needed them to, out of their own inner chaos, hurts, and wounds, which led us to develop a persona of compliance or rebellion, where we believed we needed to be perfect or to act out in order to gain our parents' attention. In my years as a therapist I have witnessed countless instances where children were forced to wear robes of compliance or defiance, not because this was who they inherently were but because they were forced into these roles by their upbringing. Most of us had to develop false ways to cope with our childhood realities, ways that started out as protecting us from the pain of parental rejection but ultimately became the chains that kept us bound to them even more.

Because the ego formed so long ago, back when we were too young to know it was even happening, we're so accustomed to thinking of this voice in our head as our identity that we don't stop to realize it isn't how we really think and feel at all, but instead is a false persona we developed to survive in our world. It's from this false mind-set, which is fearfully focused on survival, that we do most of our parenting. It is this—our false self—that creates the first seeds of disconnect with our children. It takes us away from what *is* to the what *if* or what *should* be. We veer away from our children's natural way of being and impose our conditioning, beliefs, and fears on them instead. The further we veer from who it is our children authentically are, the more we disown their true spirit. Our disavowal of who they are is the ultimate act of betrayal toward them, for they wonder, "Why is my mother not able to see me for who I am? Is this because I am bad?" or "Why is my father shaming my natural ways? This must be because I am unworthy!"

I experience countless moments in my own parenting when what I truly feel toward my daughter is so easily eclipsed by my ego's reactivity. Instead of relating to her in the way she needs, I find myself engaging in all sorts of mental scripts about her that often have nothing to do with the present moment.

For example, the other day when she asked me to give her privacy, I found myself being pulled by the voice in my head telling me I was being rejected. This turned out to be nothing more than my ego. "Why doesn't she need me?" the voice in my head demanded. "Doesn't she want my wisdom and presence?" Instead of seeing my daughter's plea for privacy as a healthy and natural desire for time alone, I got lost in the story of rejection the voice in my head was telling me.

When we get caught up in the ego like this, we can no longer really be there for our children. Our real self, which is the only part of us that knows how to be present with another person, has been hijacked by our ego. This false sense of ourselves naturally leads us to lose sight of who our children are, forcing them to develop a false sense of themselves just to survive around us. Now they too are plagued with an ego!

This is also where having a child can be immensely helpful for our own growth. A child has the ability to bring to our attention just how unconscious much of our parenting is. This is exactly what my daughter does for me. If we are willing to see it, we begin to recognize the huge difference between the thoughts and emotions we so easily get tangled up in, that basically emanate from our own sense of helplessness and rejection, causing us to react in all sorts of ways—yelling out orders, dishing out time-outs, administering "discipline" we haven't honestly thought through—and how we truly feel about our child's behavior or a situation that has arisen.

Becoming aware of this raging mental and emotional activity of the ego enables us to separate it from who we are. This is essential if we are to parent consciously. Once we are aware of how our ego subverts our ability to be present, we are in a position to consider what a truly appropriate response might be to a particular behavior or circumstance, approached not from a place of fear but instead from a place of the greatest attunement to our children's needs.

The Roar of the Ego

Once I recognized that it was my ego talking, I could explain to my daughter how the ego works in language a twelve-year-old could understand.

"When we get upset or afraid we won't be understood," I began, "we turn into a ferocious tiger to protect ourselves. This is what was happening to you. You realized I wasn't taking the time to understand you, and in your desperation you bared your teeth and showed me your claws. Of course, based on the way *I* was brought up, I thought to myself, 'How rude!' I then bared my own tiger mommy teeth right back at you. I should have known you would never go on the attack unless you were somehow feeling scared or trapped."

Maia listened intently and, letting out a sigh of relief, snuggled deeper into my arms. As she rested contentedly in the knowledge that she was understood and appreciated, I took a moment to reflect on how I had allowed myself to react so blindly to her. I had sermonized, preached, and admonished—all from a pedestal based on ego, which thinks of itself as all-knowing and all-controlling. Quite naturally, my daughter's self-protective instincts kicked in.

It's human to want to assert our perceived power. And when it doesn't come from ego but from our deeper self, to feel empowered is healthy. By "deeper self," I'm referring to the aspect of us that is unswayed by the constant noise and machinations of the reactive ego within us. For instance, we see ourselves beginning to get angry, yet we are able to stay resolute in a state of calm and ask for our needs to be met with a deep respect for ourselves and our children. Or we recognize that our ego wants to dish out a threat or a punishment, but we resist this urge and instead find another way to enforce our boundaries. If we stop to pay attention, we can *all* sense when we aren't acting in alignment with a more evolved consciousness.

When my daughter believed I wasn't accepting her feelings, her naturally powerful self spoke up. But when I reacted from ego instead of from the calmness of my own empowered essence, this triggered *her* ego, and so we became locked in a battle of egos. In the heat of the battle, it didn't occur to me that my daughter wasn't behaving in a particular manner because she was "bad," but because of a healthy need *to defend herself from my ego.* So wrapped up was I in my ego that I had failed to create an appropriate space for her to assert her own voice.

This is so important to understand. When children aren't given the space to assert their authentic voice, but are drowned out by the roar of our parental agendas, they grow up anxious and depressed. Many of our young people are so deprived of our acceptance—of simply being *seen for who they are*—that they self-harm in a variety of ways. Getting drunk, taking drugs, engaging in inappropriate sexual relations, even cutting themselves—all of these are cries for our acceptance. They are manifestations of a deep yearning to be seen, validated, and known.

Many parents may judge themselves harshly for their past errors as they read this. It's my hope that my words create awareness in parents, not guilt. One of the typical reactions of parents who start on this path of conscious parenting is to look back at their errors and feel a sense of regret and guilt. I remind parents that this reaction, while understandable, is yet another ruse of the ego to create emotional paralysis and a disconnection from the present moment. I encourage parents to realize that no parent is going to be conscious all the time. All of us experience moments of blind reactivity that cause confusion and leave us feeling helpless. This is an intrinsic part of being a parent. Instead of wallowing in how we "should" have been, we need to use these insights as opportunities for transformation. In this way, we train ourselves to be mindful and respond to our children in the present moment and bring nothing from our past that isn't relevant. Forgiving ourselves for our unconsciousness allows us to immediately enter the present moment and create the change that needs to happen.

In the situation with my daughter that I described, had I kept on believing that my way was right instead of correcting my wrongdoing, I would have crushed her natural inclination, undermined her budding self-determination, and set her on a path to devaluing herself. In the process, she would have carried within her a growing resentment toward me, which in turn would have put distance between us, marring our ability to connect at the very time she most needs me.

This is why it's valuable to practice being aware on a daily basis. With a heightened state of awareness, or what's often referred to as being "conscious" or "mindful," we become accustomed to identifying the difference between a reactive state that's coming from ego and the far more calm, centered state of our true being. As we learn to observe our patterns of emotional reactivity and how they lead us to betray ourselves, it becomes easier to break out of a reaction that's a sort of trance—and, in due course, easier not to get into one in the first place. Whenever we find ourselves beginning to react, we pause and ask ourselves, "How can I approach my child so I am fully aligned with who they are versus who I think they should be?"

To parent consciously doesn't happen overnight. It takes practice to become aware of how our ego seduces us. Thankfully, even small steps toward increased awareness can result in monumental shifts in the quality of our relationship with our children. Every step we take toward increased consciousness brings us exponentially closer to our child's heart and spirit.

How Fear Drives Our Anxiety, Anger, and Other Reactions to Our Children

Because we all passed through childhood, and given that we were raised by parents who were largely unaware of how to navigate the parenting years in a manner that would result in our growing up to be emotionally mature, we are bound to suffer from varying degrees of unconsciousness. Even late into adulthood, many of us still haven't learned to respond in levelheaded ways rather than reacting immaturely. This is why we have gaps in our emotional development, particularly around our children, since they evoke our own childhood experiences.

One of my clients, Janet, felt the pain caused by the gaps in her emotional development in an especially strong way. A thirty-nine-year-old mother, she was constantly triggered by reverberations from her childhood. "I'm failing as a mom," she said to me during one counseling session, her voice quavering with emotion. "I just don't know how to be a grown-up. I feel like I'm still a little girl inside. How can I take care of my seven-year-old daughter when I don't even know how to be an adult yet? She's going through so much at school with her friends, I worry about her 24/7. The anxiety I feel affects every aspect of my life."

I listened as Janet continued, "When my daughter cries, I cry louder than her. When she's angry, I'm angry alongside her. When her friends are mean to her, it feels like they are being mean to me. I don't know what to say or how to act. Half the time I check out. The other half I move between panic and rage."

As we talked, Janet kept repeating, "I feel so anxious, I just don't think I can do this." She was echoing what countless clients tell me. Bringing up children is a scary task, because we are always afraid we're doing it "wrong."

As parents who are trying our best to do a good job, we don't realize that it's precisely our fears for our children, which we think of as concern, that are the problem with most parenting. These fears often take the form of intense anxiety with regard to our children. Whatever its precise manifestation, our fears undermines so many of our good intentions. Fear is the reason our parenting somehow manages to produce results that are the exact opposite of what we were aiming for.

Regarding Janet's situation, we began exploring her past. Not long into our discussion, she revealed how two major influences affected her life before she turned six. The first was that her father lost his job and the family had to move in with her grandparents in a different city. The second was that her parents began fighting a lot because of the stress generated by the huge change. From this time on, she no longer felt secure. Because she had no voice in the changes imposed on her by the adults in her life, she felt powerless.

"Whenever your children trigger you," I explained, "you think you're responding from your adult self. However, you aren't. Even though you are thirty-nine years old, you go right back into the way you learned to behave as a child, reverting to the six-year-old who had no way to speak up and assert herself. It's as if, emotionally, you're frozen in time. This is why you feel out of control on the one hand, yet paralyzed on the other."

As Janet was able to bring her residual emotions from these events into consciousness, becoming aware of what was really going on inside her, she began to spot when a situation was triggering a pattern established long ago. As she learned to step back from the situation, making a conscious decision instead of being driven by unconscious impulses, her emotional reactivity subsided. Increasingly able to approach situations in a calmer, more mature manner, she found she could embrace her present relationship with her daughter without feeling assaulted by her own past.

Think about a time when you couldn't sleep because you were so anxious that your child might fail a test at school. Or an occasion when your child was crying inconsolably because she was being bullied, and you found yourself in a state of panic. Anger, anxiety, guilt, or shame—in one form or another, we all experience intense negative emotion in connection with our children, all of it driven by fear. At those moments when our fear takes over, we lose all sense of our mature self and behave in ways that leave us feeling like a failure as a parent.

Experiencing fear in the form of anxiety is just one of the ways in which we can become quite irrational where our children are concerned. Catherine, another client of mine, shared with me how she had a history of blowing up at her daughter. She still felt terrible about the first time she lost her cool with Cindy in a really bad way. The girl, who was four years old at the time, had made a mess in the kitchen after her mother told her not to touch anything. It was really quite a trivial matter, yet it struck a nerve in Catherine and she flew into a rage.

What stuck in this mother's mind from the incident was Cindy's shocked expression. The daughter was so aghast at seeing her mother morph into a maniac that her look of horror instantly stopped Catherine's tantrum. When she realized how badly she had lost it, she was appalled. It was as if she had been taken over by some overwhelming force that descended on her out of nowhere.

I agreed with Catherine's assessment that an "overwhelming force" had taken over her, but I also explained that it didn't just come "out of nowhere." The reason she was triggered paralleled Janet's experience, in that it had to do with her own childhood. Growing up in a home where her parents controlled her, she had picked up an emotional blueprint that caused her to react in the same way to her own daughter in the present.

When Catherine witnessed her child suffering as she was, she knew it was time to examine herself. As she began to unravel her past, she came to understand how what had happened in her life long ago was now running and ruining her present. Most of all, she opened herself to the precise way her child had entered her life so that she could awaken to her forgotten self. She saw how our children come to us specifically to trigger this awakening within us. Of course, the onus to answer this call to rediscover the true self lies with us.

The Part Played by Your Past

We all need to be aware that the past influences our present. It is one thing to be stuck in the past, but quite another to become conscious of how it affects us now. Endlessly regurgitating what happened to us long ago only digs the hole we are in deeper. At the same time, to the degree that we are unaware of the hold our past still has on us, it will be difficult to make sense of how we react so strongly to our own children.

The experiences of our childhood create a template upon which we build our life. From this template emerge our current patterns of behavior, which closely resemble our early life. Unless we become aware of this, we keep repeating those patterns. In fact, most of our adult experiences and relationships adhere to those patterns. In this way, the degree of consciousness with which our parents raised us is a key determinant of how well-adjusted we grow up to be.

Perhaps more than anything, becoming a parent offers us the opportunity to become aware of patterns established in childhood. Because of our children's closeness to us, they offer us a mirror of ourselves. Through them, we are brought face-to-face with what it must have felt like for us to be a child. This can be painful. What are we to do with this pain?

My client Connie expressed this dilemma most beautifully: "I feel so helpless in these moments. When I cannot get through to my ten-year-old daughter and she keeps crying or having a tantrum I feel as if I am right back there with my father, being controlled all over again. I hate it. One part of me wants to cave in like I did as a child, and the other part of me wants to scream and rage at the fact it is happening again. So I either neglect her or I punish her. I hate myself both ways, but I just don't know what to do when I feel so out of control!"

Our tendency when we feel helpless or anxious is to control these feelings by lashing out at others, in this case at our children. In psychological terms, we refer to this as "projecting" our pain onto another, so that it looks like the other is the cause of our pain. Instead of reacting to our children because of what they are showing us about ourselves, the conscious response is to look into the mirror they are holding up to us, allowing ourselves to become aware of the many ways in which we still behave like children ourselves.

The more immature we are emotionally, the more our children will present us with complexes, insecurities, and behavior problems. This is their way of saying, "Hey, parents, I'm here to show you that you have some growing up to do. Can you please get on with it so I can move on and be who I'm supposed to be? I'm doing you a huge favor by showing you exactly what you need to do in order to become a mature person. The sooner you do so, the sooner I can free myself from the burden of being your mirror."

Answering the call to look into the mirror our children provide for us is the hallmark of a conscious parent. Each glance into the mirror presents us with a chance to break free from old patterns so that we don't transmit them to our children. It takes great courage to change the script from the old to the new, but this is the only way we can awaken to a conscious connection with our children. Only from this mindful place can we help them blossom into their truest self.

Is It Your Child, or Is It You?

Have you ever screamed at your child in anger? I'm betting there's hardly a parent who hasn't at some point become furious with their child, then felt horribly embarrassed afterward.

When we exhibit rage with a child, it's like being knocked off our feet emotionally. We usually think of the child as having behaved in a way that "set us off." We tell ourselves they were being annoying, testing us, provoking us, or pushing us "to the limit." We might justify our anger by saying something like, "Now look what you made me do!" Similarly, when we become anxious, worried, or fearful, we blame these feelings on something that's happening to our child or something our child is doing.

In traditional approaches to parenting, it's always been considered the child's fault when we erupt, are riddled with anxiety, or suffer a rush of panic. "Why do you *do* this to me?" we demand when our children act in ways that catalyze any of these reactions in us.

Equally traditional are the remedies recommended for such behavior. We issue a time-out or punish a child by taking away a privilege or administering a spanking. These autocratic strategies are our default reaction when we feel outwitted or overwhelmed by our children. A client once related how her pediatrician told her, "Your two-year-old is a force of nature. You better rein her in now before she turns into a nightmare. You should start considering time-outs and punishments to control her." These old-school ways of relating to our children are deeply ingrained in us, causing us to believe we are "bad" parents and will be ineffective if we don't adopt them in our own parenting.

If we are more contemporary in our approach, we perhaps use a neutral tone of voice and choose words that we hope don't come across as judgmental. Or, if we feel provoked, we might take a time-out ourselves in order to calm down. Who of us hasn't used the "count to ten" technique? To prevent a situation from spiraling into a rage-filled fight, one parenting fad recommends wearing an elastic band around our wrist, which we snap to remind ourselves we're at risk of losing our composure.

The problem with both the traditional punitive approach and the more contemporary methods is that the effect is short-lived. It's often no time at all before we find ourselves dealing with the same issue— or, worse, a manifestation of the issue that's gone underground, such as lying, cutting classes, or engaging in a forbidden behavior out of our sight.

The reason neither traditional nor contemporary responses to children's provocations are effective for long is that they don't get to the root of the behavior. The focus of the various techniques parents read about or pick up from experts or other parents is on the particular behavior, not on the dynamics that underlie the behavior. These techniques are all about controlling children so their actions don't trigger us. We tell ourselves that if we could just get the child to "do" or "not do" certain things, we wouldn't react the way we do. It's a game in which both parent and child are always trying to stay one step ahead of the other. Needless to say, the game results in anger, anxiety, and frequently disappointment and even sadness.

Conscious parenting is a game changer because it doesn't try to change the child, just ourselves as parents. It holds that once the parent creates the right conditions, the child will naturally change and evolve toward higher consciousness. The question, of course, remains whether the parent knows how to create these conditions. Conscious parenting addresses the fear that lurks behind so many of the ways we parent, all the while imagining we are doing "the right thing," as well as how we so readily react to our children with intense emotion. Our growing awareness of the ways in which our emotional reactivity obscures our ability to connect with our children allows us to reflect upon new ways we can design mindful responses to them. From this place of conscious awareness, we can tailor responses that allow them to fully express their truest self.

How Our Children Are Our Awakeners

Our children may be small and powerless in terms of living independent lives, but they are mighty in their potential to be our awakeners.

I like the term "awakeners." It transcends the usual clichés we use to reference our children—terms such as "friend," "ally," "partner," "muse." It speaks directly to our children's potential to enlighten us and raise our consciousness to new heights. When I began to notice how my daughter accomplished this, I was in awe.

The really surprising aspect of this is that the insights our children offer us aren't so much epiphanies as they are lessons stumbled upon in the plainest of moments and the most humbling of situations. Actually, more often than not it's in times of conflict that we get to see the full range of our unconscious theatrics. This is why, instead of shying away from conflict as many parents do, or even denying the existence of disagreements in the home, I encourage parents to accept the inevitability of conflict and use the insights that emerge to awaken themselves to the growth that still needs to take place in them.

To exercise domination over our children is a huge temptation for our ego, which loves to feel powerful and in control. Can we really blame it, when it was raised in an autocratic manner and is now addicted to it? After all, who else allows us near-total control over their life? You cannot do it at work. Or with your parents or siblings or friends. Often, your ego thinks the only relationship you can have complete control over is the one with your child. That's why it tries so hard to exert it. Only with our children do we get to be all-knowing, controlling, dictatorial. If we only realized how this kind of control is actually indicative of a weak sense of inner power, we might reconsider our ways.

When we ignore the immature ways we sometimes behave toward our children, which they consistently reflect back to us, we turn down one of the most profound opportunities to grow ourselves up. If on the other hand we embrace the mirroring of our immaturity that our children offer us, we have a chance to become profoundly altered. The most ordinary, everyday interactions with them in even the tiniest matters then become a catalyst for change.

Take for example the mother who complains that she loses her temper with her children because they never seem to listen to her in the morning, which means they habitually arrive late at school. The traditional response to such a situation would be to encourage the mother to discipline her children so that they learn to listen. The problem is that parents say repeatedly in such situations, "Are you listening to me?" Then a while later they follow up with, "What did I just tell you?" Before long they are yelling, imagining that if they talk more loudly, the child will finally be attentive. What they don't realize is that it isn't attentiveness the child is learning. Far from it. The child is growing resentful and therefore increasingly defiant.

Instead of the traditional approach of giving instructions more forcefully and more often, what if we explore whether the mother is disorganized and frequently tardy? Is she herself unable to function well in the mornings? Ah, now we have shifted the focus away from what the children need to change to what the mother may now need to transform within herself.

Using this quite different approach, the mother may need to look in the mirror and ask herself, "Is my child in some way reflecting the way *I* tend to operate? Are there ways *I* need to restructure my life so I can be more organized?" Where before we had children a certain level of disorganization may have seemed acceptable, we now realize that our lack of organization is undermining the healthy patterns of behavior we are seeking to teach. We may have been able to cope with a measure of chaos, but its effect on our children is destructive.

For a mother to be somewhat chaotic in her morning routine may seem a small thing, but it's precisely these everyday patterns that end up regulating our children's behavior, not the teaching we do or the commands we issue. Until we come to terms with this issue in ourselves, our children will continue to reflect the fact that we have some growing up to do. Indeed, unless we are willing to take up the challenge of growing and maturing in the way we organize our life, these seemingly small things have a way of seeding many a dysfunctional pattern in a family.

Take a different scenario: a twelve-year-old who, as a result of bullying, was increasingly becoming a social recluse. He refused to go to school or even to play with his friends, despite all the coaxing, enticements, and threats his parents employed as they became increasingly desperate. Experts were called in to "fix" the child's problem, to no avail. At times such interventions may be necessary, but before seeking such help, what if we shifted the focus to the parents? For instance, how about investigating their history with regard to social situations?

When we explored the mother's past, she revealed how she too had been bullied and felt ostracized as a child. Consequently, she had been lonely much of her childhood. Thinking it was her fault she was forever being picked on, she experienced considerable shame. The bullying, loneliness, and shame caused her to become extremely anxious. When her son began being bullied, it triggered her own latent anxiety. Worried sick about him, she unwittingly undercut his confidence. Instead of encouraging him to summon his inherent resilience, through her excessive anxiety she caused him to withdraw.

In therapy with me, this mother learned how her son's withdrawal from life was a reaction against her own anxious reactions that were too much for him to bear, her own reactions being a remnant of events from her childhood that she had never really dealt with. In simple everyday ways, as well as more profound ones, our children are constantly saying to us, "Wake up, look at yourself, transform yourself. Do this for *you*, so that I may be free of what burdens you."

Sometimes our children awaken us to our tardiness, at other times to our obsessions and addictions. Similarly, they bring to our attention our anxiety, need for perfection, and desire for control. They show us our inability to say yes or no, and how we don't really mean either most of the time. They bring to light issues of control, our tendency to dependency, and our marital troubles. They reveal how unable we are to simply be still for very long. They show us how difficult it is for us to engage them with full-on presence, how challenging we find it to be open, how threatening it is for us to be spontaneous and playful. They especially mirror back to us all the ways in which we simply aren't authentic. It's in how our children act and react to us, and how we act and react to them, that—if we are willing—we are able to see our unconsciousness. As we learn to embrace this truth, we stop resisting our children when they act in ways we find challenging, and instead awaken to the fact that this challenge has come into our present because of something in our past that is yet to be resolved.

A Shift of Focus

The conscious parenting approach is a true game changer. By shifting the focus away from the child and onto the parent's inner transformation, it holds the potential to awaken families in deep and fundamental ways. Integrating this shift of focus in our daily lives is far from easy for us as parents. As it turns the mirror on all the ways our reactions to our children are unhealthy, it challenges us to explore our unconscious inner workings and confront aspects of ourselves that lurk in the shadows. By not allowing us to rest on "how things were done in my childhood," we are forced to discover new ways to relate to our children, moment after moment, handcrafting our responses to match the child before us. This forces us to ask ourselves, "How can I use this moment with my child to learn more about myself?"

My client Jenna, the mother of five-year-old Anna, was having a hard time with her daughter's meltdowns. Unable to find a way to communicate with Anna, she felt driven to desperation on a daily basis. Things came to a head when, after a particularly harrowing night of Anna being irritable and restless, Jenna lashed out, slapping her across her face.

Jenna was mortified by her lack of control and immediately

booked a session to see me. When we went over the incident moment by moment, I was able to see where Jenna had dug herself into a hole. She said to me, "I tried so hard to connect to Anna's feelings while she was having her tantrum. I kept asking why she was so unhappy and what I could do to help. But instead of telling me, she just kept on crying and flailing her arms at me. I continued trying to calm her down, but she just kept screaming. Finally I just lost it." Like many parents, Jenna thought she was trying to connect, when in reality she caused a deeper rift with her child.

I pointed out to her that she had missed the most essential piece of the puzzle. "You have forgotten to include the most significant details— your thoughts and feelings," I said. "Are you able to tell me what thoughts were racing through your mind or what you were feeling in your body?"

Jenna looked at me dumbstruck. "I have no idea at all," she blurted out after several moments of silence. "I was so focused on Anna that I didn't pay attention to what I was thinking or how I was feeling."

Jenna's response is typical of many parents. Focused on their children's acting out, they blindly react in the moment, with little thought to the driving force behind their reaction. Quite naturally, they often react unconsciouly, compounding the issue. Only when Jenna began to turn her attention to herself, focusing on her own internal landscape, did she realize how much she contributed to the chaos her child was experiencing. More important, she was empowered to create avenues for change.

"You were experiencing a host of feelings while relating to your child," I commented. "You were feeling helpless and out of control, frustrated and angry. All of these emotions are really manifestations of fear. You don't realize it, but the true trigger of your reactions was your own fear, not your child's behavior."

Jenna slowly began to understand what it meant to turn the spotlight on herself. In a moment of quiet reflection, she said, "Oh my goodness, I had no idea I was the one who was unraveling more than her. I just wasn't paying attention! In my desire to fix her, I was blindly reacting to her. You're right—the whole thing scared me, and that's why I lost it."

Because conscious parenting is concerned with the actual roots of our acting out—and I do mean *our* acting out *as parents*, not so much our children's acting out—it avoids quick fixes and Band-Aids. Instead, we undergo transformation *as moms and dads*. Through the repeated act of self-confrontation, as our children reflect back to us all the ways in which we have yet to grow up, we develop into the truly amazing parents we have the ability to be—the kind of parents every child born into the world deserves.

CHAPTER TWO

How the Culture
Sets Up Parents to Fail

C hildren don't need us to lead them to an awakened state, because they are already awake. Our task is to foster their natural awareness, providing a context in which it can blossom. To achieve this, parenting needs to shift from controlling our children, which is rooted in our fears and serves to impede their progress, to supporting the development of their physical, emotional, and mental capacities.

Our children need us to embolden them to captain their own ship in an age-appropriate manner. They need us to encourage them to practice their innate navigational skills at every opportunity. They do not need our fears calling into question who they are. We need to trust that once they take charge of their self-governance, they will spontaneously reach for the fullest expression of themselves and find everything they require for this to happen.

The subtle but profound movement away from fearfully attempting to motivate by controlling, to emboldening children to emerge as self-motivated individuals, fuels within them an excitement about life. Because their motivation springs from within, they will naturally develop the self-discipline needed to carry out their objectives. In this way each child becomes their own unique expression of the consciousness that underpins the rich tapestry of intelligent life.

As parents, it's vital for us to understand that as long as our children are in touch with their deepest self, with its boundless resources, they will motivate themselves beyond anything we could ever imagine. Our role in their life is to help them express their motivation in ways that are tailored to their particular makeup. This is something we can do only to the degree we keep pointing them inward, so that they learn to listen to their own desires rather than allowing others to unduly influence their decisions. Of course, our ability to help them is in direct proportion to how we do this in our own life.

I know how extremely difficult it is for parents to trust that if we simply usher our children into their own self-realization, rather than pressuring them to comply with our idea of who they should be, they will flourish. Because it goes against our conditioning, which teaches us that life is precarious and therefore we need to be in a "doing" mode at all times, embracing the role of an enlightened usher may feel uncomfortable at first. And it might make you feel that you are abdicating your role as a parent. This is because most of us were raised with the mantra "you are what you do." We feel that if we aren't trying to control or effect a desired outcome, we are not doing what we are supposed to do. Parents become obsessed with activity as an imagined antidote to our fear. We treat our children like chattel, pushing them toward a future we imagine for them. Only when we stop listening to the voice in our head and stop obsessing and regard our children as sovereign beings who are fully capable of rising to the challenge of becoming the author of their own life will they embody the vigor and courage that is their natural state.

When Caring Feels Like Control

Control is very difficult to give up. If you try to do so, your ego will bombard you with fearful messages reminding you of all the reasons you wanted control in the first place. But those messages have nothing to do with the reality of who your child is and what's actually transpiring in the present moment.

To illustrate what I'm sharing with you, let me tell you about the time fourteen-year-old Tonya and her mother, Karla, came for their first therapy session and bickered the entire time. Karla went through a list of things her daughter was failing to do. Karla said she was:

- *Not studying*

- *Not doing laundry*

- *Not exercising*

- *Not eating right*

- *Not getting A grades*

- *Not making new friends*

- *Not volunteering*

- *Not spending time with her dog*

The list went on and on. Each time Tonya attempted to defend herself, her mother launched another rant. It seemed as if there was nothing Tonya could do right. Giving up on trying to defend herself, she retreated further into the couch, until she was totally withdrawn. The barrier between mother and daughter was thick with resentment on the daughter's part and sheer hysteria on the mother's.

"I can tell how panicked you are right now," I said to Karla. "Can you identify what's scaring you so much?"

"I'm terrified Tonya won't be accepted into a college and will be left behind," Karla confessed, tearing up as she spoke. "I'm so scared she won't find a good career and be able to stand on her own two feet. I took years to find my way, so I don't want this to be the case with her." Letting out a huge sigh, she went on, "Tonya thinks I'm nagging her all the time, but I'm only trying to ensure she succeeds in life. I wish she would see how much I care about her instead of always thinking I'm the enemy."

I explained to Karla that as a consequence of her need to control, her caring was getting buried beneath a pile of instructions. Over the course of the next few sessions, I helped her change her approach to her daughter, assisting her in moving away from her fear-based tendency to instruct, which came across as desperation.

As Karla gained insight into how her anxiety was undermining the leadership she wished Tonya to develop, as well as overriding her ability to be present with her daughter in a way that would enable them to connect, Tonya began to open up. She was starting to understand that her mother wasn't operating out of negative intentions, as she had imagined. Just the opposite: It was evident that she cared deeply. As Karla continued to peel away her insecurities, recognizing how they stemmed from fear that took root in her own childhood, her connection with Tonya improved to the point that they started to have honest, heartfelt conversations.

As I have seen so many times with clients, when we parents eliminate our anxiety from the equation our children step forward to become the authors of their life. Thus Tonya developed the self-initiation her mother longed for her to gain. But she was able to do it only when her mother stopped controlling her life. Ironically, her mother got exactly what she wanted only by giving up the control she thought she needed to help her daughter.

The Clash of Time Zones

Karla is like most parents I know and work with. Swept up in a culture that demands action, they believe the only way to live a successful life is to constantly be busy and in control. In turn, this was the message Karla transmitted to Tonya.

Success in a society like ours is measured by cultural yardsticks, so that we are raised to think that life is all about pushing ourselves, optimizing, and achieving. Where our children are concerned, the focus is on scoring high marks, earning good grades, and fitting in with the "right" people—all in the hope of eventually making a six-figure salary.

Obsessed as we are with reaching goals and their golden promise of a "happy" future for our children, we constantly micromanage our youngsters' lives. As if the pressure to perform academically weren't enough, we press them to become involved in sports, social activities, dance, singing, or playing a musical instrument, among other endeavors such as hobbies and clubs, while at the same time the media and the Internet all demand their attention. Surrounded by activities, they grow up in a world focused on *doing*.

Why do we put so much stock in involving our children in all this busyness? Simply because we are afraid that they may somehow "miss out" and therefore not become what we hope for them to become—a success in the world as defined by society's standards. Or because we wish we had had these opportunities as a child and want to make sure we give our children everything that we did not have.

When people are as busy chasing from one activity to another as so many of us are with our kids, what's happening in *this* moment begins to feel somehow inadequate, even undesirable or unacceptable—and therefore invalid. We become programmed to think that it's the *next* thing that counts, not what we're presently engaged in. Then we wonder why our children have such a hard time concentrating or practicing something for long.

In fact, were you to ask me what I believe to be the root of conflict between parents and children, I would tell you that it's a clash of time zones. Parents are oriented to the future, to getting to wherever they imagine themselves to be going. Children, on the other hand, when left to themselves inhabit the present. Most of the disconnection between parent and child comes down to this rupture between a life enjoyed moment by moment and a life that's focused on moving ahead.

You may be thinking that to ignore the future would be irresponsible, and I agree with you. It's wise to plan appropriately. After all, you can't catch a plane unless you buy a ticket ahead of time and acquire the correct form of identification. But this is fundamentally different from being focused on the future *to the detriment of the present*.

When I speak of a child's ability to be "present," I'm referring to being fully engaged in whatever they are doing at this moment, including if they are doing nothing in particular. This is quite natural for young children, until we teach them to disconnect from the present by hurrying them along from activity to activity to the point that they have no opportunity to simply "be."

When our children are allowed to relish each moment without constantly having an agenda thrust on them, they come alive to their native intelligence, heartfelt desires, and natural inclinations and interests. These are rooted in a child's natural sense of the wonder of being alive and a belief in their life as a magnificent adventure, not in fear that they have to perform or life may pass them by. This is the case because the universe that birthed us arose from a potentiality that ever since has continued to express itself in an abundant array of manifestations, pouring forth untold energy on its creative journey.

Consequently, as long as we allow our children the space for their inclinations to arise from within, they will of their own accord explore their world from a state of inherent curiosity. This is why when something interests them they become engrossed in what they are doing to the point that it's as if time stops. They are rarely bored, because when they have finished a task, it's never long before the spark of fascination flares up afresh, igniting renewed energy. Even if they are just lazing around, they bask in the experience of relaxing and feel no guilt for doing nothing but simply being, fully attuned to their authentic nature.

A child raised in this way needs no pushing in order to live a full and purposeful life. No goal needs to be imposed on them for motivation, no carrot dangled before them. All we are required to do as parents is to provide a safe context in which they have the time and space to awaken to their own inclinations as a means of expressing their unique spirit—even as the universe itself, in its vast array of manifold forms, has arisen out of the stillness and silence of time and space.

The whole notion of needing to motivate our children to reach for their potential is misguided. Forcing a child, rewarding them, or using "tough love" to goad them into action produces short-term gains but ultimately backfires. The resentment that results can't possibly uplift and inspire. Whatever it may succeed in achieving will therefore fall far short of the child's potential.

What Children Really Need

What do you imagine your children most want from you? The latest iPhone? New shoes or designer clothes? A trip to Disney World? Tuition for a top private school? Every kid enjoys getting something new or going to an exciting theme park. But what all children really yearn for goes much deeper. It doesn't involve fancy clothes, the latest electronics, pricey trips, or even a high-cost education.

I believe most of our parenting failures emerge from our lack of understanding about what our children truly need from us in order to thrive. Every child wants to know three things:

- *Am I seen?*

- *Am I worthy?*

- *Do I matter?*

When children feel seen, believe they are worthy, and discern that they matter for who they are *as a person* and not just because of what they accomplish, they are able to enjoy their own sense of empowerment. This then translates into genuine enthusiasm for whatever holds their attention and focus. In other words, their *natural love of themselves* manifests in *a love of life*.

As children start out in life, their sense of their lovability, dignity, and worth is inevitably fragile. They haven't yet had a chance to become bold in their self-love and self-expression, which naturally requires time and experience. Because of this, particularly in their early days, they need us to mirror back to them how rich they are in their capacity for accomplishment and ability to run their own life. Just how much power they possess is affirmed by how *we* see them, how *we* feel about them. In other words, our connection to them is crucial at this stage of their development. It's what assures them that who they are is valid. Consequently, if we are hyperfocused on their performance, the things they sometimes say, or aspects of their behavior, we miss the opportunity to fulfill the prime parenting task of this early age—the reinforcement of their own innate sense of self. It's when this fails to occur that they then go against their authentic being and develop a substitute false self, the ego.

Parents must be in touch with our own rich inner life to fulfill this role successfully. We must be awake to our own desires, aware of our own unique bent, deeply attuned to our purpose and place here on earth. If not, we are bound to feel disconnected, bored, and likely lonely.

The result is that we will be needy, which is precisely how, as par-

ents, we so easily end up using our children to fulfill our *own* ⟨
Instead of encouraging our children to do what *they* wish to d⟨
we divert them into assuaging our sense of inadequacy, our unfulfilled
longings, and our loneliness. When we need them so desperately, how
can we accurately reflect back to them their value? All we can offer
them is a distortion based on our own distorted sense of ourselves. Of
course, through it all we assure ourselves, as the culture has taught us
we must, that everything we do is because we are so dedicated to "serving" our children.

Since children develop a solid sense of self when who they are intrinsically is seen and affirmed, it's vital that we connect with each
child not as a clone of ourselves or a fantasy we harbor of who they
need to be, but as an individual who is unique. Thus it's through our
appreciating gaze, our authentic presence with them, and our attention to them—but *not* indulgence—that they grow up with a strong
sense of self. We communicate their importance through each of our
interactions with them.

"Do you see me?" This is the big question your child is asking every day. "Can you recognize me for who I am, different from your
dreams and expectations for me, separate from your agenda for me?"

Our children yearn for us to understand them on the deepest level
possible, which I think of as their essence—their very being, which is
who they are before they "do" anything at all. They count on us to cut
through the rubble of their sometimes irrational behavior and see
them in their pristine selfhood. They need us to affirm their intrinsic
goodness, regardless of the ugly things they may say or do at times.
This is how their natural inborn belief in themselves becomes solidly
grounded instead of masked by ego.

A sense of our children's worth flourishes when the way we look
at them, the way we listen to them, and the way we speak to them
reflect just how lovable they are. This is how we empower them—
how we draw out in them their innately powerful sense of self, which
is what will carry them successfully through life. Only when we can
separate our fantasies concerning who our children *should* be from
who they actually *are* can we do justice to their original essence and
craft our parenting to allow for this essence to flourish.

CHAPTER THREE

The Invisible Triggers of Our Reactivity

B ut how should I begin this process of becoming more conscious as a parent and raising conscious children?" This is one of the most common questions I am asked. Parents want to know, "What is it that I need to become aware of? And how exactly do I become aware?"

It's one thing to say you want to change and be aware of what's happening in the present moment, but it's another to know how to do this in practical ways. The trouble is that since the path to consciousness is an internal process, identifying universal principles is a challenge that leaves many struggling to know the steps they need to take.

Because the journey of awakening is complex and idiosyncratic, I always advise, "Start with what you are observing happening right now, with what you are actually seeing moment by moment."

To this end, a common exercise I do with parents is to inquire about their triggers. I ask them to list those things that most disturb them. Naturally, they think I'm talking about how their *children* upset them, so they quickly make long lists of issues such as:

- *"I get mad when my daughter doesn't clean up after herself."*

- *"I feel upset when my son hits his brother."*

- *"I feel anxious that my daughter is never going to fit in anywhere."*

These common parental complaints illustrate how we automatically think our *children's* behavior is the starting point of our negative interactions with them. So I challenge them, "Did you notice that you pointed your finger at your child when I asked what *your* triggers are? Do you see how quick you are to blame them for your reactions?"

"Well," parents frequently retort, "should I pretend my children don't trigger me?"

I don't blame parents for their confusion. Traditional parenting models have conditioned parents to believe that if they are triggered by their children, it's naturally the child's fault. Nevertheless, I don't hold back when talking with parents about this. If a person refuses to take ownership of how they transferred my question about themselves onto their child, they won't be able to parent consciously, since this touches upon the foundation of conscious parenting.

Our childhood conditioning by our families and culture leads us to react to life in robotic ways. I go so far as to say that our children *never* trigger us. The trigger *always* lies within us, rooted in our past hurt and childhood struggles. Our children's behavior is the gust that fans the cinders within us into flame.

Parents almost fall out of their chair when I say this. "What do you mean, they don't trigger us? Everyone knows that children are engineered to trigger us!" I understand why parents are so indignant. After all, every parenting book has endorsed the notion that our children know just how to set us off. Until recently, I too thought this. It was on deeper reflection that I saw how I had allowed myself to buy into this subtle but far-reaching error that our children purposely tailor their behavior to incite us.

I explain to parents, "Our children are just being who they are. They aren't interested in inciting us to fury or causing us guilt or anxiety. Quite the opposite: They function from their own internal state, which really has nothing to do with us. However, because we carry so much emotional pain, they inevitably ignite a firestorm within us at times. None of this is intentional, but is a result of our own lack of wholeness. We are triggered not by their behavior, but by our own unresolved emotional issues."

To move away from all illusion that our children are maliciously intent on triggering us is an important step on the path of awakening.

When we dare to let go of the mainstream idea that they push our buttons on purpose, we awaken to the true extent of our own immaturity. Without having them to blame on any level, we are now forced to confront our inner lack and discover the reasons why it exists.

The culture's blind assumption that the child is to blame when parents are triggered gives parents the authority to "fix" their children, controlling them to a point where the child doesn't set them off in the same way. The simplistic notion is that if you change a child's behavior, the parent won't be triggered anymore.

The reality is that as long as we focus on changing our children—or anyone other than ourselves—we'll discover that it's akin to trying to empty the ocean with a teaspoon. Because this is how we believe parenting works, we mindlessly repeat the same actions over and over. But just as the waves of the ocean keep rolling in, so too our children's behavior continues to set us off again and again. The problem isn't the child's behavior, but why it sets us off. Unless we examine why the behavior causes us to react negatively, we will never change the patterns of interaction between our children and us—and this is true of any close relationship.

When Lena came in to see me about her relationship with her sixteen-year-old daughter, she was exasperated. "I get upset by how rude she is. I just hate her tone of voice."

I challenged her to deconstruct what she meant by "tone of voice."

"You know how these kids talk these days," she explained. "They have this demanding tone of voice that can just gnaw at you."

I pushed Lena even further. "I need to know the exact words that set you off. Unless you are able to identify the external flame to your inner activation, you won't be able to find out why it causes you to react so negatively."

Finally, Lena said, "When she orders me to do things for her without showing the least bit of gratitude, it makes me feel as if I'm her servant."

At last Lena had discovered the root of her issue with her daughter. I explained to her, "It isn't your daughter's tone of voice that's the problem. It's your inner sense that you are forced to serve her on some level. Each time your daughter speaks with a tone that's reminiscent of control, your inner 'servant' gets activated and retaliates. What if your daughter wasn't intending to enslave you, but was simply reacting to her own internal needs and feelings? If you could tap into your feelings, perhaps you wouldn't interpret her tone in terms of a trigger."

Within moments, Lena was teary-eyed. "This makes absolute sense. I grew up with a controlling mother, so I have strong reactions to any form of control or dominance. I immediately retaliate, just like I rebelled against my own mother as a teen." As Lena uncovered what triggered her, she realized her daughter wasn't to blame, which allowed her to calm down.

The fact is, if we didn't already carry pain within us from our own upbringing, we wouldn't react unconsciously. It's only when we have been sensitized in some way internally that our triggers can be enflamed by something external. For this reason, I explained to Lena, "You have an internal script that says you need to be in control, just like your mother did. This internal script has become your mantra. Each time you feel your daughter has more control than you, you react. As you begin to awaken to what's really happening, you'll begin to see how your daughter is only reflecting an aspect of yourself."

It's in such ways that our children show us what we are carrying within us. Our willingness to turn our eye inward creates the momentum to change our relationships on the external level. Conscious parenting urges us to see our children's reactions to us as a wake-up call to go within. Then, instead of acting out what we are feeling based on our past programming, thus taking it out on our children, we choose to contain our emotions and quietly reflect on what we are experiencing. Such reflection allows us to disengage from the overwhelming seduction to react from blindness, ruled by our past, and instead be fully present to the needs of the child before us.

The Roots of Our Triggers

In order to get to the root of our triggers, it isn't enough to stop at explanations such as, "I was tired that day," or "My boss was really demanding at work and I took my frustration out on my kid." Nor is it enough to say simply, "I have an anger problem I need to work on."

"But *how* do I do this?" every parent asks. "How do I begin?"

We begin by becoming aware, which is what conscious parenting revolves around. Aware of our thoughts, feelings, actions—indeed, of everything we bring to each and every moment of our children's lives.

Awareness requires us to hold a dual lens, one facing inward and the other outward. Most of us are raised only with the latter, so that our focus is on *doing*. This book is about infusing our doing with the grace and wisdom of being. We need both elements in life—the doing *and* the being, the behavior *and* the awareness behind the behavior, the action *and* the insight behind it. It's at the confluence of both that true consciousness arises.

The path to conscious parenting is a lived experience, uncovered by a willing and committed curiosity. No one can *make* someone more conscious. It's a silent and deeply personal undertaking by a person who understands that the only way they will be able to regulate themselves with balance and equanimity is by learning to be aware of how they think and the way in which they tend to emote. After all, it's from our thoughts and emotions that so much springs forth. The mind, then—meaning the beliefs we live by that drive so much of what we think and feel—is the true starting place for change.

It was only when I embarked on the process of examining the beliefs I had around parenting that I was able to initiate shifts in my life. At first I found it hard to even uncover what my beliefs were, as I thought this was just the way everyone thinks, or at least should think. As I began to sit in silence with myself more, simply breathing and being still—a kind of meditation—I began to slowly detach from my thoughts and saw how I had falsely taken them to define who I am. I still remember my first epiphany while doing this, which happened when I attended a meditation retreat to learn more about how to simply be quiet with myself. I remarked to my roommate, "I cannot believe I am not my thoughts or my beliefs!"

When I first realized that my beliefs were just constructs, and that I was in effect living my ego's ideal for my life, I underwent a mini-death of sorts. I felt myself coming apart at the seams. Everything I held dear, every pillar I had based my life upon, every limitation I had thought to be real was now coming apart under the scrutiny of my growing awareness.

Once I specifically delved into my beliefs about parenting, I was shocked at how rigid, archaic, and toxic they were. Not only were they designed to stifle my creativity and growth as a human being, but they were targeted to chip away at my child's ability to be original and creative. I later found this to be true with every client I worked with.

Our thoughts are neutral. Let's look at common thoughts: "It is raining" and "It is seven in the evening." These are just statements and therefore neutral on their own. However, once they are followed by an entourage of beliefs, they begin to get charged with a positive or negative valence. For example, the thought "It is raining" can be followed by a belief, "All our plans will be ruined," followed by "We will have a miserable time." You can see how a neutral thought quickly leads to a mood and emotional state. Or let's take the thought "It is seven in the evening." Again, on its own this is a neutral thought. However, backed by a slew of beliefs, even this benign thought can now have quite a charge. Beliefs such as "I am tired and exhausted" and "I have too many chores to do and am overwhelmed" can quickly take a neutral thought into the realm of a negative feeling.

Therefore, because our beliefs control our behavior, this is the place to start if anything is to change. It was here that I embarked on the quest to unravel my ideas about parenting and replace them with consciousness. I wished to no longer be ruled by the stereotypical templates of generations past. I began to walk a new path, one where *I* took responsibility for how I wanted to live and parent. I held the paintbrush, and I took ownership of the strokes it began to create. I was now the manifestor of my destiny, the master designer of my present. Although scary at first, the path has a way of illuminating itself quite effortlessly and seamlessly. One needs only to have the right road map, which we quickly discover was with us all along—the one directed toward the true self, with the guiding question being, "What is true to me and my child at this moment?"

The Parental Kool-Aid

All our beliefs about parenting emerge from a single source, the consumption of a potent dose of what I refer to as "parental Kool-Aid." This Kool-Aid comes in the form of seven myths the culture holds concerning how to parent effectively. You may not realize it, but when you are triggered, you are consciously or unconsciously allowing yourself to be overtaken by one or more of these cultural myths.

These myths are so pervasive and so deeply entrenched in society's accepted way of doing things that it never occurs to most of us to question them. The insidious aspect of the myths is that at the very time we are trying to relate to our child, they actually work against forming a truly meaningful connection.

Is it possible that how we have been trained to think about parenting is actually the root of all the dysfunction we experience with our children? Could it be that what we have been endlessly told is the right way to raise children actually isn't? Most important, do we dare to go into the closet of these beliefs and spring-clean all that's toxic along with everything that's unnecessary?

Despite the resistance we may experience to changing our beliefs about parenting, there's no avoiding the fact that every parent is in a profound relationship with these cultural myths. The myths define how our children are "supposed to be," which often has nothing to do with who a child actually is. It's this gap between what society holds up as an ideal and what individual children are really like that causes so much disconnection between parent and child. It's this gap that also feeds our fear that our children won't measure up and might even fail, causing us to put so much pressure on them.

Sadly, these myths receive huge support not only from society's official channels, such as the government, religious institutions, and the educational system, but also from those whose personal lives are interwoven with our own. Everyone has drunk the parental Kool-Aid—our relatives, our friends, our teachers, our clerics, and much of the parenting industry at large.

These myths, reinforced over generations, seduce us into submitting to society's dictates concerning how children ought to be raised

and how they are supposed to turn out. The collective parental p
that results is in effect a trance into which we have all fallen. I have
lectured around the world, and whether in India or Canada, Mexico
or the United States, I find parents to be under the spell of these cultural dictates. Almost universally, we act in accord with society's beliefs without examining them. Much of the time we aren't even aware
we are doing so.

If on occasion we catch a glimpse of what's wrong with the beliefs
we buy into, it can be frightening. We are afraid that if we did things
differently we would be ostracized. Not only does the thought of
veering from the mainstream scare us, but as I mentioned a moment
ago, we also fear for what will become of our children. We realize
they could pay a high price at the hands of a society that has innumerable ways to punish unorthodoxy.

Let's talk about the price of unorthodoxy. In fear of ostracism and
isolation, we follow the way of the mainstream—in this case, the
myths of what it means to be a "good" parent. If we believe the cost of
unorthodoxy is too high for us to bear, this is an indication that we
are cut off from our own inner abundance. In this case these costs
may indeed feel too burdensome. However, once we get in touch with
our inherent power, we realize that it's when we follow the mainstream with blind compliance that we actually pay the highest cost:
the price of authenticity.

Despite their fear, I find that most parents are thirsty for a new
approach to parenting. The world is desperately in need of change,
and the best place for this to start is in the home. It's there that our
children receive their template for how they are to love themselves
and others, how to resolve conflicts, and how to care for the world
around them. The home is the seeding ground for all that comes later.
If the ground isn't planted with the right seeds, our children are
likely to flounder.

For change to occur in how we parent, we need to be bold. We are
going to need to abandon the archaic child-rearing practices that
have produced generation after generation of unfulfilled humans.

Sometimes I'm asked, "Who do you hope your child will be?" This
question fosters the illusion that we have control over who our chil-

dren become. Innocent on the surface, it fuels the desire of parents to micromanage their children, turning out products of their making.

My answer to this question is always the same: "My goal as a parent is to raise a child who is firmly rooted in who she is, certain of her inherent worth, able to express herself with authenticity and be grounded in her relationship with me." In other words, it simply doesn't matter to me what career or lifestyle my child decides to pursue, as long as she is true to herself. Society's attempts to make her something different from who she is carry no weight with me.

Children who grow up to be authentic will inevitably be helpful members of society, because they will feel compelled to take care of their fellow beings and the planet on which they live, since this is how they treat their own heart, mind, and body. A person who honors their own being will guard the rights of others with great care.

When we break out of the collective parental trance and see society's parenting myths for what they are, we open the way to seeing our children as they are. This constitutes a huge breakthrough. We begin to connect with who our *children* want to be, instead of what society tells us we should want them to be. As we connect with them in a way we haven't been able to until now because we weren't seeing them as they actually are, we find ourselves understanding them based on their unique temperament, needs, struggles, and desires. But first we must understand these myths in order to break free of them.

~ Our Children, Our Awakeners ~

In my illusion I thought I was going to raise you
To be whole, complete, and worthy,
To be educated, kind, and wise,
To be a leader, empowered and free.

I was deluded to think I knew it all,
fooled by my age and might.
I thought I had it all together,
Ready to teach, inspire, and change you.

Only now, after so many moments
With you
Do I realize how foolish these ideas were,
How baseless and grandiose.

I now understand . . .
That it is *you* who is here to teach me,
To guide, lead, shift, and elevate,
To transform, awaken, and inspire
Me.

I now realize how I had it wrong,
Upside down and outside in,
It is you who are this perfectly designed clarion
To wake me up to my true self.

Part Two

Our Parenting Myths

CHAPTER FOUR

Myth #1
Parenting Is About the Child

A common question I ask in my workshops is, "What's the main focus of parenting?" The resounding response comes instantly: "The child, of course."

By now you realize the problem with this answer. The workshop crowds often wonder why I would even ask such a question when the answer is so obvious. Then they turn to protest when I explain that society's child-centric approach is at the root of much of the disappointment, worry, and dysfunction in families.

"How can this be?" audiences ask in shocked tones. "How can focusing on our children be a bad thing? Don't we need to support our children and give them every opportunity we can?"

Before parents lunge for my throat, I explain that I'm not advocating that they become self-obsessed and narcissistic, so that they are focused on themselves to the detriment of their children. Just the opposite: I'm advocating an approach to parenting that offers the maximum benefit for a child.

Much of conscious parenting is highly counterintuitive. Initially, this is not easy. However, once I explain why the old parenting paradigm doesn't work, parents begin to see the benefits of this new approach.

The Problem with Child-Centric Parenting

Today, more and more of us have become convinced we must raise our children to be *exceptional*. In fact, the parenting industry—made up of a pantheon of experts who include authors, psychologists, psychiatrists, educators, testing companies, tutors, consultants, pharmaceutical companies, and bloggers—thrives on parents' misplaced obsession with raising an exceptional child.

In my workshops I often ask parents, "What are your goals for your child?" They promptly list the standard ones—for them to be happy, successful, kind, respectful. Without realizing it, they are imparting the message that their child is lacking in some way—that these qualities aren't currently present in the child.

The reality is just the opposite. Parents aren't able to see that their child already embodies these qualities. From society's perspective, a child needs to develop such qualities for the future, whereas I'm saying that children already possess them, albeit sometimes in a masked fashion. Society's view focuses on the future. Conscious parenting keeps us firmly planted in the present.

The word "goals" itself carries the burden of planning for the future and "creating" childhood as if it were a project with a specified outcome. The push to get our children to an end point creates all sorts of tensions that inevitably spill out in reactivity, at times raising the temperature in the home to boiling point. It's only when we are able to connect with our children as they presently are, seeing them as everything they need to be at this precise moment, that we can provide them with the parenting they need. Making the seismic shift from matching our children to a fantasy to matching our desires for them to who they actually are is what conscious parenting is really about. Instead of matching the child to the way, match the way to the child.

My clients Raphael and Tess constantly pushed their young son Gavin to meet goals he was incapable of achieving. Unique in temperament, Gavin was incapable of following the "normal developmental curve" of his peers. Teachers and school counselors were pressuring his parents to get him up to par.

Naturally, the home environment was rife with struggles and disharmony. The more the parents pushed, the more stubborn Gavin got. As he grew increasingly frustrated, the frequency of meltdowns at home and school rose exponentially. Inevitably the recommendation was put forward that he ought to be on medication. Needless to say, when this suggestion was made, the parents were distressed. What was the right path for their son? If they refused medication, would this place him at further risk? Not knowing where to turn and hoping for a different perspective, they came in for therapy.

When parents are burdened with high stress, as Raphael and Tess were, the way to begin is to de-stress. I explained that the pressure on Gavin to achieve the typical markers of development was driving the family to madness. Unless the energy in the home shifted, he was at risk for psychiatric problems. After all, no one can bear to live in a pressure cooker for long.

I asked the parents to back off from pressuring Gavin for a period of three months. I didn't advocate that they back off on their boundaries or schedules at home, just the emotional pressure they were putting on him. I also asked them to reevaluate their expectations of both their son and themselves.

As they continued in therapy, this couple began to see how they had been pressuring Gavin beyond his means. So caught up had they been in the goal of getting him to a different place that they had missed connecting to him where he was. As they began to understand who he was in the present moment as opposed to who he was "supposed" to be in the future, they began noticing remarkable changes— not only in Gavin, but in the atmosphere in their home. They eventually changed his school to one that provided an environment that's more of a match for who he *is*. To this day he remains medication-free.

But what could be so bad about wanting to raise a child to excel?

Have you noticed how many of our children grow up feeling anxious these days? Modern kids are so anxiety-ridden that diagnosing and medicating even very young children has become normal.

In addition to anxiety, depression is rife among children today— not only among teens but even among children in elementary school. When our young people carry the burden of having to be a certain way in order to please their parents, they can't help but feel a high level of anxiety. Instead of being free to develop naturally and spontaneously in alignment with their authentic being, they invest their efforts in a struggle to win their parents' approval and thereby earn their love. Such children are weighed down by pressure to mold themselves to meet their parents' and the culture's standards.

Can you imagine how it must feel to constantly believe you have to live up to someone else's idea of who you should be? If you are in touch with how this felt for you as a child, you can tap into that feeling. Perhaps you found ways to hide your true self from your parents, knowing that they would not be able to understand who you authentically were.

Recently my twelve-year-old daughter was sharing with me how she felt about a boy in her grade, her latest crush. Her friend was with us. I turned to her friend and asked, "How does your mother advise you when you discuss your crushes with her?"

She replied, "Oh, I could never talk about my crushes with her. She would never understand my feelings. She thinks I should not have a crush until I am eighteen." My heart opened up, not only to her, but also to her mother, as I realized that neither will experience the delicious connection that only a mother and daughter can share as they discuss matters of the heart.

The memory of another mother comes to mind, a client who bragged about her fourteen-year-old daughter, "I am so lucky that my daughter isn't interested in boys and is an A student. She is as mature as a twenty-year-old." When the daughter heard her mother say those words, her eyes grew wide in fear.

In the next session, I asked her why she had that look on her face. She replied, "My mother thinks I'm not interested in boys, and I cannot betray her. Please don't tell her that I discuss boys with you. She would die if she knew I had a boyfriend. She is dead set against it." I assured this girl not only that I would keep her secret, but that she was normal to have a crush at her age. Yet I could see the weight on her shoulders as she grappled with the notion that she was betraying her mother's idealized fantasy of her and therefore was a failure on some level.

Ask any child and they will freely express how much, excepting for appropriate boundaries, they resent being subjected to the dictates of their parents. Their inner spirit, which intuitively knows it should be self-governing, resents that it needs to match another's idea of its expression. It is this resentment that can lead the child to grow into a teen who rebels and withdraws from parental authority. The greater the mismatch, the greater the defiance and isolation. It is imperative for us as parents to realize how we create the abyss that stands between ourselves and our children.

The Tyranny of "Too"

As we saw in Gavin's case, the more we attempt to micromanage our children's progress, the more society encourages us to become dependent on "experts" to "fix" our children if their anxiety becomes overwhelming or if they aren't performing to a certain standard. Thus it has become completely normal for parents to harbor fears that something may be "wrong" with how their child is developing both socially and academically.

For instance, many parents find themselves asking whether their child is:

- *Too shy*
- *Too quiet*
- *Too precocious*
- *Too aggressive*
- *Too impulsive*
- *Too disengaged*
- *Too unmotivated*
- *Too carefree*
- *Too meticulous*
- *Too impressionable*
- *Too unfocused*
- *Too lazy*

I call this the "tyranny of 'too.'" These and countless other expressions of "too" are manifestations of parental worry, disappointment, and even guilt about failing to parent adequately. Underneath
all of it is fear.

Such concerns can be particularly acute if a family is confronting
a situation in which a child is veering out of control. During such
times, fear becomes alarm. I realize that only someone in a similar
situation can understand the feeling of utter helplessness—and often
of sheer terror—that parents experience. Unable to make sense of
what's happening, they feel desperately alone. This is especially true
if, whether just starting out in life or already a teen, a child seems to
be slipping away from the family.

Obviously it's appropriate to be concerned when a genuinely alarm-
ing issue arises. If you are unsure of what steps to take to rescue the
situation, it can be a wise move to seek help, reaching out to educators,
therapists, and sometimes psychiatrists. However, when children are
being raised in an awakened and conscious manner, situations such as
this should be the rare exception. When they become the norm, it's because they are being perpetuated by the parents' misguided approach.

The fact is, what was once the exception has become the norm precisely because modern society's obsession with our children's future
"success," defined according to how we think it should be defined, places
a huge burden on our young people to reach for impossible standards
and an unattainable level of excellence. Such a burden is psychologically
unhealthy for any child.

Listening to the radio one day, I heard about a parent who called
the dean of admissions at a prestigious university for advice on apply-
ing to the institution for their nine-year-old. Can you imagine the pressure this child must be feeling? Especially if the child later can't meet
the parents' expectations. This may seem like an extreme case, but it's
a window into the phenomenon of child-centric parenting that's currently wreaking havoc on the lives of many of our youngsters.

Many of the expectations we have of our children are unspoken.
Despite what we don't put into words, children intuitively sense
when we wish them to be other than they are—sense that we want
them to fulfill *our* fantasies of who they will grow up to be and what

they will accomplish. Yes, some children rise to this challenge and are successful. But for every child who does, there are a host of others who buckle under the pressure.

If children are unable to meet our ideal of who they should be, either because their inherent temperament doesn't allow it or because their innate desires are so fundamentally different, our disappointment can have a damaging impact on them. Countless children suffer from guilt, and in many cases live in a state of shame, because they are unable to perform to their parents' satisfaction. This can result in children looking for ways to rid themselves of the shame they feel about being inadequate. They may start being distracted at school, experiencing angry outbursts, or even turning their anger toward themselves in the form of some kind of self-harm.

When children experience such feelings, they can't help but create a disconnect within themselves. After all, imagine being constantly told that you are supposed to be different from the way you are. How would you feel? Quite naturally, you would be confused. Pretty soon this creates a barrier between you and your father or mother, causing a disconnect that, as they push ever harder for what they believe you need to do, can become so wide that it's all but impossible to repair.

If you take nothing else away from this book, this is the most fundamental lesson on becoming an awakened family: Placing expectations on your child instead of allowing the child's own natural inclinations to emerge spontaneously may well result in an emotional Grand Canyon between you and your child. As the gap widens, a flood of anxiety will rush in to fill it—anxiety not only for your child but also for yourself.

Is Parenting *Really* an Unselfish Act?

Another aspect of the myth that parenting is about the child is the way it leads us to believe that what we do for our children is selfless, and that therefore they should be appreciative.

While there are elements of selflessness in parenting, it isn't entirely accurate that we are being selfless when we raise children. In fact, little about the parenting journey is altruistic. It can be downright dangerous to tell ourselves we are being selfless, as it creates a feeling of righteousness on our part. We then parent from a mindset of being "right," which is devastating to a child's healthy self-development.

Rather than being a selfless act, bringing a child into the world tends to start out with a heavy dose of ego. The decision to have a child often springs from a desire to fulfill an inner longing on our part, which we imagine will be solved by the fantasy of what it will be like to have a family and to be a parent.

Of course, the culture doesn't think that the desire to have a family and be a parent has much to do with our ego. Far from it—it places a martyr's halo on parents, seducing them to imagine themselves ennobled by the act of birthing a child. It's this aspect of becoming a parent, which is a product of our ego, that leads to the feeling of owning a child. This is why we hear parents say, when an issue arises such as the harm done by spanking, "No one's going to tell me what I can or can't do with my child!"

Sadly for their children, many parents hold an unchecked belief that they can do to their child whatever they feel necessary, since they are after all being selfless. When the same child later revolts against parental tyranny, the parent feels victimized—as if they are being harmed by the child. They also expect society to pick up the pieces of their unconscious parenting, usually in the form of psychological help. The simple fact is that the nuclear family isn't a world to itself, and the outcome of a parent's actions affects a wide swath of other members of society. This is why it behooves parents to set aside their ego's beliefs about their entitlement to raise their children as they please and instead seek out the best information available to help them with this challenging task.

Children who feel the pressure to protect their parents from disappointment forsake their authentic voice in order to please them. This abandonment of their authenticity can have far-reaching implications, sometimes causing them to act waywardly. These negative implications can be avoided only if a parent is aware of how unselfless and obsessed with the fulfillment of the parental agenda much parenting truly is.

Changing our relationship to this myth is paramount if we are to alter the equation from one of power and control to love and true kinship. It's this shift that enables our children to break free of the burden of thinking they need to be "raised" or "fixed" by us. Liberated from such a burden, they will fly as high as they wish to—and reap the rewards they deserve.

Dare to Raise *Yourself* First

When we buy into the myth that parenting is about the child, we readily take credit for our wonderful parenting when our children match up to our expectations, whereas we just as readily place blame on them when they don't meet our expectations.

To parent consciously is to turn this approach on its head. The focus shifts to the parent as the one who needs to be "raised." In other words, we put *ourself* under scrutiny, not our children. This is because, as we saw earlier, most of us have been raised with a high degree of unconsciousness, which has resulted in emotional damage to our psyche. It is also because the one person we do have control over and can influence is ourselves. Parenting is often most effective when we concentrate on ourselves rather than our children. This is where the best results come from.

Plagued with their own issues and complexes around parenting, our own parents were misattuned to who we were as children. I regularly hear my adult clients describe their childhood by saying, "My mother just didn't see me for who I was," or "My father was constantly upset with me because I didn't turn out to be what he imagined." To be raised with a template of invalidation inevitably shapes the way we view the world. The inner lack we live with colors every experience. Despite being late into their thirties or forties, these clients still carry the memory of feeling rejected and invalidated, and consequently bring this insecurity into their present relationships.

Not being seen for who we are creates a hunger for validation, approval, and belonging. This inner void throbs with pain. When the pain we are in goes unattended, and perhaps even unnoticed, it grows. Pain begets more pain. Unconsciousness begets more unconsciousness. The pain is like wearing a second skin—so much so that we don't even realize it has become who we are. We just think, "This is what it means to be human."

It's important to be clear that the hurt we have experienced never goes away unless we address it directly by bringing it into our awareness. Only when we awaken to the fact that we are recreating childhood patterns can we begin to address the source of our present unhappiness.

This is where having a child comes in. As adults, and now parents ourselves, we find ourselves unexpectedly triggered by an experience with our own child. What's happening is that pain from our past is being reactivated. What we buried a long time ago because we didn't know how to deal with it now rises to the surface with all the furor of a starved animal that refuses to be in deprivation any longer. It's this residual pain that causes us to react in inappropriate ways, often without realizing we are doing so.

The most potent triggering we experience occurs in our closest relationships, especially those with our children. Conscious parenting stresses how our children act as a mirror for what we can't see about ourselves. They bring to the surface the pain we haven't processed but that's now causing us to react so strongly, and often irrationally, to their behavior. Unless we take seriously what they are showing us about how hurt we have been—and how we have never really faced up to this hurt—we will raise them to exhibit the same immature behavior that reflects our unresolved pain. This is the essence of the profound journey of parenting.

Instead of focusing on either actual or perceived flaws in our children, the real challenge is for us to take the lead in the process of transformation, fully owning that the way our children behave is a direct reflection of our own behavior. Instead of trying to "fix" our children, we are asked to turn inward and examine what in our own psyche needs to be resolved.

To get a better idea of what this entails, step with me into an imaginary parent-teacher conference. The teacher says, "Mrs. Davis, since your son could use more focus, I would recommend that you and your spouse undertake a three-month program in which you focus on what it means to be mindful. This program will help you to calm down, which will impact your child's emotional state."

Or picture the following: "Mr. Jones, I highly recommend that you consult with an organizational specialist so you can learn how to manage your time better and develop some organizational skills. I've noticed you have trouble getting to our school meetings on time, and it's become clear that your habits are impacting your child negatively. He appears to be getting lost in the chaotic state of your home life."

"But I am a conscious parent!" many clients respond, indignant at the suggestion that they may need to take responsibility for some of their children's behavior. "I'm calm most of the time, and I really try to be there for them."

Earnest in our desire to be seen as "good," most of us are desperate to defend our parenting. But it isn't a matter of being a "good" or "bad" parent, which are just labels. It's a matter of an ongoing awareness that our children constantly bounce off our energy, and therefore to "fix" our kids means we should first fix ourselves. Once parents see that consciousness isn't an identity but a *way of being*, they are able to understand that there's no such thing as perfect consciousness, only aspiration and ongoing development.

Conscious parenting is a practice, a daily commitment. It's not about the label and all about one's inner state of being. It asks us to notice where our attention is directed. Is it focused outward or inward? It's the constant calibration of our attention that differentiates a conscious parent from the rest. The conscious parent may make as many mistakes as any other, but the difference is that they are able to face those mistakes and then ask themselves, "What do these mistakes say about how I need to grow?"

Rather than turning our focus inward, we can't seem to help seeing our children as a project to fix and manage. They enter the room and we immediately judge their hair, their cleanliness, their shoes, or some other thing. They can be sitting quietly, busy with their work, and we barge into their space and begin micromanaging them and directing them. In our eyes we are being caring, whereas our children feel imposed on and intruded on. Our insatiable need to direct, encourage, improve, and manage ruins wonderful moments of potential closeness.

Isn't it interesting how parents tend to pounce on their children's negative behavior, but rarely find the good in their ordinary behavior? We are so primed to focus on our own negative behavior that we naturally do the same with our children.

I always ask parents, "What's the chief characteristic of your child's misbehavior?" They might say it's anger, disrespect, or anxiety. Most parenting advice focuses on combating such behavior directly. Instead, I challenge parents to focus on the antidote to this energy, which of course is found within themselves. I ask, "What's the antidote to the energy your child is exhibiting?" They might say it's cheerfulness, helpfulness, respect, or courage. I then tell them to highlight any behavior that matches this antidote and pay no attention to the other.

"But what if my child rarely displays such behavior?" parents often protest. I assure them that this is simply impossible. It's only when we view our children through fearful eyes often cloaked in worry about their future that we can't see how wonderful they are. Every child has at least a few moments in the day when they are respectful, calm, or whatever trait the antidote to their negative behavior might happen to be. The task of the vigilant parent is to spot these times and amplify them. Soon enough, the desirable behavior moves to the foreground, while the undesirable behavior fades away.

This isn't as simple as believing that merely focusing on something will change its expression. That isn't what this strategy is about. Instead, it speaks to how our own energy changes when we focus on behavior we wish to see versus behavior we don't care for.

When we focus on what we desire, our mental state changes. Our children sense when we are lighter, calmer, freer. Like a sunflower responding to sunlight by turning toward the sun, our children move toward us. Though it may be imperceptible at first, calling for trust on our part, the shift gets under way almost immediately. Slowly, the quality of our interactions in the home undergoes a shift. Instead of the constant conflict that results from our focus on negative behavior, we start celebrating each other and enjoying each other's company.

When we spend time each day in the heart-space of "being," it allows our children to feel that we are on their team as their partner, instead of their boss. Rather than saying, "You must do x, y, z," we might say, "I hear you, I see you, I want to help you. Can you help me to help you?" Instead of saying, "You are bad because of x, y, z," we say, "You must be feeling bad, huh? How can I change what I'm doing in order to better help you?"

How many times have you bombarded your child with questions as soon as they get in your car or come through the door after a long day of school? When they give you a monosyllabic response, you take it personally and feel rejected by them. You might not say anything right away, but you subconsciously tuck away this sense of hurt in your back pocket. After a few hours and some exhaustion, the smallest thing your child might say can enflame this buried sense of hurt and bring it to the foreground, leaving both of you wondering how you got to the boiling point so quickly. What if instead of asking a thousand questions and setting up your child and yourself for failure, you simply reached out, took their backpack from their weary shoulders, and gave them a backrub? If instead of seeking something from them, you became the giver, the comforter, the loving container? Wouldn't that change the dynamic instantly?

How many parents have endured hours of battle with their children that could have been resolved in no time at all had they only asked, "Can I change something about me to meet your needs? How can I be better for you?"

The irony is that the more ungrounded and insecure we are, the more insensitive, rigid, and righteous we are likely to become. This makes sense, doesn't it? After all, how can we be tuned in to our children when we are encaged by our own mental worries and fears? Attachment to our rigid and fearful ways always gets in the way of connection. By its very nature, life demands that we meet it "as is," without fixed expectations. Otherwise we'll surely be disappointed.

Our children come into our life to present us with an opportunity to raise ourselves, growing ourselves up. Thus every moment in the parenting process serves as a wake-up call for us. The promise of this awakening is great, as it helps liberate our children from the shackles of our expectations and empowers them to develop into their most authentic selves.

When we shift our focus to raising ourselves in the light of what our children's behavior is showing us about ourselves, not only do our children become free of our baggage, but we also lessen the burden of feeling that we have to constantly police them and manage their life for them. We come to see that this is an absolutely insane burden for anyone to bear. In this way, we begin to use the parenting process to at last put our past behind us and thereby break free from impossible expectations for our children's future.

~ Affirmations to Raise Oneself ~

I fully accept that parenting is about raising myself,
    not my child.

I realize that the onus for change lies solely with
    me, not my child.

I am aware that my struggles are reflections of inner
    conflicts.

I will transform each challenge into a question that
    asks, "What does this say about me?"

CHAPTER FIVE

Myth #2
A Successful Child
Is Ahead of the Curve

Y our child will be placed in the beginner ballet class," the secretary of the prestigious neighborhood ballet school informed me. I was thrilled.

"Great! She loves to dance and will be so excited," I enthused about my eight-year-old. Then the secretary explained in a hushed voice, "Just so you know, she will need to be in the class with mostly six-year-olds. I hope that's okay with her."

I thought I had misheard. "Six-year-olds?" I repeated. "No, you don't understand. She's eight. Isn't there a beginner class for eight-year-olds?"

The woman looked at me with sympathy as she patiently explained, "Most of our kids have been studying dance since they were in preschool. By the age of eight, they are very advanced. So if your daughter wishes to join our school, she will need to start with the younger ones." I was speechless. My daughter just wanted to dance. Was she already *two years* behind? How could this be?

Both as a mother and as a psychologist, the experience was an epiphany for me. While I had been engrossed in exposing my child to mud at the neighborhood park, along with cultivating her creativity by building tunnels out of cardboard in our living room, I had apparently failed to get in sync with the parental timetable subscribed to by my peers—a timetable that involves turning your child into a professional by the age of six.

I was to discover that Maia was behind the curve not only in her social activities, but also in her academics. While I had been feeling pleased with her exposure to "enrichment," which revolved around baking cookies and cutting bunny ears out of Play-Doh, my neighbors' children had been shuttling back and forth to tutoring classes such as Kumon and sign language. Their mothers had obviously read up on "how to raise a genius," while I had occupied my child with hours of nothingness.

How did fun and hobbies, which are so essential for the early developmental years, get turned into the pursuit of a profession? Why has childhood been reduced to a mad race to the front of the curve?

Agenda-Driven Fun

When my client Erin expressed her frustration about getting her son into pre-kindergarten, I thought she was surely being dramatic.

"I cannot believe how my child is expected to be a genius at the age of four! He has to pass ridiculous entrance exams and interviews, all to get into a pre-K? And one I pay $30,000 for?" she railed. "Not only is there pressure for him to get into the school, but because he was born in August and is what they call a late baby, I am being advised I should keep him behind a year. All my friends are telling me he is going to fall behind the curve and feel really insecure. They all look at me with pity when they hear that he's a summer baby. Apparently I missed the memo about when to conceive, because all the other mothers are timing sex with their husbands so they can produce the most eligible babies for kindergarten applications."

Although Erin was highly emotional, she wasn't saying anything that isn't true about this disturbing trend called "redshirting," where parents keep children behind a year, especially boys, so that they obtain an advantage over their peers in athletics and academics. In the affluent prep school circuit, they prefer more benign terms such as "reclassifying." The rationale parents give for holding back their children is that they don't want them to feel insecure or "lesser than."

Rationalizing their motives as being in the best interest of their child, parents feel justified in playing God with the system and contouring reality to meet what they think of as the "needs" of their child. Not those needs that are natural, but "needs" that are based on an artificial standard imagined by society, which the parent buys into. Maria Montessori, who espoused a mix of ages so that older children could help the younger ones, along with building resilience through failure, must be turning in her grave.

Parents enroll their children as young as two or three in activities that are supposed to be "fun" and "exploratory" but quickly turn competitive. Excessively supervised and overly trained, our children have become the subject of rigorous pursuit by an army of parents and teachers who are zealous about eradicating the wondrous aimlessness of childhood. Adult notions of order, organization, and optimization supersede the child's natural way of learning and developing.

How did parents decide that their two-year-olds need structured activities in order for their days to be fulfilling? Most days, I could barely decipher what my toddler liked. When I started asking parents outside schools and at playgrounds how they decided on an activity, school, or hobby for their kids, the following were some of the answers I received:

- *"It was a no-brainer for me. I firmly believe that preschool is the most formative time for children, so enrolling my kids in a private full-day preschool was worth it, even if the cost rivals my own college tuition."*

- *"I just decided for my daughter that she needed to play an instrument, so I picked one for her."*

- *"Every child should be involved in a sport, especially boys. I picked the sport I loved the most."*

- *"Sending my child to a private kindergarten would allow her to be preselected for a prestigious prep school and give her a distinct advantage for college."*

- *"I am an art teacher, so naturally I wanted my child to learn art."*

When parenting is less about the child and their experience of childhood, and more about the parents' idea of what childhood should be, we have leapt the tracks of what bringing up a child is really about.

As parents, we naturally feel pressure to have our child turn out well. Of course, this pressure didn't start with our generation. In previous ages, if you were the village cobbler, you wanted your son to become a cobbler who would be as good at mending shoes as yourself. The difference today is that we don't content ourselves with our child turning out "well." We want overachievers—an outstanding child we can show off to our family and friends, as well as on Facebook.

Perhaps you think you don't buy into the trophy child philosophy. However, each time you post a picture of your child winning a medal but don't post about them losing, you add to the myth of the overachieving child. The pressure to produce a child prodigy is so contagious that we are all drowning in it. Parents are anxious, teachers are stressed, and the children we are raising are moving further and further away from their authentic nature.

A friend who is a tennis coach at a private Manhattan club said to me, "I hate teaching kids you just know don't want to be there, but their parents push them. They have a miserable time, and I loathe having to teach them. It never really works anyway."

My daughter's cello teacher almost teared up when I told her, "I want my kid to love the process of learning the instrument. She doesn't need it for her résumé or a Ph.D. My only request of you is that you focus on the love of the process." As if I had reminded her of her own true love for the instrument, she exhaled a deep breath and confessed, "I appreciate your perspective. All I get is pressure from parents to turn their children into Yo-Yo Ma."

Pushing a child to succeed early is often entirely ego-driven by the parents, who want both validation of their parenting and a living, breathing trophy of their own success as parents for all to see. The ego isn't ultimately concerned with the child's authentic nature, only with the way the child is viewed by others. For the child, this can create isolation and anxiety, the exact opposite of what parents think they are creating. Living in a pressure cooker of overzealous competitiveness does nothing to draw our children closer to us. Our children pick up on the anxiety we feel, absorbing and internalizing it, which leads them to believe the world is a stressful place. The consequences range from sleep issues to migraines and stomach pain. Children as young as six and seven are having panic attacks. Some children as young as eight find themselves labeled "oppositional defiant," while increasing numbers at all ages are being given a diagnosis of ADHD or some other disorder. While many symptons are organic, some of them are enflamed due to a parenting approach based on a fear of the future instead of a trust in the present moment.

The Curve Shows Up Everywhere

Many parents are seduced by the notion that a child's worth is measured by their performance. For a child to be ahead of the curve is seen as the measure of good parenting. As our children grow, the pressure to be ahead becomes even fiercer. Witness the number of "gifted and talented" schools in New York City alone.

As children move into middle school, many parents angle for extracurricular recognition and the scholarship opportunities that come with a child being a star performer in sports, the arts, chess, or debate. It's like turning your child into a racehorse you're betting on as a winner. You start to equate your child with the financial opportunities they might have in the future.

I shared with you what my daughter faced when she wanted to dance. The response she received concerning her age didn't dampen her desire to dance. But in all too many cases this is exactly what happens when we turn what should be enjoyable into a serious business. I think of a fourteen-year-old client of mine who decided he wanted to join the tennis club at his school. He had fallen in love with the sport while attending a professional match. His hope was that he would develop the acumen to compete with his team. When he tried out for the tennis club, he was told he wasn't qualified because he was a beginner. His mother was furious. "What do you mean, he's not qualified?" she demanded of the coach. "Is this a club, or is it the try-outs for Wimbledon?"

The coach sheepishly explained that in order to be in the club, students needed to have been playing the sport for at least three or four years. "He simply won't be able to keep up," he advised the mother. "Most of these kids have been competing since they were eight or nine." That was the end of my client's desire to learn tennis. He dropped the idea and refused to try again, even when his mother offered to start him in a program with group lessons. As she watched her son's enthusiasm for the game wane, she felt at a loss.

In no area does the pressure to be ahead of the curve show up more forcefully than in academics, often with adverse consequences. One of the brightest seventeen-year-olds I know suffered for years from severe acid reflux. Stella's condition had recently worsened into ulcers and cysts. Doctors rightly told her it was stress-related. The academic bar had been set so high that a score of 98 percent disappointed her. The physiological backlash was immediate. Her identity was so caught up with being the star pupil that she couldn't tolerate the anxiety of being anything other than the brightest and best. Indeed, if she couldn't be perfect, she believed she was a failure. Do you see how being ahead of the curve ultimately meant nothing, because she was an emotional mess as a result of trying to handle all the pressure?

Because Stella was at the top of her class, acing almost every test, naturally everyone imagined that her success came easily. They also thought her parents were lucky to have such a studious daughter. Little did they know what Stella confided in me about her academic achievements. "Do you think it's easy for me to get 100 percent on a test?" she asked one day. "When I see a score of 100, I groan inside myself. I hate it. There's no chance to enjoy the fact I did well, because immediately there's pressure on me to repeat this on the next test."

Referring to the fact that her parents had become concerned about her health, she continued, "Naturally, my parents are worried now. They know it's partly their fault. They were the ones who pushed me to excel when I was a child. They just didn't realize I would take it to such an extreme."

Stella is like millions of other children who feel that their entire sense of worth depends on the grades they get, whether they are accepted for college, and which college they are invited to attend. When the plan doesn't work out, they fall apart. How sad that our children learn to define themselves with superficial identities, not realizing that they don't need to borrow an identity at all because they already have one of their very own.

The Double-Edged Sword of "Reaching for One's Potential"

The word "potential" is a double-edged sword. While it sounds, well, full of potential, there's a danger in using it without understanding its underlying implications. To many people, potential means "you are not worth a damn yet."

When we tell a child they aren't reaching their potential, we are communicating that who they are at the present moment not only isn't who they can be, but more pointedly isn't who they "should" be. Again, instead of focusing on the abundance of grace present in our children in the here and now, we focus on the promised land of to-morrow, fixated on an idea we hold of who they should become that's based on nothing but our fantasy.

I cannot emphasize enough that while everyone can improve themself if they wish to, this isn't the same as the notion of having a certain "potential," which serves only to send a child down a slippery slope that starts and ends in the parents' own head. When this is the parents' mind-set, it leads them to undermine their children's spontaneous expression of themselves in the present moment. Who the child actually is currently is negated as inconsequential in comparison with who the child will be in an imagined future that the parents regard as all-important.

Think about this in the context of your own life. Imagine you are preparing dinner for a group of friends. You plan the menu meticulously and prepare the meal with your heart and soul. Most of your friends gush about how good the food is—except for one, whose feedback is given somewhat reticently. You wonder what's wrong. Doesn't she appreciate your food? Finally, this guest blurts out, "I can see you tried to make us a good meal. But I honestly have to say I don't think you lived up to your potential." How would this make you feel? Motivated to cook again? Delighted to hug this friend? No, you feel upset, and would think twice before inviting her over again.

When I appeared on *Oprah's Lifeclass*, one of my comments during the show touched many, and subsequently I received a lot of e-mails about it. I talked about how I was sure I would go back home and watch a rerun of the episode, almost certain that I would admonish myself for not expressing myself as well as I should have. I would critique myself for not being good enough and failing to live up to my potential. However, I went on to say that I knew beyond all doubt that I was doing the best I could with the consciousness I possessed at that moment. Because I was in touch with the fact that I was trying my best, I knew I could counter the inner critic that would surely make its voice heard in due course.

I can almost hear you protesting, "Well, what if you hadn't prepared adequately? What if you hadn't tried your best? How would you react then?"

Although a conscious approach takes into consideration the past, it's very much a present-moment experience. Because of this, it doesn't allow us to stay stuck in shame or guilt for our past lapses in awareness. Instead, ever focused on the now, it challenges us to ask ourselves, "What were my inner obstacles to getting prepared? How can I own responsibility for not having put in the effort? What can I do in the present moment to change my destiny?"

An introspective moment like this can awaken us to our motivation for what we do, enabling us to discover whether we are really in touch with our heart's desires, in which case we need to act on them, or whether we are perhaps unconsciously engaging in self-sabotage. In other words, we own that we have a choice. Either we can mope about what's happened, or we can decide to do things differently from now on. Coming face-to-face with ourselves in this way, we might say to ourselves, "I've learned from this experience. My lack of effort was in the past. This is now. What can I do in the present to ensure I maintain an aware state?" With this perspective, there is no real failure, only an opportunity for us to further evolve.

Each of us longs not only to be validated but also to be hono[r] who we are at this moment right now. When who we actually are feels unseen and unheard because we are constantly being compared with some external standard, such as someone else's notion of our potential, we feel frustrated and, if it continues, resentful. Our children especially feel hurt and diminished when we fail to see them for who they are. For this reason it's important for us to examine whether we impose our expectations on our children and, by doing so, take them out of the present moment and into a disconnected state of wanting to be someone other than who they are.

The "Unpotentialized" Child

Do you know how your children actually feel about the various aspects of their lives? Are you sure? The fact is, most parents don't.

Take nine-year-old Marcus, who began picking his skin. It became such a habit that his parents brought him to me for therapy. They described him as a gifted child who sadly was unable to reach his potential.

But how did Marcus feel? He described his life in these words: "I'm cursed because I'm gifted. Everyone keeps telling me I'm gifted, but I don't even know what it means. I hate being gifted. I always feel like I'm not good enough. Everyone wants me to be better at things because I'm gifted, but I don't know how to be better. My life sucks."

It wasn't just Marcus who was conflicted about his talents. His parents were even more conflicted because his teachers were constantly sending notes home complaining, "Marcus didn't try hard enough today," or "We know Marcus can do better." In other words, the parents were being made to feel like *they* weren't reaching for *their* potential as parents by challenging their son more.

As we also saw earlier in the case of Stella's parents, countless families experience what this family does. Believing they need to "optimize" their children, they feel guilty if they don't push them—all because of a deeply ingrained fear-driven idea that we need our children to reach for imaginary "potential."

The idea of living up to one's potential needs to be redefined. Instead of seeing potential as future-oriented, involving who our children will become, we need to break the word down into its components, getting at the root meaning. The word "potent" lies at the heart of the word. Potency isn't futuristic, but refers to the power our children already possess that will propel them into a better tomorrow. Anything that will come later is founded in what's already abundant in a child, not on something we are trying to instill. Look up the word "potency" and you will find synonyms such as "vigor," "capacity," "energy," "might," and "moxie." Each of these speaks to the abundance of vitality a child possesses in the here and now. So if we wish to emphasize a child's potential, we need to focus on the child's *inherent* powers right here, right now, not on wishful thinking about what they might someday "become."

When it comes to living in the now, young children are gurus. Perhaps it's their lack of language, especially in the first few years of life, that allows them to immerse themselves in reality, body and soul. Their ability to be in this moment now, detached from "what was" and "what might be," with all their fearful "what ifs," is a sharp reminder to us of how to engage life in the time zone in which we actually find ourselves.

When we shift from defining potential as something in the future and move into the recognition of each child's potency in the here and now, we become aware that every child is both gifted and ordinary at the same time. Perhaps we have a visceral reaction to being average or ordinary, with the thought conjuring up deeply entrenched feelings of inadequacy. Our Western culture especially wants every child to feel "special." This is quite unlike many Eastern cultures, where being unique and different is anathema. However, we need to realize that such extremes are dangerous for our children. As both stem from the ego, they fail to take into account *who our children actually are*.

Our children don't possess just one quality, but are forever and fluidly capable of many expressions, including giftedness and ordinariness. Since this is the case, they need to be free to express themselves without feeling encumbered by pressure to please us. I tell parents, "Yes, your child is unique and should be treated as special by you, but in the world your child needs to be treated just like the others."

Many parents are indignant when their child doesn't receive the red carpet treatment, but I always say, "Your child is fine being ordinary. It's your own sense of lack that needs them to be labeled extraordinary. They don't have this need—your ego does."

When we can embrace the present moment as mighty and full of moxie, we don't feel a need to project into the future. Stripped of our desperation to create the "future version" of our child, we can bask in their present. Imagine how a child feels knowing that their parents see them as just fine, instead of lacking in some way.

Sadly, this way of viewing children isn't the way of the world. This conscious approach to parenting requires an inordinate amount of courage, along with steadfastness in the face of opposition from family, friends, and the culture, as we constantly measure and compare ourselves according to impossible external standards.

When parents complain to me, "But it's so hard to be the only parent who doesn't focus on grades and doesn't push their kid," I tell them I fully understand those pressures. Then I explain that if they want to raise an authentic spirit, they need to be willing to go against the crowd. Instead of abiding by society's dictates concerning how their child should be raised, they should attune themselves to the spirit of their particular child, for it's here that all the answers lie.

Putting Things in Perspective

I like to think about our parental priorities in terms of a hand on which each finger represents an important aspect of child development. I allocate external accomplishments such as grades, achievements in sports, and the like to the pinky finger. The other four fingers represent connection—first to self, then to family, next to community, and lastly to a purpose. Sadly, we spend too much time bolstering the pinky finger as if it was the entire hand of life, ignoring the vital role of our other fingers.

It was this understanding that led me not to sign up my daughter for a single structured activity until the age of six. My friends warned me she would be behind everyone else, and I knew they were right. I replied that while Maia might be too late for the world stage they all wanted their children to star on, the timing was perfect in terms of developing the emotional resilience that would enable her to enjoy a meaningful life. "My child first needs to get a grounded sense of who she is, not who I might like her to be, before I sign her up for a string of activities," I explained. "I will wait for this sense to emerge within her. When it does, I'll take direction from her."

This approach is so different from that of a family I met while sitting on a plane flying to California from New York. The man and woman next to me had an adorable six-month-old baby boy. Getting into a conversation with them, I learned that both were police officers who had met on the job. The man said to me, "Boy, I had no idea kids are so much work. I'm so used to being in control, this has been a really hard adjustment."

"Wait till he grows up," I responded. "Now is the easy part."

"I'm leaving this part to my wife," he said. "She's into this bonding stuff. This is the part she enjoys. I'm waiting for him to grow up so I can do stuff with him I enjoy."

"Which is what?" I asked.

"Oh, play baseball," he said matter-of-factly. "My brother and I played baseball every single weekend, and I can't wait to do this with my son."

"I hope he likes baseball," I said. "But what if he doesn't?"

Speechless, he stared at me as if he had never even considered such an absurd idea.

"It does happen, you know," I said. "Just because he's a boy doesn't necessarily mean he'll be into sports."

"My son? Ah, that's never going to happen. In my family, we've been into sports for generations. Baseball is in his genes."

I looked at the little boy resting contentedly on his father's lap, oblivious of the fact that his fate had been decided for him. Not yet half a year old, he had already been defined as a sportsman by his father— and a baseball player at that—whom he undoubtedly would wish to please and be disappointed if he couldn't.

When we step back and wait for our children's inner being to show itself, we give them the inestimable gift of developing self-awareness. This allows them to accept themselves exactly as they are. Confident in who they find themselves to be, they take charge of what they want to do with their life. Because they bring their own internal guideposts to bear on each and every situation, they enjoy ownership of their choices.

This is particularly important when it comes to the one topic that arises in therapy more than any other—discipline. The traditional approach espouses all sorts of techniques and strategies to control our children's behavior. Of course, the focus is on getting them to a certain place by pushing them. Instead of supporting our children in the discovery of their capacity for self-governance, we admonish with sticks or reward with carrots, believing that fear or enticement will eventually help them to internalize right from wrong. In my book *Out of Control*, I spell out how discipline has become another means of controlling our children. In so doing, it has lost its original intent of teaching them through wise guidance.

Instead of reaching for the next disciplinary intervention, we need to turn our children's attention inward, helping them attune themselves to their feelings and motivations. As they grow in alignment with their inner being, they will begin to take greater ownership of their choices. When their choices are their own, it creates a ripple effect. Because we pave the way for them to make decisions for themselves, within reasonable limits, they naturally develop self-authorship. This movement from external to internal control allows them to think through their choices instead of being bullied into compliance by us.

Seeing us as their stalwart supporters, our children lean on us in a healthy way, seeking us out for our kinship and at times to act as their sounding board. This strengthens the connection we share with them, which bolsters their confidence and self-worth. The ripple effect expands outward as their belief in their value fuels creativity, initiative, and a feeling of empowerment. All of these positive effects emerge from a single decision on the part of the parent—to let go of our projections of who our children should be and allow them to discover what it means for them to be authentic.

The idea of getting ahead of the curve proclaims that being better and more accomplished, as defined by someone else, leads to success and happiness. But it doesn't. It guarantees neither love nor security. On the other hand, it can be a surefire path to a severe loss of self, accompanied by a diminishment of the entirely natural confidence enjoyed by a person who knows and loves who they are.

~ Affirmations to Create a New Curve ~

I dare:

* To redefine success as measured less by achievement and more by spirit.

* To allow my child to develop an ownership of life, taking their lead on what interests and motivates them.

* To allow my child to enjoy childhood with as few impositions on their time and space as possible.

* To expose my child to fun and spontaneous hobbies without turning them into competitive events.

* To teach my child that the only curve they need to follow is the one that emanates from their own spirit.

* To let my child be average.

CHAPTER SIX

Myth #3
There Are Good Children and Bad Children

We have all been influenced by fairy tales and cultural messages that tell us some children are "good" and some "bad." When I conduct workshops around the world, I often ask parents to define these terms. Inevitably they come up with similar lists.

Society considers "good" children those who don't stir the pot too much and who preferably have good manners and self-control. Good children are those who are obedient and studious, able to sit still and pay attention. In other words, when we look closely, we see that a child's "goodness" is measured by how easily the child's behavior fits into *our* life. Similarly, children are labeled "easygoing" because they make *our* life easy. Children who "go with the flow" are praised because they go along with *our* flow. It's natural that we would find compliant children easier to be with. This is why, often without realizing it, we gravitate to those children who don't challenge our ways or our deeply ingrained beliefs. We love "good" children because they allow us to feel in control. Since they don't force us to face uncomfortable issues, we reward them with preferential treatment.

In contrast to the "good" child, those children we consider "bad" are hyperactive, distracted, loud, and often defiant. When such a child doesn't conform, things can turn ugly. Children who "don't listen," hit, or show "disrespect" find themselves punished. Violent behavior is never appropriate and needs to be addressed immediately by the parent. However, stamping out this kind of behavior is often-times done in extreme ways that cause resentment and further acting out. Of course, the reason parents often overreact like this is that their child's behavior fails to honor their agenda or disrupts their sense of order.

Children as young as age one are expected to "behave properly." By the time they reach two, even the fact of being two is seen as a problem, which is why we label this age "terrible." Small children are made to feel as if their normal development, expressed at times in resistance, tantrums, and even outright defiance, is an inconvenience and therefore something to feel ashamed of.

While "good" and "bad" are the typical descriptors of our children's behavior, they aren't the only ways in which we label them. Because the ego is constantly categorizing, we have many labels, based partly on a child's behavior but also to a large extent on how they make us feel about ourselves. Labels such as "lazy," "sweet," or "shy," for example, have the potential to wear heavily on a child who hasn't yet formed a solid sense of self.

No doubt each of us remembers a label from our own childhood— one we wear around our neck like a noose, allowing it to choke us with shame years after it was given. Elena, one of my adult clients, revealed how she still remembers being called "Miss Piggy" by one of her mother's friends. She's still haunted by the shame she felt back then. Sadly we hold on to negative labels for decades, while quickly discarding the more life-affirming things said about us. The reason this happens is that our innate sense of worth has been undermined from such a young age that shame feels immediately familiar, allowing our psyche to absorb it without thinking. If instead we were raised by parents who were conscious, shame doesn't stand a chance to establish itself in our emotional foundation. When shameful comments are then projected onto us by others, we are able to discard them from awareness easily because we don't recognize them as familiar.

Just the other day, my daughter, Maia, told me her friends were making fun of how she wore yoga pants to school every day, instead of the latest brands. Her response to them was, "I don't care about your opinions of me. I love yoga pants." Had she been even slightly insecure about her appearance and fashion sense, their comments would have pierced her heart and made her feel ashamed about herself. Instead, she was able to see that her friends' comments were just their opinions and had no bearing on how she needed to dress. This is how having a sturdy inner foundation is key to warding off the unconscious projections of others.

As we were all raised largely with shame and insecurity as inner templates, labels and judgments from others carry great weight for us. The way a child is labeled by society not only affects the child but also can have an enormous impact on the parents. For instance, if a child is labeled "uncooperative" by a teacher, and the teacher complains to the parents that they need to get their child under control, the parents feel pressure to fix their child. They may even be advised to seek treatment.

Jamie still remembers how disenfranchised she felt when her son's teacher told her that her son wasn't going to succeed in life unless he was put on medication and in behavior therapy. Feeling dismal about her son's prospects, she blamed herself, thinking she was ineffective as a mother. When she brought twelve-year-old Adam for therapy, I saw a completely different picture. A bright and energetic boy, Adam had a physical need for movement and exercise. He admitted to having a hard time sitting still, but he rightly protested, "I get good enough grades. My parents are happy with them. I'm on two sports teams. I just get really bored when I sit too long. Is that a crime?"

Adam was right to feel indignant. Tired of teachers constantly admonishing him for his high energy, he had even thought about home-schooling. "It's just not fair. I do better than most of my friends, but it's me who gets into trouble because I can't pay attention or because I doodle in my book." Adam is one of many boys who, helpless to advocate for themselves, feel resentful about the labels that are slapped on them by their teachers. They long to be seen simply as they are, without any of these derogatory labels.

While our children may be lacking in certain skills and need help to obtain them, it's detrimental for anyone to presume that they can define a child's temperament with a label, especially when that label involves the word "good" or "bad." When our children's teachers fall into this kind of unconscious thinking, it's up to us to step into the role of advocates. Inevitably, having to do this causes many of us to revisit the inadequacy we felt as students ourselves in the school system. In the same way a child feels nervous and scared of disapproval when called into the principal's office, we have similar feelings, which can paralyze us instead of spurring us to talk frankly with our children's teachers.

As Jamie began to get in touch with her own inner insecurity, she was able to clearly see why she had been so hooked by the teacher's comments. As she began to unhook from her inner vulnerability, she was able to teach her son not to identify with the labels imposed by the culture around him. Since Adam was already trying to do this, he responded quickly, emerging confident in himself, accepting that he was different but not limited. Jamie slowly helped him to channel his high energy more appropriately, shifting from shaming and blaming to celebrating her son's vibrancy.

Every parent is plagued by the desire for approval from society, especially our children's teachers. When our children are viewed unfavorably, we feel personally maligned. Alternatively, we may feel ashamed of our parenting skills or angry at our children for not falling into line. Either way, the pressure from external sources skews our ability to connect to who our children really are and help them develop the skills they need to grow into their authentic selves.

Is It Defiance or Defensiveness?

A child who is willful, stubborn, and defiant challenges us to evaluate our beliefs. Of course, it's easier to label a child than to question our assumptions. When children cause us to confront ourselves, we like to put them in time-out corners and on naughty stools.

Ironically, many of these children aren't even all that willful or defiant. It's just that they are strong, and their strength of spirit collides with ours. Much of the time the problem is that, locked in our ego as we are so much of the time, it is we who are unwilling to back down when rightfully challenged. Because the culture has assigned power in the parent-child relationship to the supposedly all-knowing parent, the child is the one who gets labeled and punished.

Mika, a boisterous thirteen-year-old, was always in trouble for being "too loud" or "defiant." The more her parents punished her to try to squash her spirited manner, the more her resistance escalated. When they brought her for therapy, it was because their home life had reached a crisis point. Mika was hanging out with the wrong crowd at school and precociously experimenting with behavior that was beyond her emotional development.

After I worked with her family for a few months, it became clear to me that Mika was a child who felt disenfranchised and emotionally unmet. Both of her parents had strict rules concerning right and wrong. Because these worked well for their younger son, John, they assumed their rules must be correct. Consequently Mika found herself constantly admonished for not following the rules like her brother. It didn't occur to the parents that the difference in the two children's reaction to such rules lay in the fact John was temperamentally more timid and even somewhat docile. Or perhaps he had just learned to be more easygoing after observing how his parents treated his older sister.

When Mika's parents came to understand her need to be heard and validated, they altered their approach. They first modified their understanding of her behavior. Instead of seeing her as defiant, they now realized that she was defending herself. Just this small shift in perspective allowed them to work with her in a whole new way. Now they couldn't just pin all the blame on her but instead had to ask themselves, "Why does our child feel the need to be so defensive? What can we do to help her?" As they examined their part, they were able to release her from the burden of being "the defiant one."

Seeing Mika's actions in a different light enabled her parents to reframe her behavior. Instead of punishing her for pushing the boundaries, they learned to interpret this as a desire to be autonomous. Instead of reacting to her with admonishments such as "Don't act like that!" or "You need to stop your bad behavior!" they became aware of her need for self-governance. They said things like, "We can see how you feel stifled by our rules right now. Let's sit down together and find ways to reach common ground. We don't want you to feel controlled by us any more than we want to feel we can't speak from our heart." As Mika saw that they were more open to her need for self-empowerment, she gradually let go of her defenses and opened up to them.

As Mika's parents decreased their demands, she in turn decreased her pushback. As they backed off, she began to pull in. I often describe this energy as a dance, wherein one partner leads for a bit while the other follows. The leader isn't necessarily a superior dancer, just the one who is leading for the moment. Both parties are needed for the dance to succeed, but both dancers can't take the lead at the same time. One has to surrender to the other as much as the other has to lead with clarity.

When parents see that their children want to take the lead, they need to heed the call to back off and let go a bit. This doesn't mean they indulge their children, only that they recognize how their own energy is creating more chaos than clarity. Clashing head-on with their children's energy only exacerbates situations.

Mika's parents were surprised by how tiny shifts in their energy brought about huge changes in their relationship with her. The more opportunity they gave her to have a voice and the more they validated her feelings, the less she felt the need to express herself in risky ways. It was eye-opening for these parents to understand that their daughter wasn't "bad" when she didn't comply, but that she was in fact inordinately clear-minded and powerful. The parents' change of approach altered the entire family dynamic, moving it to a far more harmonious state.

When our children enter our life, we expect them to simply fall in line. If a child's temperament allows this, we are pleased with the result and credit our parenting skills. However, many a child's temperament doesn't allow them to conform in the way we might like. Such children have an inherent drive to stand up for themselves and take charge of their life. Parents are often ill-prepared for them. Labeled as behaving "badly," they grow up feeling that they are the problem. This leads to unnecessary shame and insecurity in such young people.

Children who test boundaries, break rules, and generate disorder often feel unheard and unmet in some way. When parents train themselves to interpret such behavior as a cry for a deeper connection, they are able to step away from the role of disciplinarian and instead become their children's champions.

Double Standards

When we focus on children's behavior as a measure of goodness or badness, we do them a huge disservice. Imagine a friend telling you that you forgot their birthday because you are thoughtless or were being mean to them. Or picture your spouse calling you "bad" and a "mess" because you were tired and took a nap before doing the dishes.

The fact is, we expect more of our children in terms of their behavior than we ever demand of ourselves, our spouse, or our friends. Talk about double standards! When our children slip up, some of us are quick to call them names, sometimes labeling them in the most degrading ways. When they fail to obey us, we reprimand them. When they forget their lunchbox, homework, or permission slip, we act like it's the end of the world. We forget all the times we've lost our keys, failed to return a phone call, or missed a deadline ourselves.

This double standard has a huge effect on our children. If we are honest with ourselves, we recognize that we make mistakes and poor decisions all the time. Yet when our preteens and teens do the same, we believe their actions are unconscionable. When we turn in a bill too late, forget to pay our credit card, or get a speeding ticket, we rationalize that we were stressed. Yet if our children turn in an assignment late, don't study sufficiently for an exam, or get a detention slip, we panic. The reality is, we're terrified that if they don't meet all the expectations of being "good," they will fail in life. We imagine that if they were truly as "good" as they could be, they would always achieve their best. All of this is nothing but our fear raising its ugly head, driving us to behave not only irrationally but also extremely unfairly.

No matter the issues we face, we parents need to ask ourselves, "How can I change the conditions in the home to help my daughter age her distractibility?" or "How can I embody more stillness in our daily life so that my son learns how to be focused?" These are questions truly worth wrestling with. They have the power to totally change the dynamic we experience with our children.

As we grow in consciousness, we see the importance of moving away from labels such as "good" and "bad." Instead of focusing on compliance and obedience, as well as how our kids make us look or feel, we begin to focus on matters such as these:

- *Did my child express themself freely?*

- *Did my child listen to their inner voice?*

- *Did my child focus on their own needs and find ways to meet them?*

- *Did my child dare to make mistakes and find ways to correct them?*

- *Did my child feel safe to tell the truth without fear of shame?*

- *Did my child follow their heart without interference from me or others?*

When we shift our emphasis away from external appearances and instead promote authentic self-expression, reprimands and admonishment are replaced by meaningful connection with our child's spirit. Instead of focusing on how to correct behavior, we become mindful of the feelings behind the behavior, secure in the awareness that once the feelings are recognized and expressed, the behavior will take care of itself.

In other words, when we let go of the duality of good and bad, along with the fear connected with these labels, we enter into the beautiful present with our children. We enjoy a real relationship with them.

∼ Shifting from "Goodness" to Authenticity ∼

Instead of:

* Obsessing over conformity, perfect behavior, and outward appearances, I will encourage genuineness in my child.

* Praising compliance, I will praise the courage to be authentic.

* Demanding obedience, I will encourage self-expression.

* Defining my child's future based on her performance, I will define it based on the strength of her spirit.

CHAPTER SEVEN

Myth #4
Good Parents Are Naturals

Perhaps because becoming a parent is linked to our biology, we believe it's a natural phenomenon. It has been seen as part of the fabric of life, without much thought given to its long-term consequences. However, were we to connect the dots in terms of how unconsciously raising a child has devastating effects both for one's own family and for society, we would realize how naïve it is to imagine that we are just naturally equipped to be parents.

I have often wondered why parenting courses aren't mandatory. After all, to marry you need a license, driving a car requires passing a test, to be a hairdresser involves training, and getting a job involves interviews. So why does becoming a parent take nothing more than two consenting adults engaging in an act of sexual intimacy?

If any aspect of life demands the highest ability to stay present, grounded, and emotionally regulated, it's parenting. These skills, among others, can be taught, but they can be integrated into our behavior on a long-term basis only when a certain degree of consciousness is present.

Take the act of yelling, for example. Every parent knows they shouldn't yell at their children. Despite knowing this, all parents are guilty of it at times. Why? Because knowing something intellectually is very different from integrating it into one's life. The former takes knowledge, whereas the latter requires wisdom and practice. Parenting requires know-how in tools and strategies on the one hand, and a certain degree of emotional maturity to implement them in an effective and empowering manner on the other. In short, parenting involves a lifelong commitment to changing and growing on a moment-by-moment basis.

Or perhaps because becoming a parent is often linked to our relationships with spouses or partners, it's seen as private and therefore out of the realm of regulatory control. Maybe because it's something people have been doing for eons, we regard it as one of those things we just know how to do. However, it's misguided to imagine that parents should instinctively know what to say, what to do, and how they should feel with respect to their children at any given moment. It's equally mistaken to imagine that parenting is something that's easy, fun, and rewarding. While some aspects of parenting are indeed all of those things, I believe this widespread cultural idea places considerable stress on parents.

Moving from the Fantasy of Parenting to Reality

Mothers especially romanticize what it means to be a mother. We imagine blissful days breast-feeding our infant or spending hours painting masterpieces with our toddler. With our older children, we imagine with blithe equanimity their roller-coaster moods and hormonal swings. Dads too fantasize about all the things they'll teach their children, looking forward to the day their children will grow up and make them proud—as we saw in the case of the father who was certain his son would want to play baseball.

Not only do many of us imagine that having a child will be the most beautiful experience of our life, but we may even see it as a way to right the wrongs and disappointments of our own past. We don't realize the extent to which, in reality, raising a child is hugely challenging. There are decisions to be made every day—decisions that often leave us feeling confused, if not overwhelmed. Is our toddler's bruise just a bruise or a broken arm? Is our teen's refusal to go to soccer practice something she needs to push through, or is it coming from her deeper self, which means she should quit?

You may wonder, "Will I ever get to enjoy my child as I was promised I would?" This is especially the case when our children don't turn out to be anything like what we imagined. What if we don't know how to connect with them or plain don't understand them? What if their temperament clashes with ours? What if they aren't like we were as children? It isn't a given that parent and child will naturally like each other, let alone enjoy each other. Genes don't carry such a guarantee.

When the gap between our fantasies and reality becomes too wide, it can feel as though our world is crashing down on us. When we encounter the hardships of the parenting journey and realize how unprepared we are for its twists and turns, we may feel we are in a no-man's-land. Why didn't anyone warn us? Why didn't anyone tell us that this journey would not only require us to have physical super-powers such as going without sleep for the first few years, but also demand an advanced degree in Buddha-like wisdom? Given the shock of how much our life needs to change to meet this challenge, we may feel ripped off. As one fantasy after the other gets knocked down, our ego takes the beating of a lifetime.

I can still remember the mighty fantasies I harbored pre-parenthood. I envisioned myself as holier-than-thou, placed on a pedestal of superiority, raising children who were nothing short of prodigies. My fantasy children would pull me through the Louvre begging to see more paintings. Of course, they would also be keen meditators and yogis, clamoring for me to teach them about spirituality.

When I finally became a parent and realized that none of these fantasies was going to come true, I saw how truly ill-prepared I was for this journey. The only mother I was equipped to be was the mother of my fantasy. I didn't know how to be the mother to the child before me.

If only I had been informed that the early years of parenthood would involve a tremendous learning curve during which I would experience immense psychological, physical, and financial strain. I thought I was the only one who felt this way. The shame that ensued ricocheted through me, causing me to isolate myself and hide what I was experiencing. I chalked it up to being inadequate as a mother, if not totally unsuited for this daunting responsibility. I had no idea that what I was going through was normal and that my experiences were commonplace.

The bubble of idealism that mothers especially like to imagine themselves in because they are so afraid to be seen as limited has got to burst. It's time we shared our experiences in an honest way, allowing the next generation of parents to enter this journey appropriately prepared for what it requires.

The fact is, *parenting is not natural.* It isn't something we are just going to know how to do. There's a misguided notion that parenting is linked to morality—that if you are a good person, you will be a good parent. If only it were so simple. Being a good parent has nothing to do with how nice or good we are as people. Parenting is a skill that takes years to acquire. Just as physical fitness requires a daily commitment to being aware of our thoughts concerning food, along with disciplining ourselves to exercise consistently, so it is with parenthood. We need to make prospective parents aware of the depth of this commitment so they harbor no illusions about the hard work it takes to raise children consciously.

Instead of being told that being a parent is second nature, it would be more helpful if we were told that it would feel like entering a foreign country where no one speaks our language. Rather than assuming we will experience an instant connection to our child and great love, we need to know that building the foundation for connection and learning to love takes time, can be messy, and involves emotional roller coasters along with moments of hair pulling.

Prospective parents would benefit from knowing that our children don't come into our world to make us feel good about ourselves, but that they will do just the opposite much of the time.

Even when a second or third child enters a family, each addition requires the parent to divest themselves of assumptions based on their experiences with their earlier children, because what worked for one child may not work for the next. Neither will what may have worked in our own childhood necessarily work today. Only when we can embrace the unlearning and relearning aspects of parenting are we ready to raise our children in the manner their uniqueness deserves.

~ Making the Shift from Fantasy to Reality ~

I will make the shift from:

* Believing I should be a natural at parenting, and instead understand that I will feel like a novice a lot of the time.

* Desiring perfection in myself or my child, and instead focus on growth.

* Wanting parenthood to be easy and predictable, and instead accept that it's natural to find it stressful, overwhelming, and exhausting.

* Pressuring myself to intuitively know it all, and instead realize that conscious parenting is a muscle I must build.

CHAPTER EIGHT

Myth #5

A Good Parent Is a Loving One

I can still remember my grandmother telling me that I would make a wonderful mother because I had such a loving heart. She convinced me that warmth and openheartedness were the key ingredients of good parenting. Consequently, before I became a parent, I assumed that if a child misbehaved, it was simply because they didn't come from a loving home.

After years of working with families, then becoming a parent myself, I now realize that my assumptions were not only simplistic but seriously misguided. Since then, I have redefined my understanding of what love is, as well as my understanding of what it means to be a caring and devoted parent.

Love is undoubtedly the bonding element between humans. Unless something happened to us in our past to squelch our natural feelings for our children, love will most assuredly characterize our connection to them. Even though, as we've seen, it isn't always selfless, parental love defies boundaries, which is why our children evoke a fierce loyalty in us and a willingness to sacrifice ourselves for them.

Nevertheless, despite our love for our children, the harsh reality is that we often act toward them in ways that are anything but loving. They experience us as constantly complaining about them, correcting them, and being angry with them. The consequence is that many of our children live in fear of disappointing us, if not in terror of us.

It's hard to admit that as a result of the way our fear drives us to behave toward them, our children frequently experience us as the antithesis of loving, ranking us at the top of their list of those they fear and ultimately grow to resent. It's for this reason that they often talk to someone else about how we make them feel, while never sharing their thoughts with us. We wonder how they can feel so alienated from us when in our mind all we do is love them.

Love Is Only a Beginning

Almost everyone I know claims to be a loving person to some degree, at least toward their family members. Yet families fight tooth and nail, lie to each other, gossip about each another, and undermine each other. The fact is, with love comes stress and strife, often at extreme levels.

Have you ever wondered why we sometimes hate the one we say we love the most? It's because while love is an admired sentiment, it tends to be contaminated by the ego with its neediness, which is what breeds the fear that causes us to be controlling and possessive. This inevitable distortion of love occurs because of our attachment to those we have this feeling toward. Our attachment to them creates a symbiosis, whereby instead of relating to them just as they are, we now relate to them based on how they make us feel.

With our children especially, our feelings about ourselves entwine with their own feelings about themselves. It's because we feel afraid for them that we then seek to control them. However, *what we are really trying to do is control our own fear.* Our inability to extricate ourselves from their lives creates all sorts of projections onto them, which muddies our ability to raise them to be who they really are. Our fear catapults us into worry about the future, which inevitably ruins our ability to be present with them in the here and now.

It's a myth that if we love our children enough, we'll be able to give them what they need. Just because we love our children doesn't mean we know how to be present with them, attuned to their inner world, and able to help them realize who they are. It certainly doesn't mean we know how to navigate our own anxiety, control our reactivity, or harness our reason and objectivity so we can be of help to them.

Despite our purest intentions, our love easily stops being loving and instead becomes heavily tinged with fear, which spawns a need to control along with possessiveness. In fact, pure love can be hard to find. Even when we experience such love, it's only the beginning of what's needed to parent effectively.

Children need parents who are not just loving, but who embody a way of being that's attuned to them. They need parents who are fairly well organized, who can remain consistent in their approach, and who are able to stay calm in the face of stormy emotions. They need to feel that their deepest emotional and psychological needs, not just their physical needs, are being met joyfully and graciously.

In order to be this kind of parent, we need a whole lot of tools in our emotional toolkit, only one of which is love. Being focused, joyful, emotionally literate, firm yet flexible, and relatively stress-free are just a few of the other tools that are essential for effective parenting.

What this means is that if we are to supply what our children need in the manner they deserve, we must evolve to a level where our inner world is fairly quiet, our sense of self intact, and our awareness acute. Love certainly has a role to play in parenthood, but it's only one aspect of raising a child who thrives.

When Love Doesn't Feel Like Love to a Child

"My dad is always railing against me," Sam, a boy of sixteen, shared with me when his father brought him to therapy. "In his eyes, I'm always doing something wrong. First he told me to join the hockey team. Then when I joined, he didn't like the position I played. Next he told me to join the football team, which I did. Now he badgers me because he doesn't think I play well enough. If it isn't sports, it's my homework. If it isn't my homework, it's my attitude. I can't keep up with him. There's always something I'm supposedly doing wrong."

Phil, Sam's father, couldn't believe his ears when he heard his son say these things. He had no idea that Sam harbored such feelings. Phil could have sworn that no one loved his son more than he did, and he felt he had sacrificed countless hours to improve Sam's odds of becoming a success, pouring money and energy into every pursuit he thought the boy would relish. So how did all this love on the part of Phil translate to so much agony for Sam?

I have counseled innumerable families in which children feel invalidated, hurt, and consequently resentful of their parents. I have seen shades of this in my own relationship with my daughter. I might believe I'm operating out of love, whereas she perceives my behavior as anything but loving.

We don't realize it, but this pattern of relating to our children is less about them and more about our own unconscious conditioning. Our own childhood feelings of being unheard and invalidated cause us to manipulate our children to meet our present need to feel empowered and heard. As our children also operate out of this need, there's inevitably a clash of spirits.

Skylar, a twelve-year-old, spent her entire first session with me in tears. "It feels as if my whole existence is about making my mother happy," she confided. "Yet no matter what I do, it's never enough. There's always something more I should be doing. If I screw up in any way, she acts as if the world is coming to an end." Skylar's sentiments echo those of a hundred or more children I've interviewed and counseled. Most children feel they are on earth to live a life that matches up to their parents' standards, in return for which they hope to receive their parents' love.

As they yell at or punish their children, parents claim, "I'm only doing this because I love you." Our intention may be to love, but it doesn't mean it will be received as such by our child. On the contrary, much of the time when we think we are being loving, it's experienced by our children as control. Our ability to tune in to how our love is being received is therefore a crucial element of parenting.

Understanding the difference between our intention and how it's being received by our children is an essential element of conscious parenting. Our children have little regard for our intentions, instead tuning in to how our interactions make them feel. It's at the feeling level that dysfunction occurs. Only when we tune in to our children at *their* feeling level, not our own, are we able to meet their spirit as it manifests moment by moment. For this to happen, we must step outside of ourselves and become aware.

Love without awareness—love absent parental consciousness—quickly turns to neediness and self-absorption. In fact, if we are honest, we would have to admit that this feeling we call "love" is often how we feel about *ourselves* when we are with the other person. It has to do with whether the other makes us feel as if we are lovable and worthy. Such love is therefore highly conditional.

Herein lies the trap of all traps. Disguised as love for the other, much of our love is really all about love for ourselves. This is because most of us enter relationships searching for that "feel-good" sensation we get from another. We love those who awaken this in us, whereas we either don't care much for or even despise those who don't. For example, we love our children, especially our infants, for the way they make us feel needed, wanted, loved.

Traditionally, true love has been all about the object of our love. I challenge this idea. Love for another has to begin with love for ourselves. Until we love ourselves, every relationship, even those with our children, will feel conditional, forced, and ultimately unfulfilling because it's based on what we need from the other instead of on simply sharing ourselves with them in the way they deserve.

As you think about the love you have for your child, as well as the challenges that interfere with actually being loving in practice on a daily basis, you might decide to alter your perspective. The way we express love needs to speak not only to how our children make us feel, but to whether we act toward them in ways that honor who they are as individuals in their own right—yes, even when this makes us feel anything but good. In this way, love for our children goes beyond telling them we love them and how much they mean to us. It gets absorbed by them on a cellular level through our daily presence in their life and the way we respond to them, especially when they perhaps least appear to deserve it.

Our children need us to respond to them as if we are meeting a person for the first time. They need us to switch from a focus on molding them in the name of love to one of creating space for them to show up as they need to, even when they are being irrational and unpredictable. Children want nothing more than to feel they have our permission to express who they are at any given moment. No, I'm not talking about mindlessly indulging them, but rather about creating the conditions for them to express their whole self. When we give them this freedom, they experience a vast, unbounded spaciousness in which to discover themselves and ultimately flourish. They feel our love as love, not as control born of our fear.

It's our sacred calling to always pay attention to the signals our children send us, so that we become aware of the fear that underpins our affection for them. When we are able to embrace our children wholeheartedly as they are, we will connect with them at the deepest levels.

Rethinking Our Ideas About Love

As we embark on the path of conscious parenting, it's imperative that we bring all aspects of our living and loving into conscious awareness. We need to ask serious questions such as, "What do I mean when I say I love my child?" and "What's my love comprised of?" Our definition of love needs to be clear and consistent, moving away from what *we* need in order to feel secure, to what our children need. It's important to be careful that our responses emerge not from our fear-based conditioning, but from a desire to provide what our children require in order to blossom into their truest selves.

Love, as I define it, is the ability to fully see, accept, and honor the other person for who they are. To love someone consciously is to harness the ability to step outside of our own self and consistently connect with the other. It means we don't ask the other to love us back, and neither do we set conditions for how they should love us if they choose to do so. In other words, our feelings don't come into the mix.

This may sound like I'm advocating self-abnegation and even self-deprivation. Far from it. This definition of love challenges us to honor ourselves so that we feel fulfilled in ourselves to the extent that the other is set free from contributing to our fulfillment.

The opposite of self-denial, this understanding of love allows us to enjoy an expansive self-love that brings us a feeling of wholeness. This in turn permits the other to bask in their own self-love. When we love ourselves at such depths, we emanate trust and a feeling of fulfillment toward all those whose lives we intersect with, especially our children.

To love ourselves consciously means to be in constant communion with our inner light, while showing great compassion for our dark side. It means we know our flaws and limitations intimately, so much so that we are constantly self-mothered and self-soothed. This allows all our parts to become integrated in a wholeness, so that we no longer see ourselves as wounded, hurt, and therefore needy.

When we undertake the task to love ourselves with such deep insight, it's only natural that we emit the same energy to all those around us, especially our children. We are now able to love them for their flaws *and* their glory with equal affinity and profound compassion. Instead of being fearful for them, as if they were lacking, we see them as all that they are. In other words, our appreciation for our own humanity translates into an appreciation of theirs. This frees our children from having to prove themselves worthy of our approval. Instead of being afraid we will reject them, they tune in to another frequency altogether, that of self-acceptance.

Until our ability to live in a state of self-love is honed on a daily basis, our children will perceive our love for them as control and possessiveness based in fear. This is why when parents come to me for counseling and speak of their great love for their children, I remind them that *love and fear cannot exist in the same moment.*

This isn't an easy concept to absorb, so let me illustrate what I'm talking about by telling you about Russell, the father of sixteen-year-old Sean. Russell was filled with fear regarding Sean's future at college. He was terrified that his son would make bad choices and even drop out. Although Sean was an average kid in most ways, Russell seemed to think his son was largely a failure. I need to mention that because Russell had pushed himself to reach extraordinary levels of accomplishment in his career, he had a different definition of success and failure than most.

During one of our sessions, Russell was beside himself with fear. He described a recent fight between the two of them. "Sean hates my being down his throat. He sees my lectures as control. I keep saying to him that I'm only pushing him because I love him so much."

I challenged, "What would happen to you if Sean stayed the same? What if he was to never become who you want him to be? Would you still love him?"

Russell retorted, "Of course I would. What a silly question!"

I then asked, "So why can't you love him right now?"

Russell rationalized, "Because he isn't doing what he's capable of."

I stopped him right there. "The minute we explain our intentions with the word 'because,' we are no longer in a state of love. We have strayed into something conditional. Love isn't conditional. It doesn't need a certain set of expectations to be met before it can be expressed. Sean doesn't feel love from you because all he hears from you is disapproval. If you love him, then you need to love him for who he is at the moment. Once you begin to truly operate from acceptance, he will start taking you in. Your fear for him is yours, not his. Unless you are able to soothe your fear without asking him to do it for you by measuring up to your standard, you will be unable to connect to him."

Like many parents, Russell struggled with this notion. He couldn't see how his good intentions could be perceived as anything but loving. It was only after some time in therapy that he began to uncover how his own parents had raised him with a high degree of conditionality, which meant that acceptance in his family was synonymous with achievement. He began to realize how he really didn't even feel love for his ordinary self at all, only for his extraordinary self. This began a turnaround whereby he was at last able to engage his son on entirely different terms. Now, instead of saying "You are not this" and "You are not that," he began to communicate with Sean from a new perspective, one that was really okay with his son's unfolding and ready to see his worth in all its abundance however it happened to manifest.

The place to start loving our children involves acceptance. This doesn't mean we endorse their rude behavior, their lack of motivation at school, or even their bad habits, to name a few common triggers. It means we accept that they are their own individuals in their own right. It isn't our job to judge them, but instead to encourage them to tune in to their own worth. Children who are tuned in to their worth will naturally shed behavior that doesn't bring them into close communion with us and lead to their highest expression. Children who are treated as worthy by their parents will naturally steer away from behavior that leads to disconnection. There may still be conflict, but there will always be great and deep connection.

Some parents manifest their ideas of love in opposite ways than Russell. Instead of being controlling, they bend over backwards to please their children. They raise their children without clear boundaries or limits. Unable to say "no," these parents equate love with being "nice," which means never allowing their children to feel uncomfortable. These children grow up unable to tolerate discomfort of any kind. They learn from their parents that it is "bad" to feel bad and, as a result, often turn to addictions to avoid any discomfort whatsoever. Once again, we can see how our ideas about love inhibit our ability to be truly present to what our children need from us.

～ Moving Beyond Love into Consciousness ～

I will transform:

* The basis of my love from fear to trust.

* My love from self-absorption to connection.

* My way of showing my love if it doesn't feel like love to my child.

* My love from need to consciousness.

CHAPTER NINE

Myth #6
Parenting Is About
Raising a Happy Child

As much as we may strive to raise successful children, which so many today regard as the holy grail of being a good parent, our default wish is that our children should be happy. What we don't realize is that chasing after happiness actually has an adverse effect on children. This is because we have been bewitched by the idea that happiness is something to be sought after like the pot of gold at the end of the rainbow, discovered as a reward for all our trying and striving. This view of happiness leads to unending discontent.

The idea that "I need to be happy" or "my child deserves to be happy" comes from a sense that the present moment is somehow lacking. In other words, we see our life through a lens of scarcity, noticing all the things we *don't* have instead of the abundant way the universe provides for us. And so, as the Declaration of Independence sanctions, we set off in "the pursuit of happiness," not realizing that this can never bring us happiness. On the contrary, it's the breeding ground of discontent and disappointment.

You can see this when you travel. When things go according to plan, you feel content and "happy." However, if your flight is delayed or your passport gets misplaced, you suddenly become unhappy. In other words, your state of being is dependent on the variables of life, which as we all know can be unpredictable and at times beyond our control.

Some take conscious parenting to mean that we are lovey-dovey with our children all the time and try to indulge their every wish so that they stay contented and comfortable. On the contrary, this kind of parenting is fear-based and rooted in unconsciousness. Conscious parenting, on the other hand, doesn't have any fear of making our children uncomfortable if this is what they need to feel in order to grow, or saying no to them if this is what they need to hear to serve their highest good. This approach of parenting doesn't seek the easy way for either parent or child; it seeks the way that is most tailored for their growth, period. The focus is always on what makes our children grow to be their most resilient and empowered selves, not what makes them happy or comfortable in any given moment. Inherent here is the awareness that life doesn't always provide pleasure or comfort, nor should we want it to. Without the jagged edges, we simply wouldn't grow.

I tell clients, "Life is inherently unpredictable. To expect it not to change on a dime is the same as expecting rain not to be wet." Despite knowing this, it's usually only when something goes wrong that we realize just how attached we are to the belief that everything should go smoothly.

What are we to do at such times? Well, suppose we were to embrace the idea that happiness can be found in the very uncertainty we wish would go away. It's possible we might find ourselves in an eternal state of happiness. The problem is that, without our realizing it, we equate happiness with the *outcome* of events, not the process. We see the end result of the event as the measure of happiness. This conditional nature of our relationship with life is the reason we are unable to tap into an internal state of bliss that's always available to us.

While we may not know exactly what happiness looks like, at the very least we tell ourselves it means freedom from painful experiences—that we are comfortable. Though we know there are no guarantees, we believe that the more successful a person is, the greater their chance of escaping pain. Thus we steer our children toward achievement at a young age as a way to inoculate them against pain, telling ourselves that if we can get them started young enough, they will be successful and eventually have a better chance at happiness.

Along with programming our children to strive for success, we want them to have an identity that involves seeing themselves as successful, since not knowing where one fits in can result in insecurity and even lead to being ostracized. In line with this, preteens and teens often identify as types such as a drama kid, a geek, an athlete, or a "popular" kid. We assume our young people will find security through these external identities. That they should be allowed to just "be" doesn't enter our head. One cannot just *be*.

The truth is, we can never escape from the possibility that we will experience pain. Potential hurt lies in wait at every turn. Even as adults with a measure of control over our life, we can't avoid being hurt at times. Friends betray us, a spouse leaves us, our place of work fires us, a tornado blows our town to bits, a drunk driver plows into us, or a flood or fire devastates our home. Pain is an inescapable aspect of being alive.

We regard getting hurt as "bad" because it forces us to adjust and cope. Faced with the unexpected and unwanted, we may have to make new friends, go through a divorce, find a different career, or develop a great deal of resilience to cope with what's happening to us. This can appear herculean. We feel as if we are simply unable to elevate ourselves in the manner asked of us and are terrified we will fall apart.

Conditioned to depend on life working out in a particular way, we appear helpless when it doesn't. At such times we may feel too paralyzed to recreate ourselves. Only when we separate the internal from the external do we realize that who we are internally can continue to adjust, and in fact flourish, despite our external situation. When we arrive at this realization, our inner being looks at life's challenges with vigor instead of victimhood, valor instead of fear.

What if dancing the waves of life, riding its ebb and flow, is the actual point of life, as opposed to the avoidance of these things? What if the art of living meaningfully lies in embracing both the peaks and the troughs? How different might your children's lives be if they learned from you how to immerse themselves in each experience that comes their way, so that they actually welcome the twists and turns, the times we feel hurt and the times we enjoy glory?

The challenge is to see the pleasure and the pain of life as holy—equal in terms of the opportunity they present us. If we approached life this way, and showed our children how to do so, we would stop searching for happiness, knowing that the process of engaging whatever comes our way holds the greatest fulfillment.

This shift in awareness means that instead of a C grade signaling doom for our children, we encourage them to enter into the feeling this grade brings them, sitting with it for what it has to show them about themselves. We help them realize they aren't defined by it, but that on the contrary they have the capacity to learn and grow from it. Is this a subject they need to work harder at? Do they need help? Or do they simply have less aptitude for it, and therefore need to accept this and, when they are able, choose a different route through life?

The key is to teach our children to stay in touch with their inner power and not feel defeated by how life presents itself to them. In doing so, we help them see that they have the ability to turn any situation into an opportunity for greater courage and adventure. It is only when we parents fully embrace the power of pain as a portal for transformation that we will allow our children the freedom to explore their own relationship with it.

Engaging Life "As Is"—Being Versus Doing

Children inherently know how to engage life as it is. They cry and throw tantrums, but they don't attach their sense of worth to what may be happening. Unless taught otherwise, they are ready to pick themselves up when life doesn't go their way. It's for this reason that it isn't uncommon for a parent to say during a difficult time, "They are children, they will adjust." We realize that children are able to tap into their joy of living no matter what the circumstances. The reason for this is that children are wired in a completely different way than we adults are. They accept the "as is" of life in a manner we have forgotten.

What does it mean to accept life "as is"? It means to notice that every moment holds the potential for both the good and the bad, the happy and the sorrowful, pain as well as pleasure. I think of it as non-pain versus happiness, because to label it as "happy" or "unhappy" distorts the value of the experience. When children cry, they cry. When they laugh, they laugh. They don't create scripts about how happy or unhappy they are with their situation. They feel their feelings, then move on. This ability to be flexible in the dance of life is lacking in so many of us adults. Our categorizing minds don't allow us to engage life as it presents itself to us. We simply don't know how to shift and change with the tides of life as children intuitively do. Stuck in old templates, we are unable to manifest creative ways to adapt and come up with mindful responses to life's ebb and flow. Fearful of letting go of the known, we cling to the illusion that life is under our control. When life, and especially our children, challenge this illusion, we feel ill-equipped to cope and we unleash this helplessness onto our children through anger or anxiety. If only we were able to embrace life for what it is, instead of how good or bad it makes us look or feel, we would ease into its unpredictability with greater grace.

The point is not to judge life based on how it makes us feel, but instead to fully explore its rich tapestry of both light and dark moments. Instead of running after a particular way to feel, as people do with a drug to which they are addicted, we let go of the expectation of feeling differently from how we feel, choosing to experience the "as is" of this moment.

When we raise our children to strive for something outside of themselves so they can feel more empowered—a particular grade, or an accolade for some achievement—we send the message that the process of life is less important than the outcome. They learn to think that their life is meaningful only when they are achieving, not when they are simply being themselves in each and every moment.

By training our children to be outcome-oriented, engaging life based on whether a particular experience makes them feel good or not, we teach them that if an activity doesn't qualify, they should avoid it and look for an experience that promises happiness. Thus, because of our fear that they might experience some kind of pain, they miss out on the immediate *experience* of life. How sad that instead of teaching our children to get in touch with their resilience so that they transcend painful experiences, we dump our fear onto them and thereby teach them to avoid pain at all costs.

When our children are forced to experience unhappy feelings, the situation is interpreted by not only the child but often also by the parent as "something going wrong." Then, in both our mind and our child's mind, a drama plays itself out starring fear and despair. All of this occurs because the child doesn't realize that life simply *is*, and that all they need to do to live a meaningful life is engage in the experience with full-on presence, empowered by the knowledge that they have within them the resilience to cope with whatever may come their way.

When my sixth-grade client Ramona was having problems with her friends at school, her mother, Jane, couldn't bear it. As Ramona struggled with her complex emotions, at times she would cry—a valuable experience for a preteen to work through. Her mother repeatedly attempted to short-circuit her daughter's feelings by intruding with comments such as, "I'll go to the school tomorrow and find out who the mean kids are. I hate to see you upset like this and will tell the guidance counselor to fix this situation immediately."

When Jane discussed this incident with me, I suggested, "Is it possible to allow your daughter her feelings without the need to rationalize them or change them? It hurts you to see her be rejected because you are equating rejection with her worth. What if you separated the two? Perhaps then you could show her that being rejected by peers is an inevitable fallout of friendships but has nothing to do with her worth as a person. Not everyone is going to be nice to us or even like us. Nor should they. They have every right to their own values, opinions, and feelings about us. This is their prerogative. We don't have control over how others behave toward us."

Jane protested, "But it hurts her feelings!"

I agreed. "Of course it does. And you are trying to help her avoid being hurt because you think it's tied in with her worth. However, her feelings are born out of a belief that her worth is tied in with how socially approved she is, when that really has nothing to do with who she is."

The goal of having our children fit in is a misguided one. Instead of pushing our children to fit into a social clique, it would be far more beneficial to them if we taught them to set clear boundaries with those who are not caring toward them. We should help them discern qualities within others that are a match for who they are, versus trying to get them to fake qualities within themselves to fit in with others. After all, isn't this what most adults have trouble with, establishing clear boundaries and staying away from those who ill-treat and disrespect them? It all starts with the fact that we teach our children to socialize without giving them the tools that will help them develop healthy relationships later in life.

Jane couldn't believe that she had been one of the key instigators of her daughter's misery. She said, "I thought I was doing the right thing by pushing my daughter to make friends and be part of a group. I thought that would make her happy. Now that you have shown me that this focus on friends is actually eroding her sense of self, I can free both her and myself of this heavy burden I have placed on us."

Together, mother and daughter awakened to the insight that our sense of worth is not borrowed from the friends we have and that the more they allowed themselves to fully feel all of their experiences, the stronger and more courageous they would become—and consequently the more capable they would be of handling life's ups and downs. The goal was no longer to "fix" the painful situation, but to deeply engage it. Ramona developed resolve and resilience as a result of this experience, which helped her gradually to stop depending on her friends for her self-worth and sense of identity.

Learning About Happiness from Children

To understand true happiness, we need only to observe young children. They are masters at embodying happiness without chasing after it. Leave them to play outside, and in no time they will find delight in the most ordinary aspects of nature. Dirt fascinates them, squirrels intrigue them, and things like sticks, acorns, and rocks keep them busy for hours.

Youngsters are able to access a state of joy almost instantly. If they get caught in a downpour, they delight in the sensation of being drenched. If it's hot and humid, they relish the stickiness. They have no need to preface experiences with how "successful" they will be at them. They accept life, as is, without begrudging it when it doesn't deliver according to "the plan." Between birth and the age of four or five, they are able to capture the experience of sheer bliss. I don't think most people are capable of happiness to anything like this degree after this age. This is one of the reasons why I call our young children our greatest teachers. If we are willing, they can lead us back to what we have lost.

Because they are as yet untainted by mainstream culture, young children don't look for happiness outside themselves. They don't wait to be happy until they are rich, thin, pretty, or in the "right" social circle. Unencumbered by guilt over the past and fears or fantasies about the future, they fully experience their life in its "as is" state, without the need to label or judge their experiences. They cry when they want to cry and sing when the urge inspires them. When they are ready to stop crying or singing, they just do.

A whole lot of "doing" may be the hallmark of adulthood, but "being" is the domain of childhood. It's this complete surrender to reality that allows young children to be free, exploratory, and adventurous. Aren't these the qualities we want our young people to have when they grow up?

To incubate these strengths, we need to allow our children to do what they do best, which is to simply be themselves. When we step out of the way, they naturally develop their own desire to manifest their dreams—all without a constant din from us about what they ought to be doing.

～ End the Chase for Happiness and Engage in the "As Is" ～

> I pledge to:
>
> * No longer look for an experience to be other than what it is.
>
> * Not need an experience to make me happy but instead to make me grow.
>
> * Not look to what I didn't receive but instead to introspect on what I chose to give.

* Stop interpreting experiences based on outcome but instead interpret them based on process.

* Resist judging life or myself for not being perfect and instead to embrace the wholeness of the imperfections.

CHAPTER TEN

Myth #7
Parents Need to Be in Control

I rrespective of whether we birth our children or adopt them, the journey of parenting them from when they are young inevitably leads to feelings of possession and ownership. For this reason, in no other relationship are we as invested as the one we share with our children. While this investment is the precious hallmark of parenthood, it brings with it land mines we need to be aware of from the outset, the most important of which is the sense that we are in control of them.

I can still remember the epiphany I had when I was in labor. Having taken all the Lamaze classes available and read all the literature I could lay my hands on to prepare for parenthood, I thought I was well armed for the twists and turns of delivering a child. However, it became clear to me early in the delivery process that no matter how much I thought I knew, my sense of control was only an illusion. Complications in labor pushed me to give up my idealized fantasy of having a "natural" birth, forcing me to accept medication I had sworn I would never succumb to. In agonizing pain, my mind fought the fact that I needed help with the delivery. I breathed, I pushed, and I cried. I wanted to give birth my way, darn it, and I was going to fight tooth and nail for my fantasy.

It eventually dawned on me that my unborn child had other plans for me. The realization that she was going to enter the world her way wasn't something I was prepared for. She wasn't comfortable with the labor and wanted her mother to change course. The harder I tried, the more she resisted, ultimately excreting meconium inside me as a show of her discomfort. It was then that the doctors told me I needed a

C-section. I couldn't believe it. "What, me?" I thought. "Surely I can do this the natural way!" I begged for more time, hoping to turn things around. My doctor allowed me a bit longer, but eventually sternly warned, "Your child is unsafe at this point and we need to go into the OR." My husband saw my pain and understood how disappointed I felt. He also knew that he needed to wake me out of my stupor and change the way I was experiencing this labor. "You have to accept this process, you have to think about her," he urged me. "This is not about you and your fantasy. This is now about her."

That moment, along with a million more since then, opened me up to the fact that parenting our children rarely goes according to our preordained plans. We are not "creating" who they will grow up to be in any way, shape, or form, only ushering them into life and through childhood in order for them to define their own life. In our misguided belief that we are responsible for who they are to become, we fail to appreciate the nature of the partnership we share with them.

Understanding the Limits of Our Control

Amy, a mother of three children under the age of seven, bemoaned in therapy, "On the one hand you tell me I'm responsible for everything my children do, then you tell me I have no control. So what do I really have control over? I'm confused!"

"Yes, you are responsible for how you are around them," I replied, "and no, you have no control over them. The art of conscious parenting lies in understanding that our ability to control our children is limited at best, and certainly undermined by our belief that we have any. Our mandate is to be in charge of their safety and well-being, but this has a clear limit. If we aren't aware of this limit, we will make the mistake of believing we are in control of who they intrinsically are."

Like many parents, Amy didn't know how to define her role with her children. Feeling responsible for their success and happiness, she assumed that she needed to control their moods, behavior, and choices. It was only when she began to delve into an understanding of the limits

of her "job description" that she could see how she had mixed u̶
ing her children with controlling them.

The only control we have, as parents, involves *our own* feelings and reactions, together with the conditions we set in our home. Our problem is that we don't really know how to control ourselves or the conditions we create in our home, which steers us in the direction of controlling our children instead.

Our children come to us with their own unique blueprint. This implies that they come with a particular temperament and way of relating to the world. Some come with boisterous energy, whereas others are calm and quiet. Some come with angst and colic, whereas others glide and float. We don't get to keep the qualities we like in our children and discard the ones we don't. Certainly we can help them develop the qualities that are most in alignment with their true self, but not through control and imposition. They are who they are. It's only when we accept this about our children that we will be able to attune to them and meet their emotional needs. Surrendering to their inherent nature, which includes their talents and their limitations, is the forerunner to endowing the relationship we share with them with respect and meaningful connection.

When we realize that our control is limited to ourselves and the environment in our home, we shift the onus for any changes that may be required from our children to ourselves. It's our responsibility to take full ownership of what has been placed in our charge. Once we accept that we create the conditions our children live within, we can begin to ask ourselves questions such as:

- *Am I setting the environment up in a manner that promotes harmony or disharmony?*

- *What am I doing or not doing that leads my children to behave in a particular way?*

To illustrate what this means in practice, we can't force our child to love brushing their teeth, though we are certainly responsible for creating the conditions that help them to see brushing as a vital aspect of daily life. We pave the path, and they choose how they walk with us on it. As long as we keep our energy focused on paving the path in line with their temperament, we will have done our job well.

One of the statements I made on *Oprah's Lifeclass* resonated with many in the audience. "We cannot control our children," I explained. "We can only create the conditions for them to rise." What this means is that we need to stop expending our energy on trying to control who they are and how they turn out in the future. As long as we keep our focus on this, we will engage in a losing battle. The real challenge is to keep our eyes on the parameters that are truly under our control— ourselves, and the way the home functions.

Reframing the Concept of Control in Order to Raise Real Humans

We tend to forget that before they are "our children," the children we are blessed with are first and foremost human beings. In our obsession to turn them into a product of our parenting, we can become oblivious of the fact that they are here to walk their own unique path.

Because our children are smaller and younger than us, we unconsciously—and sometimes not so unconsciously—take this to mean they are less knowing and even less human than we are. I doubt any parent would actually say children are less human, and yet we frequently act as if they were by ignoring or overriding their uniqueness.

An important aspect of this is not to deprive children of their experiences, which they have a right to even though those experiences might be painful. We can't allow the strong emotions that some of our children's experiences evoke in us to cloud the fact that they are on their own journey, not ours.

We don't have the right to dictate how our children express their humanity. On the other hand, we are privileged to show them the importance of being true to themselves by embodying what they value. Our job is to embrace them, celebrating them as their life unfolds. In this way we honor each child's particular relationship with their own humanity, including not only their amazing strengths but also their limitations.

If your child is shy, does it really mean they are deficient in some way and need to be pushed to become assertive? Or would it be better to allow them to simply experience their shyness? In the same vein, if your child fails a test or a grade, is it really because they are lazy? Or is it because there's value to experiencing their limitations in a particular subject?

Letting go of control over our children is probably the hardest spiritual task we face as parents. It's particularly challenging when we feel pressure from other parents, as well as from teachers, to make our children toe the line. When our children do not subscribe to developmental norms, we often feel judged by others, especially other parents. These judgments create scarcity, which pressures us to clamp down on our children with control. We believe the more we control, the more we can change them. Little do we realize that we create the opposite effect of cementing the behaviors even more.

I think of Madison, the mother of an atypically developing seven-year-old girl. "You are being challenged to reframe your idea of control in a big way," I told her. "More than with a typically developing child, you are forced to confront just how little control you really have. In order to let go of your desire to control the outcome of your child's life, you are going to need to move away from seeing yourself as her mother, per se, and see yourself more as her spiritual mentor. For this to happen, you need to first see your child as a spiritual being."

Madison reacted with fear: "What do you mean by this? I am her mother. I don't know how to be anything else."

"Our rigid attachment to our role of mother or father can keep us stuck at a superficial level," I explained. "Even though our culture has endorsed the role of parent, attaching to these roles ultimately limits our ability to fully connect to our children as spiritual beings. If we embraced a wider perspective, connecting to our children spiritually, we would recognize that life is about more than helping them simply grow up. It's about the fact that each of us is given a lifetime in which certain challenges present themselves to us and we must work through them. These are going to be different for everyone. To work through our particular challenges, we need our loved ones to help us.

Your daughter doesn't need to feel as if her challenges mean something is wrong. She is simply asking to accept herself just the way she is. When you help her embrace her challenges instead of resenting them, you may realize she can't be who she is without them. She needs you to accept her limitations for what they are, then from this place of acceptance to help her grow into her fullest expression within the context of these limitations. When we can see our children for what they came into this life with and honor this as an intrinsic part of their nature, we will be able to help them transform in the manner that *they* need, not as *we* think they need. This is what it means to be their spiritual mentor."

Madison slowly began to unpack the subtle but profound difference between controlling our children's limitations, trying to get them to conform, and accepting our children so that they have an opportunity to integrate their limitations on their path to transformation. Once she understood the power behind this different way of seeing her daughter, she saw immediate shifts in their relationship, reporting with excitement, "We don't fight over homework anymore. I used to have great anxiety about homework, insisting that she complete every piece of it. Now I tell her to try whatever she can and celebrate her accomplishments. When she sees I'm accepting of her struggle, she beams with pride and actually tries harder than I have ever seen. I cannot believe that I was the one who was blocking her path all along. I thought by pushing her I would help her to change, but now I see how I was diminishing her capacity."

Our children automatically sense our acceptance or lack thereof. When they feel that we understand their basic temperament, they release the energy they had stored to protect themselves from our criticism. This release of energy brings about a renewed commitment to their own growth and expansion. When we understand the power of our role as our children's spiritual mentor, we honor the throbbing spirit within them that longs for actualization.

~ Moving from Parent to Spiritual Guide ~

Instead of:

* Seeing a child, I will see a spiritual being.

* Identifying myself as a parent, I will identify as a partner.

* Holding my child to my standards, I will help them create their own.

* Holding them in dependency, I will liberate them to autonomy.

* Treating them as "mine," I will usher them to their own selfhood.

~ Redefining Behavior ~

Our sacred task as parents is to redefine
Aggression against our control as a defensiveness,
Lying as a reaction against our rigidity,
Anger as a rebellion against our disconnection,
Defiance as a barrier to our resistance,
Anxiety as an avoidance of our judgement,
Distraction as a reflection of our own inner chaos,
Sadness as a mark of our own unworthiness.

When we see our children's acting out
As an
Impetus for our own awakening,
We absolve them of the burden of having to fix
    themselves.

Instead, we embody the change their behavior
    triggers in us.
In doing so . . .
We become emotionally integrated
And
Set our children free.

Part Three

Understanding
Our Reactivity

CHAPTER ELEVEN

Raising the *Real Child*

If I hadn't embarked on a journey of awareness early in my twenties, I would never have been aware of the effect of my inner world on my external reality. Like so many, I had no idea that I didn't actually know my *real self.*

Tuning in to one's inner world and who we really are is an art, something that needs to be honed over time. If only this were taught in schools, our world would be an entirely different place than it is today. We simply wouldn't have all the dysfunction, the crime, and the violence with which society is riddled.

It was having a child that awakened me to the realization that my essential self had gotten lost in the process of growing up. And what a rude awakening it was! Although I had been practicing mindfulness for an entire decade before becoming a parent, I found myself ill-prepared for the onslaught of new triggers my child evoked in me. Just as a new exercise class makes you aware of muscles you were unaware of, so it is with the parenting journey. No matter how enlightened you think you are, having a child unravels you in ways you couldn't have prepared for.

This makes perfect sense if you think about it. You have never met this being before, and yet you are entrusted with their care. You are supposed to be in complete control, but quickly realize you can never control this person. You are supposed to feel an undying affection for them, and perhaps you do. But it's also quite likely that they trigger in you all sorts of complicated feelings that rapidly deflate the bubble of love. Truth is, you simply don't know how you are going to think, feel, or react to your child, because each moment with them is entirely new. This is why the practice of mindfulness, which teaches you to enter the present moment as if it was new, is particularly valuable in parenting. While it doesn't create immunity against being triggered, it at least helps you realign yourself with a state of presence, which is the best way to understand why you are triggered.

I am often asked whether I get triggered by my child, as if writing books on parenting must mean such things never happen to me. I always say, "I'm not immune to being reactive, and in fact I never feel disappointed when I am. I'm not above anyone else in my humanness. However, the discipline and art of mindfulness has served me well in that I'm able to regain my center a lot quicker than before I became aware. It has also allowed me to dispel all illusion that it's my child's fault when I react. The only difference in my parenting and anyone else's parenting is that my eyes are turned toward my inner process. I don't see my child's behaviors as triggers. I see my own wounding as my trigger, and her behavior as just the match that enflames it. This allows me to always keep the mirror shining on my inner process. Instead of pointing a finger at her, I turn the spotlight within."

How I Began to Awaken

Allow me to share with you one of the weaknesses in myself that I encountered as I began to be aware. In my early years as a parent, I found myself simply unable to create a boundary. I would start out strong, but if she was insistent, I would cave almost instantly. My toddler had the power to bring me to my knees in moments. The rhythm went like this: "No, no, no . . . yes." I saw the effects of this inconsistency in my daughter's behavior. She quickly learned that to get her way, she needed only to push harder and Mommy would give in. This created a negative cycle between us. I knew I was the cause of this mess, and the only solution was to figure out the reason I was so inconsistent.

We don't have to look far for the cause of our insanity. I simply had to turn to my upbringing, which had conditioned me, as it did most of the women of my generation, to be more comfortable in the role of pleaser and accommodator. Stepping into the role of the boundary-maker and saying no was unfamiliar to me. I felt uncomfortable being an enforcer. I knew what was right and what was wrong, but something was blocking my ability to communicate this to my child. What was the root of my hesitance to assert myself? Why was I so afraid to hold a limit? It was only when I delved into my past and became aware of how *I* was conditioned that I could get to the root of my fear.

Notice that I am not blaming my upbringing or my parents for this. Understanding what enflames our inner wounds is important and fundamental to stopping our outer reactivity. But we need to come to this understanding without judgment or blame. Our parents were on their own path, and the important thing is to understand how it affected us.

As I uncovered the layers of my psyche, I became aware of my deep desire for approval. This seemed to be a central motivator in my interactions with others. Was I liked? Was I seen as the good one? I began to be mindful of how this longing for approval trumped my will to do what was right. Somewhere in my childhood, I had an unmet yearning to be seen as good, and it was this unfulfilled striving that was dictating my present relationship with my child. As a way to have this unmet need met, I had created a false self—an ego whose persona was that of "the pleaser." This inauthentic version of myself was standing in the way of my ability to parent my child in the manner she required.

When I saw my daughter unhappy with me, this reminded me of displeasing others growing up. As I had not yet resolved these old disappointments within me, I was unable to tolerate those feelings when they arose in the present moment. Quite unconsciously, I would capitulate to her demands just so I could preserve the image of myself as "the good one." This is how sneaky our old patterns are, sabotaging us in the most insidious ways, paralyzing our ability to respond to our children as they need us to. My daughter needed her mother to be clear and resolute. When she intuitively absorbed that I couldn't be this for her, she embedded the message that a no wasn't really a no and that she could get her way through demands and persistence. In turn, I found her to be unrelenting, further enflaming my inner triggers, causing me to cast her as "the bad one." Although I knew this pattern was unhealthy and not her fault at all, I had no power over my participation in it until I began to uncover why I was engaging with her in the way I was. It was only when I took ownership over my part in the dynamic, and saw how it was the driver of the disconnect, that the relationship went back into alignment and began to flourish.

Children raised by parents who live in their false self grow up in contaminated spaces filled with polluted emotional energy. Instead of the parental energy being attuned to the child, it's muddied by voices, messages, and beliefs from one's past or one's culture—things that often have nothing to do with the child in front of us. When parents aren't aligned with their own truth, but are instead conditioned by the unconsciousness of their ancestors and society, they project these beliefs onto their children. Unable to see who their children are, they blindly act according to past mandates, without even knowing they are doing so.

Instead of creating firm boundaries for my daughter, my inconsistency pushed her into an unhealthy pattern of entitlement and grandiosity. This was not her natural choice; it was a reaction to my inconsistency. Somewhere in her psyche, she learned that her mother was not going to take a stand unless she raised the volume on her demands. Of course when she did, I immediately castigated her, causing confusion in her. So you see how we unconciously create the "bad" behaviors in our children that we then punish them for? In this case, it was only when I got to the root of my unresolved need for approval that I could break this pattern successfully.

When a child's self is not allowed to develop into its authentic form and flourish as it should, an emptiness begins to grow within. It is this emptiness that causes all the trouble, as the child intuitively longs to fill this hollowed-out feeling—painfully, I might add, since the ego's dysfunctional behavior to get attention is a poor substitute for truly valuing our real selves. Beginning from when we weren't permitted to heed our authentic voice as a child, we learned to ignore our true self. As who we really are became buried, we began to experience an internal disconnect, which led to a feeling of discontent and a life that, to varying degrees, is in disarray. The fact is, not knowing our real self feels awful. We know something is off, though we can't place our finger on exactly what's wrong or how it came about.

When we feel this way, our instinct is to blame it on others or on our circumstances. Just as our parents did in their moments of unconsciousness, we project this feeling onto those around us. The mantra becomes, "It's someone else's fault if I feel bad, and I will make them bear the brunt of my feelings." We either turn our wrath on those around us or, in the case of depression, turn it against our own self.

The flip side of this is that the reason our children are able to rattle us the way they do is that we too aren't in touch with our solid core. Like our children, we are operating out of the feeling of lack created by our missing self. In the absence of our real self, we rely on our ego for an identity, which of course consists of layers of programming picked up in our childhood. You can see how, until we are grounded in our core, our children will inevitably trigger our insecurity and the drama that results, as they are thrusting an awareness of our missing self in our face, which is painful for us and must be deflected in some way. Of course, as all acting out begins from a mindset of lack, our reaction to our children's behavior only perpetuates the dysfunction that already abounds in the home.

Every time we react stormily to our children—and by this I mean like a storm cloud, in that we are overwhelmed by dark bursts of energy—we glimpse just how disconnected we are from our deepest self. The beauty of our children is that they mirror this storminess back to us. The more we storm, the more they thunder back and show us how we are engaging with them from an ungrounded state.

However, don't misunderstand me: Storms with a lot of thunder don't necessarily mean rage or violence. Sometimes reactivity can manifest in the most silent of ways. Dysfunction doesn't always mean yelling or tossing insults at one another. Sometimes it occurs in subtle ways, requiring a high level of awareness to catch that it's happening. Watching innumerable families on my therapy couch, I have become painfully attuned to these subtle shifts in energy. A mother unconsciously grimaces, and her son instantly slumps his shoulders in reaction. Or a father tightens his fist and his children immediately know to stop in their tracks. Sometimes the most nuanced reactions have the most profound effect on our loved ones. I am reminded of one teenage daughter who described this perfectly when she said, "When my mother becomes silent, it's louder than a yell and scarier than a beating." Only when we dare to awaken to these energetic shifts in ourselves and watch their domino effect on our children's state of being will we enter a more conscious state of being and parenting.

I firmly believe that the deep attachment we have to our children is one of life's most powerful ways of pushing us to this level of awakening. How wonderful that our children have such an effect on us as to cause us to consider doing such painfully introspective inner work. In its unique juxtaposition of intimacy and detachment—they are in one sense ours, and yet they do not belong to us—we are offered a glimpse into what many wisdom traditions refer to as "surrender." This involves fully giving of ourselves to the present moment without imposing conditions or control for the future. It's in this gray space, when the many manifestations of the present moment are embraced with vigor, that we learn to live a courageous life. Our children, who are masters of living in the gray, show us how to live free of our past. They teach us that while life may rarely follow our plans, we are fully capable of equipping ourselves to meet its challenges. When we undergo this metamorphosis, life takes on an unsurpassed glory. As we liberate ourselves from attachment to rigid ideals and future goals, we are able to engage with ourselves and our families with spontaneity, joy, and a feeling of lightness.

Recognizing the Call of the Lost Self

Leila, a forty-one-year-old mother of two young children, experienced crippling anxiety that expressed itself in the form of a relentless paranoia about leaving her children alone with a nanny. "I know it's abnormal and extreme," she admitted, "but every time I think of leaving my five-year-old and two-year-old with a stranger, I panic." She came for help because her inability to entrust her children to a caregiver was getting in the way of her ability to take care not only of herself but also of the children.

In Leila's case, what she felt as a result of her crushed spirit took the form of stress. She was tense and exhausted to the point of burn-out. As we explored the roots of this in her past, she talked about a particularly traumatic incident when her parents left her with a nanny for over four months because they had to travel abroad for work. As she related this story, she was amazed at the similarities of her past to her present situation. She had been about the same age her five-year-old was now, and her mother had been a few years younger than Leila currently was. History was repeating itself in the most un-canny way.

I said to her, "Your reaction to leaving your children with a nanny is extreme because of what happened to you as a child. Because those scary feelings were left unprocessed, they are easily triggered by the present situation. Given your past, it's only natural you don't trust caregivers. It's a reflection of a deeply rooted lack of trust where your parents are concerned."

People often ask me, "How can I get in touch with my lost self?" Well, we are seeing how we find it right here in Leila's situation. Through what was occurring with her children, she was beginning to recognize how her lost self—her crushed spirit—was trying to get her attention. She was starting to understand that unless she began to pay attention to what was happening deep within her, as was mir-rored for her by her children, and learned to take care of her needs in a healthy way, she would continue to act out through all sorts of dys-function.

Beneath the ways we feel bad, our lost self is always present in our reactivity to others. If only we were prepared to see every emotional reaction we have as a sign that our lost self is peeking through, we would absolve others of fixing us and instead turn our attention to soothing ourselves and tuning in to ourselves. Rather than judging others for triggering us, we need to express gratitude for the situa-tions that allow who we really are to reveal itself, for this is our golden opportunity to go within and integrate that which has never been ad-dressed.

As we engage in this process, it's important to realize that our ego—our surface layers—played an important role in our upbringing, helping us cope with threatening situations. For this reason we shouldn't resent these aspects of ourselves. At the same time, when what were meant to be temporary defenses become rigidified, so that we are no longer able to access our authentic self, we find ourselves imprisoned in reactivity as a result.

Examining our many layers needs to be undertaken progressively, starting with the broader generalities passed on to us by the culture, the myths we learned about how to live and how to parent. We then go deeper, unmasking those layers formed in our family of origin. Beneath these layers we will find our real self in all its purity and beauty.

Befriending Our Lost Self

Aspects of our lost self always accompany us until we claim them. The more aware we are of them, the less we will act in dysfunctional ways, and the same is true of our children.

Having said this, I need to point out that awareness of our lost self is fundamentally different from engaging with its distorted manifestations. To see the difference, take a situation in which we feel rejected by a friend. A typical unconscious reaction to this feeling of rejection could be any one of the following:

- *Call out our friend on it.*

- *Feel bad or sorry for ourselves.*

- *Stop talking to our friend.*

- *Talk badly about them.*

This kind of engagement isn't awareness. It's simply an escalation of our reactivity. Just because we are talking about the incident doesn't mean there's any enlightenment around it, or any insight.

So what would awareness look like in this case? When the feeling of rejection arises within us, this is the sign that our lost self has been activated and is expressing itself through the emptiness we feel. At this point we make a pivotal choice, to look either outward or inward. By looking inward and becoming present with the void we are feeling, instead of blaming or reacting to the one who triggered this feeling in us, we begin to find ourselves. "Hello, lost self!" we might say. "Welcome. Tell me about yourself. You are here to show me something about myself in this moment, and I'm curious. I'm ready to learn from your presence." This is the key difference between being aware and thinking we are.

The crucial point is that rather than talking ourselves *out* of a feeling, we hold it in our awareness, observing it in its "as is" state. Thus when Leila asked, "So how do I get rid of this fear?" I reminded her, "You can't get rid of fear by willing it to disappear. The only way it will naturally fade is by holding it in your awareness, which means you neither wallow in it, act it out, or suppress it."

I showed her a way to do this. "Instead of telling yourself not to be paranoid, simply allow the emotion to rise within you," I said. "Note it and let it sit beside you. Understand that it doesn't define your present moment. It's from the past and therefore needs to be gently guided away from the foreground of your present experiences. Unless you become aware that all your reactions stem from the past, you will constantly be deluded into thinking someone or something is causing them."

It's imperative not only that we become aware of our lost self, but also that we begin to notice how our adult life is constructed around its experiences. In essence, we keep recreating the same situations from childhood, as if this will somehow give us a chance to revisit what was left on the sidewalk.

Leila knew exactly what I was talking about. "I have literally re-created my own abandonment over and over by operating out of a deep distrust," she admitted. "The more I distrust, the more things I find to distrust, which leads me to feel betrayed over and over. The more I feel betrayed, the more fearful I become."

I explained to Leila how we create entire scripts for our life based on our unmet needs and pain from the past we haven't addressed. The more we operate out of the sense of lack caused by the void where our true self ought to be blossoming, the more we create circumstances that reflect this back to us.

The traditional approach to parenting doesn't get this at all, which is why it majors in control. The parental Kool-Aid teaches us to annihilate our anxiety, rather than being aware of it and learning to accept it, by controlling those who make us feel bad in any way. In Leila's case, she had spent years blaming each and every caregiver who entered her children's lives. No one was good enough for her. Little did she realize that her own fears were creating unrealistic expectations of those who worked for her, which led to their inevitably failing.

As we move away from the traditional paradigm of parenting, we accept our inner lostness as simply part of the process of growing up. As we do so, we allow ourselves to become aware of our true self's many faces and start to integrate them into our life. We feel neither sorry for ourselves nor superior, but simply accept ourselves as a work in progress, allowing life's lessons to show us the many ways we have yet to grow from within.

Discovering Your Family's Emotional Blueprint

Though very young children are in touch with their core self, they don't yet have the sophistication to protect this in the face of their parents' unconsciousness. They aren't equipped to understand a parent's words, actions, and reactions as manifestations of the parent's own programming long ago. They don't understand that Mommy gets mad because *she* feels inadequate, which is the result of not being in touch with her essential self, or that Daddy shames them because *he* feels insecure in his work life. All they see is anger directed at them, which causes them to believe it's because of them. Neither do they understand why their mommy or daddy never spends time with them or plays with them. They see only their parents' distraction or disinterest, and as a result they believe they are either not likable or not fun enough.

Since a child is incapable of forming an accurate assessment of a parent's emotions, the child unconsciously absorbs these emotions. Slowly, these emotions replace authentic feelings and become a blueprint for how the child will cope with life as they grow up. Similar to how cultural myths affect our thinking, this family emotional blueprint supplants our original one and begins to govern how we express ourselves. Unless we learn to decode it, we will automatically pass it on to our own children, burdening them without even realizing we are doing so.

How this decoding can be accomplished can be seen in the case of my client Victor. A normally calm father, he began finding himself increasingly irritated when his seven-year-old son would cry after losing a Tee-ball game or when his sisters teased him. The thought of having a weak son triggered rage in Victor, causing him to berate his son mercilessly. "Toughen up, son. You're being a wimp," he repeatedly told him. "There's nothing to cry about. You're being ridiculous."

Although many men have this attitude when their children cry, especially a son, Victor's reactions were at times so extreme and relentless that his wife became fed up with his lack of empathy and his impatience. It became such a problem that she threatened him with divorce if he didn't let up. This brought them into therapy.

Victor shared with me how he grew up in a poor neighborhood in Brooklyn, New York, where he had to deal with gangs and street violence on a daily basis. He was constantly dodging drugs, bullets, and other dangers. His mother, who was single, worked at night, leaving Victor not only to fend for himself but also to care for his younger sister. Consequently Victor absorbed an emotional blueprint that involved squelching his feelings in order to maintain a fight-or-flight status. He had learned early that if you let your defenses down in a dangerous world, you might not survive.

Victor grew up determined to leave his history behind him. To achieve this, he became an attorney, leading a successful life in Manhattan. Still, despite his conscious effort to free himself from his past, he was never able to recover from growing up as that scared little "tough boy" he once was. Squelching his feelings had enabled him to mask them with a façade of strength, but this front could never remove the insecurity, fear of abandonment, and terror of being killed that were deeply ingrained in his psyche. Consequently, each time he saw his son cry, he was reminded of the fear he had tried to erase but that was still very much alive inside him.

When his son complained of something that was troubling him, Victor was unable to take his experiences at face value. They were always colored by his own childhood. It was as if he were saying to himself, "If my son cries over losing a baseball game, how would he possibly survive on the streets of Brooklyn?" This caused him to respond to his son as if he were responding to his own young self, telling him, "Stop crying, or you will really have something to cry about."

When Victor made the connection in therapy, he broke down, shuddering. Tears streamed down his cheeks for the young child he was never allowed to be and the many ways in which he wasn't allowing his son to be just a child either.

For one reason or another, most of us find ways to compensate for our childhood pain. We stop trusting and instead become resentful. We also swap our innate self-worth for a feeling of shame. Layer by layer, we cover up our authentic self, growing one hard shell after another.

Have you ever seen a Russian nesting doll? It consists of a wooden doll containing a series of smaller and smaller dolls. In a similar manner, we form deeper and deeper layers of our own psyche as we cover up who we really are in reaction to what's happening to us. The Russian dolls increase in number year by year as we learn to create false personas in more and more areas of our life. Compensating in this way may allow us to survive our childhood, but it impedes all true growing up.

It takes becoming parents ourselves for us to discover how immature we really are. We realize that on the inside we're still carrying around bucketfuls of charged, limiting, unresolved emotions. Only when each of the layers has been brought into the open do we reach a point where we no longer need to protect ourselves from the things that frighten us—the things that drive us to control our children.

Albert, another client, learned this the hard way. His son Thomas had completed his calculus homework and asked his father to check it for him. When Albert went over the material, he noticed that Thomas had done very little rough work in order to solve the problems. The

answers looked as though they had been typed without any effort behind them. He immediately asked Thomas, "Did you cheat?"

Thomas was appalled that his dad would suggest such a thing.
"No, Dad," he replied, incredulous. "Why would I cheat? I know all
the answers."

When Albert reported this to me, it was with a sense of considerable shame. "You won't believe what I did next, Dr. Shefali," he related. "I gave him a new set of problems to prove to me he didn't
cheat. When he began crying in protest, saying I was being unfair, I
refused to listen. I was convinced he had cheated and wanted him to
prove me wrong. Well, he did the new problems and got them all
right. Again, he had little need to work them out on paper. I can't believe I accused him instead of praising him."

I call these moments treasured opportunities for growth. I'm not
a masochist who enjoys uncomfortable confrontations, but often it's
these intense moments that present the greatest opportunity for
growth and understanding. Far from judging parents when they engage in such unconscious behavior, I guide them to see these events
as bejeweled invitations to investigate the residual pain from their
own childhood—the pain of missing their lost self.

When I asked Albert to remember how he behaved around homework as a child, he immediately admitted, "I was a slacker, cutting
corners any way I could. My friends and I always freeloaded off each
other. We had a pact that only one of us would do homework at a time.
The others would copy it. I was constantly ridiculed and punished by
my father. He made me feel ashamed for not trying hard enough, so I
often lied to him."

As Albert connected with his deep shame over his own lack of effort
and his dishonesty, he was able to see how he had projected these feelings
onto his son. Now he understood why he was so activated by Thomas.
Because he had never really faced up to his past behavior, he was fearful
that his son was following in his footsteps. When feelings from our past
haven't been integrated, they float around inside us like balloons, ready
to pop the moment they are pricked. When we can release ourselves
from the burden of our parents' unconscious pain, we give ourselves the
opportunity to begin walking toward our own freedom.

Sometimes I'm privileged to hear how this approach helps children understand their own parents better. I recently received a letter from a fourteen-year-old who felt compelled to reach out after watching my episode on Oprah's *SuperSoul Sunday*. She had battled with anxiety and depression most of her time on Earth and had tried to end her life several times. She described her relationship with her mother as "tortured," explaining that the show illuminated her mother's own pain and inner torture. For the first time, she was able to separate her own pain from that of her mother. She wrote, "I can finally be free to find myself. I no longer need to feel responsible for the way she feels."

To find ourselves—this is the key to living a fulfilling life. It's how we bring our children up to enjoy their own ability to experience fulfillment, instead of inheriting the distorted emotional blueprint from our past, that's the hallmark of conscious parenting.

The realization that our worth doesn't depend on anyone or anything external but rests solely in our essential self allows us to enter a deep companionship with our inner truth, relying on it to be our radar. The last sentence in this teen's letter to me captured this perfectly: "I can now search for who I am without all the guilt and anxiety I have been buried under all these years. It is now time for me to be me."

CHAPTER TWELVE

What's *Really* Behind
Our Reactions

We have seen that our beliefs stem from our culture and our families. While these are idiosyncratic, we all have one universal underlying emotion that drives our reactivity, be it with our spouse, ourselves, or our children: fear. This fear creates a schism within us, cleaving us from our authentic self, cloaking our true being in self-deception and the falseness of the ego.

Think about all the times you may have been depressed, anxious, or confused. It's quite possible you were scared about confronting something or someone, were afraid of the outcome of a situation, or were terrified to lose the admiration or approval of someone you esteemed. When we feel fear, we instinctually cover it up with a host of reactions. These range from self-doubt to retaliation against another. Typically fear leads us to harbor falsehoods about ourselves and others, such as, "I'm not good enough," "My child is a failure," or "I'm incapable of making a change in my life." In fact, anytime we are critical of ourselves or others, we are operating out of fear.

At first it may not be easy to see how fear is the driver of our reactions, since it is a master of disguise. It wears many masks, such as anger, frustration, inauthenticity, control, and sadness. While we may certainly feel justified reacting in these ways in certain circumstances, it's important to understand that fear underpins each of these expressions. Sometimes it leads us to protect ourselves from negative influences, whereas at other times it keeps us stuck in negative cycles.

Whenever fear hides behind our various masks, it causes us to displace onto others what we are feeling, perhaps through blame, anger, jealousy, or control. Alternatively, we might displace it onto ourselves through self-sabotage, bouts of depression, or self-harming. Either way, we are attempting to cover up the fact that we dread ever feeling our fear full force. Indeed, the thought of it triggers a sense of panic.

Where there's no fear, we never react. Instead, we formulate a mindful response to the present moment. The difference between reacting and responding is huge. Whereas the former is a knee-jerk, unconscious, highly emotional, habitual way of addressing an external situation, the latter is thoughtful, calm, deep-feeling, and has no emotional backlash. Fear undergirds all the cultural myths we have been talking about and underpins each emotional pattern we pick up from the family in which we were raised.

Our children are the perfect catalysts when it comes to awakening our fear. Deeply attached to our children as we are, they frequently trigger our primal need to protect them. Because we constantly fear for their safety, happiness, and well-being, we are in a constant state of reactivity to them. If we aren't afraid they will grow up to be a failure, we are afraid they will grow up to be disrespectful or unkind. If we aren't afraid for their future, we are afraid of how we will live without them if something happens to them, or of how we will live with ourselves if they experience a trauma. No matter the reason, fear abounds in our reactivity to our children. It's what leads us to yell at, scream at, or hit them. It's also what causes us to shame, humiliate, or guilt them.

Typical Pathways for the Expression of Fear

We can practically map a direct path from a child's behavior to our emotional reactions, revealing the way our emotional blueprints have influenced us. Let me show you what I mean:

> *Child's behavior: Doesn't listen to you.*
> *Your reaction:* Rage, threats, punishment.
> *Underlying fears:*

"I don't have any control over my child."

"My child will grow up to be a monster."

"I am ineffective as a parent."

"I don't feel heard. My voice doesn't matter."

Child's behavior: Violates curfew.
Your reaction: You are upset but are unable to create boundaries.
Underlying fears:

"My child is selfish and inconsiderate."

"My child will be angry with me for creating limits."

"I don't feel heard. My voice doesn't matter."

Child's behavior: Is upset because they are rejected by peers.
Your reaction: Overinvolvement and interference in their social life.
Underlying fears:

"My child will feel insecure if they don't belong in a group."

"My child will feel lonely and ostracized."

"My child will be lost without a peer group."

"My child will not be liked."

Child's behavior: Is upset because they failed a test.
Your reaction: Anger and punishments.
Underlying fears:

"My child will not attend a prestigious university."

"My child will not be successful or happy."

"My child's sense of self will crumble."

"My child will be left behind and will not amount to much."

In these examples, notice how the way we've been coded emotionally comes to the surface in direct response to the fear our children awaken in us. It's as if the feeling of fear sets off an alarm that instantly triggers our emotional blueprint. By causing us to say or do something defensive or protective, the reaction that follows provides a temporary respite from our fear.

However, the longer we harbor feelings of fear, the thicker our layers of self-protection become—layers added to our pseudo-self, the ego, created when we weren't permitted to be true to ourselves. These form a barrier against emotional pain. It's these layers that we need to work through until we get to that last little Russian nesting doll. Of course, had we been fortunate enough to have parents who were able to help us work through our feelings and integrate them as we were growing up, there would have been no need to create these layers of protection in the first place. Imagine how free we would feel without all this baggage.

When we operate from the highly defensive and reactive state engendered by our fear, we can't enjoy a meaningful connection with our children because we are unable to see the real child before us. Instead, feeling overwhelmed and in a state of near panic much of the time, we attempt to assuage our raging pain by reacting to our mental distortions of our children. Parents who are racked by their own unprocessed emotions can't attune themselves to their children's feelings because they are under siege from their own.

The Core of Our Fear

Once we see the correlation between our emotional reactions and our fear, we are likely to catch a glimpse of a more powerful feeling that underpins the whole shebang. This concerns our sense of worthiness, which at its deepest level involves our understanding of our place in the universe. In other words, our personal fear is a microcosm of the universal self-doubt that plagues humankind as a species.

To get a clear picture of what's going on inside us, it will help if we explore aspects of our core fear.

Fear of Being Unloved

Somewhere deep within us, we all desire to be loved. To the degree that this desire goes unmet in childhood, either we will chase after ways of fulfilling it as adults or we will closet ourselves away from all possibility of being loved in more than a surface manner. The latter is the reason many of us grow up in homes where feelings are left unexpressed. Whatever you may be experiencing emotionally, you don't show it. The emotional distance generated by such stoicism leaves children feeling that they have no moorings.

It's our unfulfilled longing to feel loved, appreciated, and validated that leads some of us to find this soul-food in all the wrong places. If the hunger is extreme, we use substances to fill our inner void. The chemical effect of drugs, tobacco, or alcohol temporarily assuages the pain of our emptiness.

Parents who feel empty inside and therefore hunger for love interact with their children out of neediness instead of real caring for the child as a unique individual. When we parent from needing to feel loved, we tend to make decisions that will alleviate our own neediness rather than decisions that are truly best for our children.

Unresolved fear that we aren't truly loved contaminates every aspect of parenting. Such fear tends to show up in one of the following ways:

- *You try to overplease your children, buying their love.*

- *You find it difficult to create boundaries with your children.*

- *You find it hard to be consistent and firm.*

- *You interpret your child's natural pushback as rejection.*

- *You see your child's reactions as a personal attack on you.*

- *Nothing your child does is good enough, which reflects your own inner feelings of lack.*

- *You find it hard to separate your child's identity from your own because yours is so shaky.*

- *You get into a rage with your child because, not being in touch with the infinite resources of your core being, you are running on empty.*

We see several of these manifestations of fear in the case of Annabelle, a client who was raised in a family in which her parents were emotionally unavailable to her. Her parents' relationship was contentious, their marriage rife with conflict. Naturally, Annabelle absorbed their unresolved pain, along with the feeling of chaos that was all around her. Consequently she grew up insecure, anxious, and obsessed with whether people liked her. When she finally married, it was to a passive man who ceded all his power to her. Needy of validation, she dominated their home life by controlling everything.

When her youngest son was diagnosed with a learning disability, Annabelle had a hard time adjusting to him. He lacked the shine and luster of the kind of son she needed in order to feel competent as a mother. The more he struggled in school, the more she unraveled internally. When he began to manifest symptoms of ADHD, which led to a host of behavioral issues, she was simply unable to cope. Telling herself life was victimizing her, she became depressed and withdrew. Because she made her son's challenges all about her, she fell apart instead of using her strengths to help him.

Annabelle was coping in the only way she knew, which ultimately meant rejecting her youngest son completely. She sent him to boarding schools and paid for professionals to take care of him. It was only after entering therapy that she was able to identify the connection between her own sense of not feeling good enough and her experience with her son. She was able to recognize how feeling rejected by her own parents caused her to reject him.

Parents who are either aggressive or neglectful operate out of fear. The slightest show of imperfection or limitations on the part of their children leads to rejection. Perhaps you find it hard to have empathy for such parents. But if you could only recognize that this syndrome arises from the deep internal hunger such parents contend with on a daily basis, you might begin to understand them.

Annabelle's case resonates with all of us on some level. If our inner being isn't grounded in a state of perpetual love, our insecurities will flare up all over the place. We will take personally things our children do or don't do, and we will catastrophize situations. As our children absorb our insecurity, they will realize they can't be themselves around us. Their life then becomes one of treading on eggshells.

Facing up to how empty we feel inside takes courage, patience, and commitment. If the need to feel lovable wasn't met in our early years, the void we experience can crush our ability to trust others, let alone cherish them. This is why it's so important to help our children feel both loved and lovable each and every day by raising them consciously. We can start by fully accepting our children, just as they are, right now. As we do so, their original, authentic self blossoms, leaving no void within to cause all the problems so many of them experience.

Fear of Conflict

As noted earlier, because of the emotional blueprint we inherit from our family, many of us are afraid of dissent and conflict. This is because whenever we engaged in conflict we experienced consequences that ranged from shaming to punishment, and even to abandonment. As a result of being invalidated by our parents in this way, we resolved to avoid conflict at all costs. The emotional pain was too much to bear. Instead of getting into an emotional collision, we adapted to what was expected of us.

Perhaps your childhood was different and you never saw your parents fighting. Consequently you never had the opportunity to observe how they resolved their differences in a healthy manner, which means you likely didn't develop the skills needed to navigate your way through conflict. For this reason, you probably concluded that any degree of conflict is undesirable.

Girls in particular are typically taught to avoid conflict by not being assertive where their needs are concerned. This is why when they grow up to be mothers, many have a hard time making their needs known and their boundaries clear. This inevitably leads to misunderstandings between their children and themselves, as well as with their spouse.

Since conflict is a normal part of human interaction, those of us with an emotional blueprint that causes us to avoid conflict find we are ill-equipped to help our children deal with it. Because we are so activated by conflict, we lack the competence to help them deal with important elements of childhood such as honoring boundaries, dealing with sibling rivalry, and coping with the inevitable ebb and flow of life.

This fear may show up in your own parenting journey in one of the following ways:

- *You can't say no to your children with any consistency.*

- *You jump in preemptively to rescue your kids from tough situations.*

- *You can't tolerate sibling rivalry and constantly intervene.*

- *You feel guilty for saying no, then overcompensate in unhealthy ways.*

- *You can't set firm boundaries with your children.*

- *You become a pushover, pleaser, and doormat to your children.*

- *You overindulge your children by buying them more than they need.*

- *You allow your children to manipulate you, and in turn grow to resent them.*

- *You're scared of your children's big feelings.*

- *You feel overprotective of your children when they experience painful feelings.*

- *You hover and control your children's lives to shield them from pain.*

- *You talk excessively, rationalize, and lecture instead of just saying no.*

- *You don't establish healthy boundaries with your spouse or friends.*

- ► *You tire yourself out doing things for everyone because you can't say no.*

- ► *You live in constant fear of being disapproved of or labeled "difficult."*

Diana's father had an explosive temper. She grew up terrified of his chaotic emotions and the conflict attached to them. As she witnessed her father's fits, she simultaneously absorbed her mother's sense of helplessness. Needless to say, the emotional blueprint she took with her into adult life led her to marry someone just like her father, a successful but emotionally volatile man. Fortunately for her, his work took him on long-distance travels, so he was scarcely home.

When Diana and her husband became parents, she found herself raising her three children pretty much alone. The pressure of this caused her to fluctuate between rage born of frustration and passive helplessness. Because she avoided defining clear boundaries, her children pushed for them by acting out. Our children always manifest behaviours designed to wake us up. Whenever Diana's children crossed a line or got into trouble at school, she unleashed a slew of punishments. Life for the three youngsters swung like a pendulum between a lack of any structure and complete lockdown.

Mothers like Diana are often misunderstood as being irrational and wishy-washy. Society deplores the way their children grow up either entitled or anxious. The reason a mother is like this is that she lost touch with her own center when she was a child. Yes, a person can "act strong" from ego, but the "strength" such a person exudes isn't at all the same as the calm steadfastness that originates in our solid core. When strength flows from our essence, it causes us to have a powerful presence.

When Diana entered therapy, she began the process of uncovering her fear of conflict. She saw that her reticence to establish boundaries with her children came from the fear of rejection she had experienced in her own childhood. She saw how she had in effect become her mother, helpless instead of standing up for herself and asserting her wishes. As her sense of her own self gradually emerged, she was able to establish the boundaries her children yearned for.

If you struggle with setting firm boundaries and are afraid of conflict, you deprive your children of the chance to find the balance between honoring their own needs and those of another. Boundaries are essential if children are to understand their limits and discover ways to cooperate with people in the journey of life. Without parents who can lead the way, children feel rudderless and may well run amuck.

When the thought of establishing boundaries makes us anxious, children can't help but absorb our anxiety. When they do, they will push the envelope, trying to get us to set a limit—something you can readily see in children who engage in risk-taking behavior early in life. Alternatively, they will become riddled with anxiety because there's no one to step in and put an end to their mind's whirling thoughts.

Our children need us to contain them, but not control them. Their true self knows they require this, and it needs to happen on both a behavioral and an emotional level. Even though our children need to feel secure in the knowledge that we will contain them if their behavior goes too far afield, and they practically beg for such containment, we can do this for them only if we have addressed our own fear of conflict and need for boundaries.

If we are to contain effectively, it's vital that we develop both the yin and the yang of our humanity. Although we generally divide the human species into male and female, we all share both masculine and feminine characteristics when it comes to our inner self. Because we become a complete person only when we connect with our internal qualities, it's up to each of us to enter into a harmonious relationship with our feminine (yin) and masculine (yang) characteristics.

When it comes to parenting, many parents follow typical trajectories for male and female roles. Fathers are often overdeveloped in their masculine aspect and underdeveloped in their feminine aspect. In mothers this tends to be reversed. As a result, it isn't uncommon for fathers to be in charge of discipline, whereas mothers are typically associated with caretaking and nurturing. While there are many men and women who don't fit into these cultural norms, our societal expectations and emotional blueprint push us to subscribe to them in the way we raise our children.

Many mothers I work with have a hard time expressing autonomy and leadership, or even asserting themselves, especially with sons. They find it difficult to establish clear boundaries in the home and feel guilty when they have to say no. Used to being something of a pushover instead of exerting their authority and letting their authentic voice be heard, they allow their children to run roughshod over them. This dynamic is healthy for neither the mothers nor for their sons and daughters. At the same time, in my practice I also counsel many fathers who don't know how to be emotionally available to their children or partner because any display of real feeling threatens them.

Both mothers and fathers lose out on vital experiences due to their inability to accept and integrate their masculine and feminine aspects. I frequently have to tell moms, "Place less emphasis on some of your feminine qualities and enter more of a masculine stance." I say the reverse in the case of many men. Our ability to enter into a balance between masculine assertiveness and feminine nurturing is vital in the parenting journey.

Women who are afraid to assert themselves are notorious for giving of themselves well beyond healthy limits and not knowing how to ask for their needs to be met and their boundaries respected. This inevitably results in resentment. Similarly, men are typically cast as those who are good at maintaining boundaries and receiving respect for their space and time, but not so adept at giving of themselves emotionally. Our children react to both these energetic templates, frequently disrespecting their mother but fearing their father. I realize that these are sweeping generalizations, and yet I see all the time how detrimental they are when it comes to raising children to be whole individuals.

Our children need to learn that they possess the capacity for both yin and yang qualities. This principle underpins all the other principles we have touched on, for it speaks to the unity of all things. It shifts our focus from the illusion of our separateness and opens our eyes to the oneness of everyone and everything. In so doing, it challenges us to transcend the outer form and enter the formlessness of our inner being.

To encourage the development of our children's capacity for both yin and yang, we need to support the development of these energies. For example, when our girls are assertive, instead of shaming them or pushing them to "tone it down," we need to channel their power wisely. When they show signs of autonomy and leadership, instead of tempering these qualities, we need to encourage them. When they make comments like, "I don't think I'll get married," or "I want to run my own business," we need to allow them to dream without interjecting our prejudices or concerns into the equation. Our girls need to be allowed to be limitless and grand, fearless and strong, capable of reaching any frontier they desire and are willing to work toward.

Similarly, when our boys cry, we need to encourage them to connect with their heart. Feelings need to be seen as a strength to be celebrated and supported. When they show signs of gentleness and domesticity, instead of putting them down, we need to back them up. Boys have the ability to be tender, caring, empathic, compassionate, and giving. They need to know that the more they connect to their heart, the more courageous and masculine they actually are.

When we spend time with our children, we need to ask ourselves, "What's the balance that's needed here? Is my child veering more into the feminine? If so, how can I help introduce the masculine? Or is it the other way around?" A conscious approach doesn't discourage the natural propensity of the child. It's meant only to create expansion within the psyche so that there's a rounding off, a balance.

It's time for our men to inhabit more of the feminine principle, becoming contemplative, tender, gentle, and feeling. If they do, they will approach conflict differently and peace will become a reality. It's equally time for women to inhabit more of the masculine principle so that they engage in greater self-advocacy, embracing their ability to speak up, stand against, and march forward.

Our children will naturally own these complementary aspects of their psyche when they see us doing the same. They need to experience their father's comfort with his feminine traits, as well as their mother's comfort with her masculine characteristics.

When the mind is integrated in this way, the balanced energy spills outward, creating cohesion in the external world. We can create a world that advances and prospers according to masculine principles, but that also nurtures the earth and its creatures in line with the feminine. Neither principle should have the power to outdo the other. There will be a natural pull to the center. It all starts with becoming conscious.

Fear of Saying Yes

When we grow up in families in which feelings aren't expressed openly, and love and validation are often withheld, we feel afraid to give of ourselves with fearless abandon. When a lot is being asked of us on the emotional level, we find it hard to say yes and plunge in. This is because we believe in the idea that love is in scarce supply. Because we believe there's not enough love to waste it, we protect ourselves from giving away too much.

The root of this perception is that our own parents weren't available for us in generous and abundant ways. Somewhat different from the fear of not being loved, our fear of saying yes shows up as self-absorption rather than need. We find ourselves withholding instead of being generous with our giving, including giving of our time and affection to people.

When we have children, we can feel overwhelmed by their constant demand for our attention. How can we engage at this level if we never experienced such ourselves? In the face of our children's limitless hunger for us, we feel weighed down. We find it difficult to grapple with the fact that they need so much from us—that they expect us to give our attention to them with complete abandon. The needs of an infant are especially overwhelming. It's for this reason that parents begin to train their children to sleep when they are as young as six or seven weeks old.

Of course, some parents opt to escape. By immersing themselves in everything from work and social activities to personal crises, they become emotionally unavailable to their children, thus reenacting their own childhood experience.

Fear of close engagement may affect your relationship with your children in some of the following ways:

- *You find it hard to stay open to their feelings without interjecting yours.*

- *You find it hard to give them your undivided attention.*

- *You find it hard to play with them and enter their world at their level.*

- *You find it hard to be spontaneous with them.*

- *You find it hard to see their demands on you as natural, not an imposition.*

- *You find it hard to give to them without conditions.*

- *You find it hard to put your own wishes aside and give to them wholeheartedly.*

To illustrate, Keith grew up with a mother who was heavily invested in her career in television and often left him and his younger brother with a nanny. His father was also a workaholic and hardly ever home. Because he failed to attach to a primary caregiver, Keith wandered through childhood without an anchoring sense of self. Though his needs were excessively indulged on the material level because he was a member of a privileged family, the simple warmth and nurturing he really needed were denied him and therefore never lit the emotional coals within him.

Because Keith didn't experience his heart being touched as a child, it began to close up—like a muscle that atrophies from lack of use. Emotional connection simply wasn't a part of his life. He learned to survive on possessions and status symbols, placing value on these commodities instead of the currency of connection. Unaccustomed to authentic connection based on warmth and caring, he treated women the same way. When he became a father, he was unable to go beyond the role of material provider. Consequently, his children never really got to know him and imagined their father regretted that they had been born.

Many of us may have grown up with parents we sensed didn't really know us on a heart-to-heart level. They somehow seemed distant. As a result, we find ourselves threatened by emotional closeness, mistakenly believing it to be suffocating. When we become parents ourselves, our children's needs feel unfamiliar and intrusive. Instead of tuning in to them, we reject them. Instead of welcoming their displays of affection and their need for us, we turn away from them, leaving them with a sense that they aren't worthy of our attention. It's only when we can see their hurt as a reflection of our own buried pain that we allow ourselves to face up to our past and at last mature into the parent we need to be.

Fear of Being Autonomous

In many families there's a clear distinction between parents and children. This is particularly the case in traditional hierarchical families in which children are taught to follow the instructions of their parents and be obedient. Such families have the potential to foster a dangerous level of enmeshment and the dependency it breeds.

When children are discouraged from having their own voice and following their own leadership, they grow up dependent on their parents' authority. Because they seek their parents' approval on most things, they rarely exercise their potential for self-governance. If they happen to exercise their own sovereignty on occasion, they are often shamed or threatened, which causes them to fall in line. When these children grow up and become parents, their passivity and dependence continue and they are unable to exercise clear and empowered leadership.

This may show up in your life and family in any of the following ways:

- *You are unable to create a clear vision for your family.*

- *You are unable to allow your children to have their own life.*

- *You control your children and don't allow them to be free.*

- *You make your children overly dependent on you.*

- *You interpret differences of opinion or interests as betrayal.*

- *You guilt-trip your children if they choose a path that differs from your vision.*

- *You shame your children for having their own mind.*

- *You cling to your children, preferring enmeshment to clear boundaries.*

Betty grew up in a home where she was taught to be quiet, gentle, and compliant. She was considered a "very good girl" and prided herself on her abilities all the way through college. She even became the doctor her parents wanted her to be, never once thinking of doing something *she* wanted to do. Then Betty became a mother herself. Following the emotional blueprint she grew up with, she raised her daughter to be just like her.

On the surface the family looked TV-ready. No one would have guessed that Betty was experiencing emotional abuse by her husband. Scared to let anyone know, least of all her daughter, she hid all signs of the abuse. When her husband cheated on her, she pretended she didn't know or care. When he started controlling their bank accounts and credit cards, she abdicated all control to him.

It was only when her daughter left for college that Betty began to crack, sinking into a deep depression. When the daughter saw how her mother was falling apart, she suffered tremendous guilt. At one point she even came home for a semester to help her cope. Betty found it difficult to emerge from the weight of her crumbling marriage and empty nest. She turned to food as solace. When her weight reached extreme proportions and her health began to suffer, she finally sought help.

It took years for Betty to discover her true self and find her voice. It was only late in her fifties that she dared to divorce her husband. Even then, she was paralyzed by fear of being on her own. She's still in therapy, now approaching her mid-sixties, grappling with issues of autonomy and struggling to find her way among the rubble of her lost self.

Staying in one's marriage for so long, not giving up, appears admirable on the surface. To the public, a person may seem as if they are extremely family conscious, devoted to their spouse and children. In one way this is a beautiful quality indeed. However, upon closer examination, it becomes clear that such individuals are defined by their family relationships, preferring to maintain the "idea" of a family or a marriage at the cost of their own well-being. In the end, they find themselves unable to stand on their own two feet.

If children of such parents reject the blueprint and flee, they end up feeling guilty like Betty's daughter. This crushing of personal initiative results in a subtle but perceptible loss of motivation, zeal, and sense of purpose. It's only when we, as parents, find the strength to be our own person in our own right, without depending on others for our meaning, that we can allow our children to fly free, fearlessly exploring their limits.

Fear of Unhappiness

Many of us grow up in homes in which there's a great deal of anxiety around being unhappy. Instead of times of unhappiness being seen as a natural aspect of being human, we feel guilty for feeling down. Consequently, we do everything possible to avoid things that might trigger unhappiness. We have bought into the illusion that life isn't supposed to be unhappy.

When we resist experiences that cause us to feel unhappy, we teach our children to be afraid not only of their natural human feelings but also of the ebb and flow of human existence. Our children then grow up believing that unhappy feelings must be avoided at all costs.

I can't tell you how many times I have heard parents tell a crying child, "Oh no, you are feeling sad. Maybe a cookie will help?" When I ask these parents how they made a connection between sadness and food, they look at me as if to say, "Isn't the connection between sadness and food obvious?" In the same way we use food to manage our pain, we use smoking, drinking, drugs, television, and even exercise to numb us lest we feel sad. If children are discouraged from honoring those times when they aren't their usual happy self, they become detached from their actual experience of their life. We believe we are protecting them from pain when we are robbing them of the opportunity to build muscles of resilience.

Let's take a look at how this fear of any intimation of unhappiness interrupts our ability to help our own children with their emotional growth:

- *You try to cheer your children when they seem sad and jump in to fix their pain.*

- *You belittle them for feeling vulnerable.*

- *You fail to be empathic when they have feelings that make you uncomfortable.*

- *You don't teach your children how to cope with pain, only how to avoid it.*

When Gabriel was nine years old, he recalls, he returned from school crying about being bullied. He ran into the house to look for his mother, yearning for her comfort and reassurance, but his father and grandfather were the only ones there, playing cards at a table. Unable to hear his feelings and enter into an empathic connection with him, they admonished him for being "wimpy." They also joked about him being worse than his younger sister, who would have just beaten the bullies up.

Gabriel remembers hanging his head in shame. He pledged to himself he would never show his father his tears again. Absorbing the message that it was unmanly to express emotion, he went to bed that night and hit his pillow as he told himself repeatedly how "stupid" he was for being such a wimp.

Today Gabriel still struggles with having empathy for himself or others whenever he sees tears. His wife often complains about how he can walk over her like she's a heap of dirty clothes when she's crying or upset. She can't understand how cruel he can be. His children spark considerable impatience in him, which results in his yelling at them or threatening them. It's because Gabriel was never validated for his authentic feelings that he can't connect with painful feelings in his children.

Constantly running from their fear of unhappiness, and consequently the fear of failure, individuals like Gabriel are often the unhappiest of all. Although it's well masked, they are extremely anxious and fill their days with all sorts of activities to avoid having to deal with the pain of being disconnected from themselves. Eventually everything crumbles around them as they are forced to face that which they have avoided all their life.

Children raised with such a template learn quickly to bury their sadness and put up a façade to make their parents happy. Such children then often express their real feelings in the form of physical complaints like migraines, stomach cramps, and earaches. Or they start failing in school. Paradoxically, these unhealthy ways of expressing their pain increase their anxiety.

Fear of Not Being Worthy

Many of us grew up in homes that left us with an emotional blueprint of not being good enough. We were constantly compared with others. When we didn't measure up, we were made to feel bad. We saw how important money, beauty, and status were to our parents and absorbed these as the criteria for success. We learned early that to simply be ourselves was far from adequate.

The sense of not being good enough tends to affect the way we, as parents, engage with our children in the following ways:

- *We teach our children to depend on their grades to feel good about themselves.*

- *We obsess over our children's looks and teach them to rely on them.*

- *We try to control our children's friendships and place value on popularity.*

- *We display low levels of self-esteem by putting ourselves down in front of others.*

- *We have excessive concern about our body image and social status.*

Mary remembers clearly how her father used to relate stories of how at work he prided himself for never making his bosses angry with him by rocking the boat. Even though one boss repeatedly humiliated him, he never disrespected his authority. The stories he shared instilled in his daughter a fear of standing up for herself. In this way, Mary came to believe she was less important than others, especially those in a position of authority. As an adult, she has a hard time protecting herself in situations in which she's being maligned or mistreated. When one of her closest friends betrayed her trust by stealing money from her, Mary finally woke from her trance and realized she needed professional help. Through therapy she began to realize she had a pattern of attracting people in her life who took advantage of her and who never fully treated her as an equal. She traced this pattern back to her own childhood conditioning, when she never felt worthy of nurturing or respect.

When Mary and others like her become parents, their children feel anxious about being themselves. From the way in which their parents slump their shoulders, hide from life, and fail to assert their authenticity, they pick up the idea that they are less than others.

Fear of Not Being in Control

The parenting industry has sold us on the idea that to be a good parent, we must be in control. We take being in control to mean we should control our children's lives at all times, whereas what we actually need to be in control of is our own emotional reactions.

Operating mainly from anxiety, we have a hard time stepping back from our children and giving them the space they need to make mistakes and grow from them. It's important to recognize the vast difference between being a dedicated parent who is present for our children and the kind of micromanagement and nagging that result from anxiety and obsession.

This fear of losing control can show up in your relationship with your children in any of the following ways:

- *You find it hard to allow your children to make their own mistakes.*

- *You feel you are abandoning your children if you give them autonomy.*

- *You feel your children will crumble if you aren't around them at all times.*

- *You feel that without your presence, your children won't thrive.*

- *You place inordinate pressure on yourself to meet their every need.*

- *You exhaust yourself trying to manage their decisions and activities.*

- *You take everything they do personally and don't allow them to flounder.*

- *You see them as a vital part of your success and take great pride in your role.*

Cathy was raised on a diet of control and perfectionism. When she had her own children, they became her project. She signed them up for the best activities and challenged them to succeed in everything they did. However, her youngest daughter, Karyn, opposed her mother's regimented ways and fought to claim her authentic voice by rebelling. As a result, Cathy and Karyn were experiencing severe conflict when they came for therapy.

It became apparent as we talked that Cathy had an extremely hard time easing up on her daughter. But because Karyn wasn't going to have it any other way, Cathy had no choice but to let go. Reluctantly, she began to see how fear-based her approach to parenting had been. As her awareness grew, she was appalled to realize how much she had done to push Karyn away.

Such parents mask their anxiety by presenting themselves as devoted. It's only when their children begin to act out that they are forced to stop and pay attention to their fear.

Children of such parents are often besieged by anxiety and fear of failure. In their desire to have a say in their own life, they are likely to react either by becoming critical of themselves and self-sabotaging or by defying and rebelling. Either way, these children are racked with both guilt and shame because they constantly feel like they are doing something wrong. Their sense of being excessively parented is often ignored until the situation reaches an extreme level of dysfunction.

Fear of Being Ordinary

Raised in an overly perfectionistic culture, we feel we are "lesser than" if we aren't special in some way. You can't begin to imagine the countless times I've heard parents complain, "But he doesn't excel at anything." Or a child may beat themselves up, saying, "I'm only average at sports." Without our conscious awareness, we have allowed ourselves and our children to define worth in terms of a sense of perfection, specialness, and extraordinariness. When we fall short of these exalted qualities, we feel worthless and consequently insecure. Our ordinariness causes us great anxiety, resulting in our overcompensating in some way.

When we become parents, our children's limitations trigger our own anxiety to the extent that we find ourselves acting out in the following kinds of ways:

- *We are relentless in pushing them to excel at something.*

- *We shame them when they fall short of excellence.*

- *We micromanage their performance and fear failure.*

- *We overstress competition and teach them that life is all about winning.*

Caroline, a studious, diligent thirteen-year-old who excels in all her studies, comes to mind here. Obedient and polite, she's pretty much the dream child. Her mother brought her to me because she suffered from a debilitating migraine every time she had to take a test. The migraines had become so severe that she often had to be excused from taking the test with the other children. Given that she was the top performer in her class, no one could understand why tests triggered her migraines.

Taking the traditional route of killing the symptom, Caroline's parents pumped her full of painkillers. Other than sedating her, they had no idea how to address the situation. When over-the-counter medications proved inadequate, they took her to a psychiatrist who could prescribe a medication strong enough to quell her anxiety.

Soon Caroline began having migraines related to issues that weren't academic. If there was a piano recital in which to perform, she would get a migraine. If there was a party to which she had been invited, yet another migraine would appear. Her parents were flummoxed. She was an overachiever, so why was she so afraid to succeed? Since she had never failed, where was this fear coming from?

When it was clear that medications weren't going to eradicate the problem, the family came to see me. I soon realized that Caroline was suffering from the burden of perfectionism. So great was the pressure to be extraordinary that she was buckling under the strain. Unable to allow herself to be average at times and slow down, she kept pushing herself until her body forced her to ease back.

Unless the parents acknowledged their role in their daughter's anxiety, nothing would change. Having become accustomed to Caroline's success, they were in denial that they had projected a fear of failure onto her. "She has never failed," her mother protested, "so how could we have caused her fear of failure? We have never had to reprimand her for bad grades. I just don't see how we could have created this."

I explained to her parents that just because Caroline had never been reprimanded for failure, it didn't mean she wasn't intuitively aware of how important her success was to them.

"Of course success is important," the mother retaliated. "We always celebrate Caroline's successes with her. Shouldn't parents do this?"

"Certainly we can celebrate," I concurred. "But when a child intuits that we are attached to their success and realizes it means a lot to us—perhaps even more than it means to them—they internalize this in the form of anxiety. It isn't our place to enjoy or celebrate our children's success more than they do. Their success is theirs to enjoy and celebrate. If it means more to us than it does to them, we send them the message that we take their success personally. Once they realize this, the 'good' children that they are will drive them to seek to make us feel good by succeeding. Caroline's migraines are the price she's paying for taking on the burden of making you feel good."

As her mother began to see how she had based her entire family's sense of worth and happiness on Caroline's extraordinary achievements, she began to change her approach. It was only after many sessions of working with Caroline's parents to help them recognize the toxicity of their perfectionist culture and recalibrate their expectations that they were able to release her from the pressure of fulfilling their dreams for her. Ironically, their desire for their daughter to perform so perfectly stemmed from their own feelings of inadequacy.

As parents, we naturally want to celebrate our children's successes. But in doing so, we can easily give them the message that failure is unacceptable. The ego is insatiable. When we give it free rein, it breeds anxiety in our children as they seek to impress us.

Fear of Scarcity

If there's a mother of all fears, it may well be fear of scarcity. Somewhere in our emotional DNA, we harbor a belief that the universe's resources are in short supply, so that there is insufficient goodness in the world, insufficient wealth, a shortage of beauty, and far from enough love. Because of this belief, instead of becoming more expansive as we grow older, we define goodness, wealth, beauty, and love more and more narrowly. The more we view our world throu~~gh~~ myopic mind-set, the more we see scarcity.

If we view wealth principally in terms of money, only the rich appear to have sufficient amounts. This narrow definition of wealth makes it hard to feel blessed unless we are loaded with cash. However, if we come from a mind-set that sees how abundant the universe is, we understand wealth in other ways, including having a wonderful family, good health, and deep friendships.

Similarly, if we look at beauty from a perspective of scarcity, we will define it in traditional terms and compare ourselves with an impossible standard. Doing so, we will find ourselves constantly feeling as if we're lacking in some way. But if we are able to approach beauty from the perspective of abundance, we realize that it comes in a vast variety, not just the narrow spectrum defined by the Miss Universe contest. In this light, we find things like our perky nose beautiful instead of annoying, our freckles interesting instead of distracting, our curvy figure pleasing instead of perturbing.

Do you see yourself and your children through a lens of what's missing instead of what's available? Do you enter a situation and notice all that is right with it or all that is wrong? Your answer will have a huge effect on how you raise your children. It also reflects the degree to which there's an emptiness inside you where your essence failed to flourish, since we see lack in the external world only if we already feel it within us.

When children are young, they are completely unaware of the concept of scarcity. They see abundance everywhere, so that the world is their playground. They love to explore their many interests, strengths, and talents. Because of this, they are accepting of their limitations. They realize that if they aren't good at one thing, there's plenty more they can enjoy. In fact, they experience no shame in admitting they aren't good at something until they learn this from us. Neither do they form an opinion of how beautiful they are compared with others until society begins to categorize them. They aren't ashamed of their body or their mind until they collide with society's opinions.

Abundance isn't about living large and spending a lot of money. Abundance is a state of mind. It involves a deep trust in the organic flow of the universe and our place in the scheme of things. It's a way of looking at events, people, and ourselves that sees the whole rather than just parts. Weaknesses and limitations are both accepted as aspects of the whole.

Have you ever thought of abundance as including limitations, loss, pain, and even death itself? When we come from a mind-set that sees abundance everywhere, we don't interpret life's natural processes in terms of deprivation and loss. Rather, we see everything as contributing to the 360-degree circle of life. All things are understood as lending a rich texture and invaluable nuance to our existence. We understand that within the whole, other elements may be at play than those we are aware of. Just because we don't see the positive aspects of a situation doesn't mean they aren't there. When we experience life from this perspective, every experience is welcomed in its "as is" form. We trust that whatever happens carries within it the possibility of increasing our wisdom and thereby helping us grow.

A fear of scarcity may come up in your everyday life with your children when you experience reactions such as the following:

- *Your child gets a C grade and you panic.*

- *Your child puts on weight and you put them on a diet.*

- *Your child feels stupid and you hire an army of tutors.*

- *Your child suffers rejection by a teacher or a friend and that upsets you.*

- *Your child forgets a folder at school or loses their phone and you yell at them.*

- *Your child gets caught with drugs and you ground them for the foreseeable future.*

Zach was a master at living with a mind-set of perpetual scarcity. Although he grew up in a household of relative comfort and privilege, his parents were both first-generation immigrants who suffered from low self-worth. Lacking a sense of their own value, they saw scarcity everywhere. Thus Zach grew up believing the world is an unsafe place where unless you have a do-or-die mentality, you lose in the game of life. This caused him to become overzealous and extremely competitive.

Zach's career as an investment banker masked his inner hunger, which is of course what drove his craving for more and more money and greater status. Even though he had become a millionaire by his early forties, he couldn't free himself from a feeling of deprivation. No matter how much others told him how privileged he was and how blessed, he was never really able to absorb this.

When Zach's children were born, he pushed them to excel at everything they participated in. Buckling under the pressure, his younger son began experiencing social anxiety. To Zach this was the worst thing in the world, and he brought him into therapy. Slowly he began to understand how he had lived his life under siege from a deep sense of lack. Through meditation and other mindfulness practices, he was at last able to experience grace in the ordinary things of life. His willingness to uncover his fear allowed him to embrace his children as they were, enabling them to feel secure.

Children raised with a mind-set that perceives lack and scarcity everywhere are crippled by fear, which breeds insecurity and an inability to feel empowered. They don't trust the more painful aspects of life to open up opportunities for growth, and neither do they believe in their ability to transcend difficult experiences. Constantly guarded and defended, they battle their way through life, dueling with circumstances instead of flowing with them.

Entering Trust, Abundance, and Empowerment

As we grow in the insight that much of our reactivity with our children is influenced by fear, we can learn new ways to cope with it. The goal is not so much to divorce ourselves from fear altogether as it is to learn to navigate its waters when it threatens to overwhelm us. Instead of seeking experiences that are fear-free, we boldly embrace all situations we find ourselves in, knowing that we are psychically resourceful enough to handle the fear such situations may bring up within us. In this way, we are no longer afraid of fear and begin to see it as an ally in fostering a greater sense of joy and fulfillment. The universe is no longer divided into pleasure or a lack of pleasure, being fearful or not fearful, but is instead integrated into a holistic experience measured by how deeply we become aware of ourselves, how much we grow, and how in touch we are with our heart.

CHAPTER THIRTEEN

Transforming Fear into Consciousness

A s we become aware of the undercurrent of fear in all our re-actions, especially to our children, we are offered the oppor-tunity to dissect our old ways of thinking and relating to the world, replacing the archaic with more evolved ways of respond-ing to the present situation.

Our childhood blueprint inherited from our parents influences our emotional responses to almost everything:

- *How we deal with money.*

- *How we cope with stress, change, boredom, rejection, betrayal.*

- *How we regard our body and those of others.*

- *How we feel about hard work, success, and failure.*

- *How we feel about food.*

- *How we handle conflict, boundaries, risks, and challenges.*

- *How we navigate friendships and intimacy.*

- *How we manage self-governance.*

- *How we handle leading versus following.*

When I first realized that I had an emotional "chip" implanted within me about every major area of my life, I was shocked. It was just mind-blowing to me that literally every idea, opinion, and judgment about myself and others had been fed to me by my family and culture. On the one hand, this meant I was already knee-deep in the muck of their conditioning by the age of ten. Undoing these imprints would probably take the rest of my life. On the other hand, it was liberating to realize that I could indeed undo whatever imprinting didn't work for me. This was an epiphany—terrifying and invigorating at the same time!

I can still remember the first time I realized that I wasn't defined by my parents, my culture, or anything I had previously identified with. Don't take this to mean I was shunning their influence in my life—that isn't what I'm talking about at all. What I'm about to describe is how I came to understand that my sense of self isn't dependent on others and isn't defined by their ideals.

I was twenty-two years old and had moved to San Francisco from India a year prior to beginning my master's in drama therapy at the California Institute of Integral Studies, one of the most forward-thinking institutions I have come across. It also was around this time that I formally started my training in Vipassana meditation and began to seriously practice mindful awareness in my everyday life. Like any foreign student, I had spent my first year abroad immersing myself in a new culture, soaking in new ideas and ways of living, vigorously dismantling old ways of being and creating new ones. My moment of epiphany occurred on a bus ride. I remember watching two lesbian women in love in the seat before me and thought about how this would never be acceptable in my culture. All of a sudden, my entire world rocked before me. A single question seared my awareness: "Why am I defining myself by my culture's standards?" Embedded in the question was the permission to release myself from the shackles of my childhood that had been chaining me without my conscious consent. My mind was reeling. If my culture wasn't right about who and how we should love, perhaps it wasn't right about a host of other things. Maybe everything I thought was the right way to be was actually wrong! Right there in that moment, I began to shed my attachments to all the checkboxes I had previously so zealously adhered to: woman, successful, psychologist, daughter, and Indian woman. As you can imagine, this process of molting the old identities was as liberating as it was deathly intimidating. Who was I without these roles and beyond these identities? What if I were rejected by my family? How would I tolerate their disapproval? Could I dare to recreate a new sense of self?

I am blessed to have been raised by highly attuned parents. Despite their open-mindedness, my childhood was inundated with underlying cultural dictates that tailored my belief systems on a subconscious level. Among these was the idea that I needed to return to India, preferably marry an Indian man, and fit into the confines of the society I was raised in. When it was time for me to divulge to my parents that I had none of these plans, I was scared of their reaction. I finally mustered the courage to confront my father. "When you sent me to America, you hoped I would change and grow, right? You didn't just want me to return as a carbon copy of how I went, correct? I have now changed. I can no longer come back and be the 'good Indian wife' you hoped I would become. I just cannot. Please forgive me."

When I started to cry, my father choked up too, then responded, "You are absolutely right. It would be selfish and narrow-sighted of me to send you to America and expect you not to change. I see how wonderfully you are growing and learning. How can I discourage that? I don't want you to worry about the traditions of our culture anymore. I want you to follow your heart and do what's right for you."

When I later reminded my father of this story, I told him, "Do you know that in that moment, you handed me the keys to my freedom?" From that moment on, I began a new life—one that was no longer encumbered by my past, but that I was instead fully free to design myself. That moment revolutionized my life, and this is why I do the work I now do.

Because I see how our families can unconsciously bind us to cobwebbed ways of being that allow us to be only a speck compared with the grand individual we can grow into, I am passionate about setting children free. My father now says to me, "When I set you free, I was really setting myself free. Your freedom has changed us all. It's because you are living your destiny that we feel the courage to live ours. You have changed your mother, your friends, and everyone you touch. Although I had no idea that this would be the far-reaching effect of that moment in time, I'm glad I had the wisdom to follow your lead and get out of your way."

Such a simple act indeed! If only all parents could remember to do this. By getting out of our children's way, we allow them to find their own voice and forms of self-expression. In their self-discovery, they liberate and transform the world. While not every child has parents who are as understanding as mine were, every child needs to come to their own realization that they are far greater than any identity—yes, even those of son and daughter—that they have affixed to themselves. Even if their families never change, this profound awareness can move mountains in a child's inner world. Regardless of our parents' willingness or unwillingness to join us, there comes a point in all our lives when we need to take the reins of our journey in our own hands and begin to steer the way. The first step, of course, is to become aware of our family blueprint and how this continually influences us.

When we interact with those we are the closest to, the way we've been coded emotionally springs to life unbidden, sparked by some pressure or fear we feel from the external world. Instead of fighting this or being defensive about it, we need to see it as an opportunity. Rather than chastising our children for showing us these unintegrated aspects of ourselves, we need to feel gratitude that finally, after all these years, we have a chance to integrate these relics from the past so we can now be our authentic self.

Emotional patterns die hard, but with practice we can learn to observe when we are buying into our blueprint and use the occasion to respond thoughtfully rather than reacting emotionally. As we do so, we in effect revisit our past, picking up the pieces of that tiny inner self we left broken on the floor—a little piece here, another there, until slowly we put back together the lost child that's our authentic self. By so doing, we become grown-ups not just in terms of our chronological age, but also in emotional maturity.

When fear is gently removed from the driver's seat and befriended, we learn to integrate it into our life rather than either blindly following its lead or pretending it doesn't exist. As we allow it into our awareness, it naturally quietens. Using an approach of "Yes, and," we allow it to exist without it stopping us dead in our tracks. So, for example, we say to ourselves:

- "Yes, I'm afraid to visit that new place, and I can find ways to feel safe."

- "Yes, I'm afraid to speak at the meeting, and I can find ways to prepare."

- "Yes, I'm afraid to confront my friend, and I can find ways to connect."

When fear is seen simply as a stepping-stone to finding creative solutions, we don't begrudge its existence or get seduced by its power. By seeing it as an intrinsic part of life, we don't sensationalize it in any way. When it loses its charge, it folds into our life in an organic way, expanding our ability rather than diminishing it.

Fear can be transformed into consciousness. It requires us to be bold in our willingness to explore it. Accepting that fear is an inevitable aspect of the human experience allows us to avoid getting stuck in it. Then we repurpose it so that we live more compassionately toward ourselves and others.

Emerging from the Shadows of the Past

You'll be glad to hear that we don't have to go way back into our childhood to excavate the roots of our fear. Instead, we watch it arise in the present moment. It's this awareness of how patterns of behavior driven by fear repeat themselves that initiates the process of setting us free. As we uncover what's really going on inside us when we act out the emotional equation, our defenses wither and the integration that follows reverberates all the way to our core, reaching the tiniest doll in the Russian doll set. Our growing awareness of how the past influences the present allows us to shed stereotypical ways of being and reacting and instead create carefully attuned responses to all of life as it manifests in the here and now. Old patterns fall away, exposing an unscripted, spontaneous, and original response to the present moment.

It must be noted that our emotional patterns are inherited over generations and can be broken only through present-moment awarenes⁣

The power and beauty of this approach to living and parenting is that we don't need to artificially force memories from the past into consciousness. Instead, we simply observe what's occurring in the present moment. Chances are that if we find ourselves reactive and overwhelmed, it's because some aspect of our past is interfering with the present—either an emotion that was left dangling and unintegrated, or a fear-based myth we were conditioned with that's now paralyzing our ability to act in an empowered way.

My client Toni's situation illustrates the power of generational patterns to repeat in families. Living with two teenagers who were unruly, untidy, and disorganized, Toni was spending all her days nagging them and begging them to clean up after themselves. She complained that her house was a pigsty and that she was embarrassed to have guests home. I said to her, "You keep complaining as if you are taking action. There is a vast difference between complaining and taking action. Complaints are passive. Action is active. What is your fear about taking action?"

At first Toni was bewildered. "What action would I take?"

I said to her, "What would you do if you found something in your living room that didn't belong to you?"

She immediately responded, "If it belonged to a friend, I would immediately return it—and if I didn't know who it belonged to, I would discard it." As soon as she said these words, she knew what I was about to suggest. She jumped in: "You want me to put their stuff back in their rooms or else discard it, correct?"

I could see this brought up anxiety in her, which I addressed. "You appear anxious. Can you tell me why this prospect is so threatening to you? After all, it seems to be the only logical thing to do in this situation."

She answered, "It's not just stuff. It's food in the fridge that lies there for days on end. I try to respect them, but then I suffer."

It was clear that Toni was confusing respect with fear. I said to her, "You are not operating out of respect. You are operating out of r. Unless you make a commitment to a sacred space of well-being ur home and ensure that it's stronger than your desire to be the ommy, this pattern will continue."

After a few moments of silence, Toni slowly shook her head and admitted, "I am just such a weakling. I don't know how to stand up for myself. I am so afraid they will reject me. I am turning them into monsters, and I'm making myself their slave. I need to put an end to this. I now realize how my complaining is just my way of staying stuck." Toni went home after our session, collected the things that her children had left all around the house, and put them in a garbage bag. When they returned home, she gave them two choices: either place them where they belong, or she would donate them. Once they saw that their mother wasn't going to tolerate living in a mess any longer, they got the message and began taking greater care of their belongings. While this one step didn't magically change their habits, it helped give Toni a path toward reclaiming her sense of power. As she so wonderfully articulated in a subsequent session, "I was crippling my children out of my fear. My own thirst for being approved of and liked by them was teaching them it was okay to live in a pigsty. The most dangerous thing I was teaching them is that it's okay to violate another's space and privacy. My own desire to be liked and accepted by them was trumping my duty as their parent."

Once I saw that Toni was able to create change in her life, I gently probed further into her psyche, helping her unravel where these fears were coming from in the first place. As she explored her history, she uncovered how her insecurities started when her parents divorced and her father moved out of their family home. She remembered feeling unworthy and responsible for the breakup. She said, "My house didn't feel like a home anymore. I felt guilty that I chose to stay with my mom and felt as if my father always blamed me for that choice." When I asked her more about her parents' divorce, she explained, "My mother was raised by a very controlling and critical father. She was attracted to my father because he was the opposite. He was carefree and easygoing, an artist at heart. My mother was the opposite—perfectionistic, timid, and anxious. As their marriage progressed, she became more and more paranoid and controlling herself. The more my father went out with his friends and enjoyed life, the more anxious she became. Eventually, her jealousy and need to control his every move drove him crazy, and they finally divorced."

It was at this point that everything made perfect sense to me. I gently illuminated for Toni how her father's abandonment was driving her fear of rocking the boat in the home. As her childhood home never felt the same once her parents divorced, she perpetuated this sense of displacement in her own home by allowing her children to lay siege to her personal space. Her lack of self-worth led her to believe she wasn't good enough to demand respect and own her space at home.

Once Toni began to see how her current problems with her children didn't just begin in her own childhood but instead had trickled into her generation from many generations past, she began to appreciate the power of awakening in the present moment. She saw how, if we dare to ask ourselves why our current situation is overwhelming us, the present can be a powerful portal for transformation. The reasons for our fear lie rarely in the present or our children's behavior, but almost always in the emotional patterns of our ancestors.

If we could only grasp how generational our fear-based patterns are, we would realize that they stem from our past and are unrelated to the situations we encounter in the present, other than the fact that these situations bring them to our attention.

Each of our fears began a long time ago. Although we interpret our children's behavior in light of our fear, the two actually have nothing in common. Once we recognize that our children's behavior is completely separate from our fear, we are able to help them as they need us to, guiding them instead of reacting to them, ushering instead of threatening. As with most emotional elements in our life, the sooner we look fear in the eye and face it with courage, the more likely it is to wane naturally. The longer we avoid or deny it, the more toxic it becomes, infecting our life with its negative energy. The quicker we recognize it as it arises in us, both in our psyche and viscerally, the sooner it will quiet and calm itself down. When we try to shove it under the rug, it mutates into anger or sadness, which causes it to loom larger.

By untangling our fear-driven emotional patterns from our chil-
n's actions, we are left with concrete behavior we can now ad-
head-on without the drama we've been accustomed to. Quite

simply, the child's behavior calls for a response suited to the behavior—minus all anxiety, emotion, and fear.

Taking our own sense of self-worth out of the mix enables us to be mindful and therefore effective with our children. With reactivity out of the way, we address each situation from a calm state and in a balanced manner, responding as the behavior warrants, thereby effectively transforming the circumstances that cage us.

Letting Go of Fantasy Parents

A large part of becoming awakened and growing up as our children need us to has to do with letting go of our attachment to, need of, and dependency on our own parents. As much as we can stifle our children from becoming independent and free, we can smother ourselves in the same way. By binding ourselves to our own parents for approval, permission, a sense of belonging, and love, we keep ourselves small and childlike. This symbiosis of selves ultimately leaves little room for each to grow and thrive. It then gets projected onto our children, enslaving them to our parental fold beyond what's healthy.

The only way we can ultimately free our children from dependency is if we have freed ourselves from our own parents. This doesn't mean we can't enjoy fulfilling and empowered relationships with them that are more like kinships and allied friendships, though it does mean that we let go of needing them to parent us any longer. I firmly believe that while our parents will always be our parents in terms of the respect this title deserves, their time for parenting us—being there for us 24/7, providing for us financially, and bolstering us—must eventually come to an end. If we continue to "use" our parents for aspects of our life that we should really be providing for ourselves, and they allow this, we not only bind them to us but also inhibit a wonderful process of growth for ourselves.

Sue, a forty-seven-year-old client, constantly complains that her parents are never there for her anymore. "My mother is so selfish. She never wants to be a grandparent to my children. She's always either with her friends or traveling. My father is constantly working or playing golf. I miss my parents and want them to be a part of my life like they were when they were young."

Sue was having a hard time individuating from her parents because, being differentiated from their role as providers and caregivers for their children, they were forcing her to come to terms with her need to be dependent far beyond what was healthy for her. I explained to her, "While you love your parents and this is wonderful, you need to ask yourself if you are missing them because you feel incapable of launching out on your own. Your parents clearly love you and have always been there for you. They are now choosing to live their own lives, as they should. Their responsibility as your caregivers has passed its expiration date. They are free to chart their own destiny, a right they have earned."

Sue admitted she had never thought about it in these terms. She had unconsciously assumed that her parents were going to forever parent her and hold her up when she failed or fell. When I helped her understand that it was now time for her to parent herself and be her own best ally, she reluctantly shared, "I guess I'm scared because I don't trust that I'm capable of doing so. I need to learn to believe in myself more, I guess."

Sue is not unlike most of us. Conditioned to depend on our parents for guidance and anchoring, we feel lost without them. At least Sue was one of those blessed to have experienced her parents as grounded and present. It was for this reason that she was more quickly able to tap into her resilience and tune in to her own inner adult. It was because she had a wonderful imprint from her childhood of being soothed, protected, and cherished that she was now able to do these things for herself.

Many aren't as blessed as Sue and didn't have parents who were at least present during their childhood. Millions of adult children feel lost, waiting for their parents to begin parenting them as they yearned for during their childhood. I think of Josh, a fifty-one-year-old father of four who still longed for the approval of his mother. He was deeply enmeshed with her, and they engaged in fights as if he were fifteen. When I challenged him concerning his need to seek her opinion on every decision, he responded, "I keep trying, you know. I keep hoping that today will be the day she wakes up and tells me how much she loves me." Ensnared by his desperate need for his mother's unconditional love, he involved her in every aspect of his life not because he consciously desired her input but because he was stuck in his childhood dependency on her.

I helped Josh see the dysfunction in this pattern. As he began to awaken to the toxic effects of such enmeshment, he asked, "So does this mean I will never have the kind of mother others have? A mother who is my biggest cheerleader and unconditionally supportive? Don't I deserve such a mother?" Josh's plea came straight from his heart.

Encouraging him to shift out of victimhood, no matter how legitimate he felt it was, and instead enter into a brutal appraisal of his situation, I explained, "If you keep yourself stuck in wanting a dream version of your mother, this pattern will never end and you will never be free. Instead, you need to accept that your mother will likely never become that mother. She is *this* kind of mother, not *that* kind of mother. The quicker you release her from your fantasy of what she should be, the sooner you will learn to appreciate her for who she is—albeit not the 'mothering' kind of mother you seek. In other words, even as we need to set our children free from our expectations, we also need to set our parents free beyond a certain age."

Liberation can come about only when we let go of our fantasies concerning others and accept them for who they are—yes, even our parents. Especially after we reach adulthood, we can no longer blame them for what they didn't give us. We need to take responsibility to raise ourselves to a higher level of maturity. Is it painful, and in some cases even tragic, that we need to do this in the absence of ever having that presence in our lives? Absolutely. But this doesn't give us an exemption from doing the work of growing up. We embrace the reality of our parents' unconsciousness for what it was and where it came from in their own upbringing, then release them from any requirement to fix us. Their time and opportunity for fixing us has long past. Now it's a responsibility we must own for ourselves. This is our gift to ourselves.

Josh struggled with this, as I would too. But as he slowly realized that his mother didn't owe him anything anymore, and that in fact the damage would only get worse by his insistence that she did, he began to release himself from needing her to fulfill his longing. As he did this, he found himself creating a more loving relationship with himself, as a consequence of which his dependency on her lessened. Soon, without the unconscious demands Josh had placed on the relationship, they both began to enjoy themselves as the adults they were, each releasing the other from the promise of the past that never came to be.

As we awaken, we realize that our parents were subjects of their own enslavement as a result of their unconscious upbringing. They acted the way they did toward us because they too were bound by fear and a feeling of lack. They certainly didn't intend to be purposely malicious or unconscious, but acted the way they did because this was what they learned from their own parents and other childhood influences. When we are able to hold this insight in our awareness, we can release our parents to follow their own path as they need to.

Enlightenment comes from letting go of our dependency on others to fill the void we feel within. As painful as it can be, we sometimes need to do this with our parents as well. Understanding them as human beings first, and only then as parents, helps us move forward on our own path of awakening and the liberation it brings.

Separating Love from Fear

Our relationship with our children is as rooted in fear as it is in love. Perhaps it's because of our openheartedness toward them that we are more in touch with all that could go wrong with them. Because we care about them so much, we know that our well-being is in many ways tied to theirs. Quite often, fear and love are enmeshed, with one merging into the other, detracting from the purity of both. It would almost be easier if we could simply say, "This is fear," and "This is love." Instead, we are often left with a feeling that looks like this: "Because I love my son so much, I help him with his social life and arrange his play dates for him," or "I insist that my daughter do well at school because I love her so much that I want her to succeed." Although from the vantage of the outsider I can assure parents that their fears come from her own past conditioning, it certainly doesn't feel this way when you are the parent experiencing this.

An exercise I have found helpful involves asking parents to stop themselves each time they find themselves overwhelmed by a wave of reactivity. Although it's hard to do in the moment it's occurring, I ask them to journal their feelings and thoughts. I then ask them to list all the fears that are arising within them.

Francesca and her eleven-year-old son Nate kept getting into power struggles over the smallest of things. Their latest conflict occurred when Francesca found him on his iPad instead of studying for a test. She lost her temper and grounded him for the weekend. Nate was livid at the prospect of missing his best friend's birthday party, which happened to fall on that weekend. He pushed his mother, screaming at her to leave the room. In the scuffle, she lost her balance and fell against the closet, hurting her shoulder. When she saw the bruise on her shoulder blade, it was a visceral signal to get help for a situation that had too often escalated beyond her comfort zone.

When I asked Francesca to list her fears, she wrote these words about her son: "Failure, weak, loser, distracted, underachiever, aimless, wanderer." Once again, we can see how paralyzing our fears can be. It's no wonder Francesca overreacted to Nate. Anyone who had these fears swirling within them would lose their mind!

I then asked Francesca to write about her love for Nate. She wrote, "I want the best for him. I want him to succeed because he deserves it. He is bright and smart. He is kind and loving. I want nothing but the best for him." As Francesca wrote these words, her entire demeanor changed. Her facial expression softened and her shoulders relaxed. It was clear that she had evacuated the head-space of worry and fear and entered a new place—a heart-space of expansiveness and freedom.

I asked Francesca to imagine the scene again. This time, instead of reacting to Nate out of fear, she should repeat the same words that she had written in her journal. As she reimagined the scene, she immediately saw how different the outcome would have been had she taken this approach. She said, "Nate wouldn't have felt so cornered. He wouldn't have felt the need to be so aggressive. Of course he wanted me out of his room! I was accusatory and mean to him. He just wanted my negative energy out of there."

Francesca began to understand how vastly different the energy of fear is from that of love. While they both appear well-intentioned, only one achieves the goal we seek. While the former creates emotional plaque, the latter frees the other to find their own relationship to their present moment.

As we move on this path of conscious awareness, we notice more quickly when we oscillate from love to fear. As we begin to catch ourselves, we can rein in our fears, allowing the space between our children and ourselves to be filled with nurturance, attunement, acceptance, and most of all a true kinship.

Let's look at one more example of how fear gets in the way of love. One of my clients, Margaret, obsessed over the fact that her fourteen-year-old daughter Debbie was more of a tomboy as opposed to a girly-girl. Debbie never wore a dress or skirt, never fixed her hair, and did none of the usual feminine activities. "I'm so afraid she's never going to grow out of this," Margaret lamented. "What boy is going to be interested in her? And when is she going to be interested in boys?"

It was clear that her mother was unable to recognize her daughter's stellar qualities because they didn't fit with her idea of how a girl should behave. Because of the mother's rigid, narrow image of how a girl ought to be, she failed to celebrate her daughter's essential self.

Debbie was actually not only a lovely child but also quite an exception. She didn't cave in to what her mother for fourteen years had been trying to turn her into. Instead, she had retained her sense of the kind of woman she wished to grow into. The price she'd had to pay for her authenticity was to be seen as defective by her mother, from whom she longed for approval.

Each of us is unique. We come bearing qualities that are idiosyncratic. Effective parenting is the kind that honors our uniqueness, including our idiosyncrasies, without making us feel we are defective if we don't measure up to some artificial standard.

Margaret isn't a bad mother. On the contrary, she has a lot of love for her daughter and was coming from a place of concern. She simply failed to see that beneath her concern lay a deeply rooted anxiety about her ability to tolerate the possibility that Debbie might not fit in with what society deems feminine.

In effect, bringing Debbie into treatment was more about Margaret taking care of her own insecurities than about helping Debbie. There was nothing wrong with Debbie. The problem was simply that her differentness triggered such great fear in her mother that it overshadowed her mother's love for her.

When the ratio of fear to love is skewed, such that fear wins, our approach to our children creates an effect that's the opposite of what we hoped for. We wonder how this came to be. As we saw in the earlier example of Francesca, our children react to our anxious control with opposition, leaving us feeling as if we were the victim. Such is the power of fear to pollute relationships and transform often benign situations into angst-ridden cesspools of misunderstood intentions and muddied emotions.

When I got to the core of Margaret's anxiety, I uncovered how she herself was severely ridiculed as a child for being overweight. Stung by all the bullying, Margaret was traumatized, collapsing under the stigma of being "the fat girl." Her own mother had been unable to help her in any sustainable manner, and in fact colluded with her daughter's anxiety by buying her an exercise machine and enrolling her in the latest dieting program. Margaret had been carrying this underdog anxiety for years, burying it under a strictly controlled life of endless diets and plastic surgeries. She thought she had dealt with the issue. It was only when I showed her how she had been covering up her anxiety that she began to realize how she was projecting this onto Debbie.

"Debbie isn't the problem," I explained. "Debbie is fine and whole just the way she is. It's your unresolved anxiety about your own inability to fit in that's being activated. You buckled under the pressure as a child. Now you're afraid your daughter won't be able to cope any better than you could."

I asked Margaret to list her fears. She wrote just one sentence: "I don't want her to suffer like I did." When I asked her to list her love for her daughter, she wrote, "She is strong and brave. She is far more secure than I ever was. I hope she never buckles under pressure like I did." When Margaret got in touch with how her fears had nothing to do with her daughter's present reality, except that it reminded her of her own past, she was able to see how much more damage she was causing because of it. She said, "I am trying to help her avoid experiencing rejection from her peers. But in trying to control this, I am the one who is causing her the most rejection." As she recognized the paradoxical nature of her actions and how she was creating her own worst nightmare, she stopped in her tracks and began to untangle from her fears.

Each one of you reading this can relate to Francesca and Margaret. We have all experienced moments of sheer panic, when our reactions are all about fear-laden control, as opposed to understanding and connection. Our children stay awake doing homework, but our fear that they won't get enough sleep causes us to bark or yell at them instead of empathizing with them. Or our child doesn't manage to master the skill of potty training on time, but instead of entering deep patience and teaching them this skill, we find ourselves riddled with fear that they will be rejected from kindergarten and will wither away at home, isolated and friendless. Or take the example of a child being rejected by his or her peers, which is a hot button for us all. Instead of allowing our children to experience this very natural occurrence, we micromanage their social life for fear that they will be ostracized, giving them the feeling that if only they were different, their friends wouldn't reject them.

It's crucial for us to be aware when our love for our children is obscured by fear. Only moment-by-moment awareness can illuminate this tendency and allow us to detach from the cascades of anxiety that besiege us, and instead enter a state of openheartedness, where we can recognize our Achilles' heel but not inadvertently project our pain onto our children.

A New Path Lights Up Ahead of Us

As we move away from the shackles of fear that were passed on to us from our ancestors, replacing those old imprints with new and enlightened patterns, we liberate not only our children but also ourselves. To the extent that we do this successfully, we begin to enjoy our children and ourselves for the boundless and limitless beings that we are.

The path toward the liberated and awakened self is never smooth or straight. It is strewn with potholes, boulders, and landslides. Just as an artist spends months, even years, painting a masterpiece, relying on the creativity within and exercising the discipline required to patiently add stroke upon stroke, so it is with the process of awakening. The liberated self doesn't emerge overnight. It arrives as layer after layer of our ego gets peeled off and replaced with mindfulness and the wisdom that comes with it. Given that we are asked to face all our fears, the price of awakening may seem high. However, if we keep moving forward, one step at a time, the rewards of such an undertaking soon reveal themselves. Our days begin to be permeated with an irrepressible joy and a sense of purpose that engages us with intense present-moment awareness.

~ The Gift ~

May you be blessed with a child . . .

Who defies you
So you learn to release control,
With one who doesn't listen
So you learn to tune in,
With one who loves to procrastinate
So you learn the beauty of stillness,
With one who forgets things
So you learn to let go of attachments,
With one who is extra-sensitive
So you learn to be grounded,

With one who is inattentive
So you learn to be focused,
With one who dares to rebel
So you learn to think outside the box,
With one who feels afraid
So you learn to trust the universe.

May you be blessed with a child . . .
Who teaches you
That it is never about them
And all about you.

Part Four

Transformative
Parenting Skills

CHAPTER FOURTEEN

From Expectations to Engagement

The fear at the root of every emotional reaction is more often than not connected to the threat that an expectation will be unmet. Either we have an expectation of being treated in a particular manner, or we expect our children to behave a particular way.

By definition, expectations are rooted in the future and are often at odds with the present. We expect things to be better than they are. We expect better results than what we are seeing. We expect more progress and growth than we are getting.

Expectations are often tacit reminders that we think the present is in some way lacking, and that the future can be better. As this shifts our awareness from who our children are in the present moment to what we imagine we desire them to be, it causes a deep divide between our children and ourselves.

If you stop to think about it, the notion that we should expect things of any person, especially our children, is ludicrous. When we hold the belief that we should have "clear expectations" of our children, we are unaware of the embedded subtext behind this heavy-handed sense of entitlement. I believe that the only person we can hold clear expectations of is ourselves, for once we create clear and consistent boundaries in the home, children naturally subscribe to these without undue distress.

However, because the parental Kool-Aid has condoned a dictatorial approach, encouraging us to believe we are superior to our children, we feel free to impose our expectations on them in a random, unchecked manner. We begin to believe that everything about them is our business. It's as if we want to own their every thought and micromanage their every action. We don't seem to realize that it's one thing to be caring and committed, but quite another to treat our children as our possessions.

When we treat our children as if they were our possessions, our expectations of them inevitably lead to anger and disappointment when they fail to live up to the ideals we have for them. Because as parents we believe we have the right to demand things of our children, even if what we expect of them falls outside their interests and perhaps even their native capability, they suffer from the burden of having to become something they really aren't. This forces them to abandon their true self, which is the most damaging trauma any child can experience, since it involves self-betrayal.

To illustrate how damaging our expectations can be even when they are well-intentioned, let me tell you about the time Emily took her three boys, ranging in age from six to ten, on a trip from New York City to Los Angeles for the first time. To make the holiday exciting for them, she packed their schedule with one enriching activity after another. However, instead of champing at the bit, eager to see all of Los Angeles, the boys resisted their mother at every turn. Their fussing and fretting created havoc for Emily, who spent the entire trip alternating between yelling at them and feeling guilty for doing so. Because she was deeply conflicted about wanting her boys to participate in the amazing opportunities she had planned, but could see that they just wanted to have fun doing things more age-appropriate, she had a miserable time.

When Emily and I explored her triggers in therapy, she said, "I can't believe my children are so ungrateful and unappreciative of what I do for them. I'm so disappointed that they are so self-absorbed. Any other child would be thrilled to be in their shoes." Like many parents, Emily had created for herself a story of how she was being victimized by her ungrateful "brats."

At the root of Emily's disgust with her boys lay a desire to offer the best of the world to them. This desire originated from her own experience as a child. "I worked so hard to make a fun trip for them," she said. "The least I expected was that they would be excited like I was.

When I was a kid, I yearned to go to Disneyland and see all the at-tractions. Why aren't they able to appreciate things like I did?"

As we explored Emily's thinking more deeply, she slowly began to understand how her expectations of the way her children "should" feel and act were intruding upon the way they actually felt. I in-quired, "Did you ask them what they wanted to do? Did you involve them in the plan? Did you make sure it was fitted to their stamina, interests, and level of maturity? Perhaps you expected too much of them, when all they wanted to do was hang around the pool and relax?"

It was hard for Emily to shift gears and tune in to the emotional place her children were operating from. So married was she to her expectations that she couldn't fathom how they could have a com-pletely different experience from hers. It was only when she began to realize how heavily invested she was in her agenda for them that she was at last able to emerge from the trance she had been in.

I knew she was beginning to think clearly when she finally suc-cumbed and said, "I see how I was pushing them to do things. They were so happy to be on the beach and in the pool, whereas I was forc-ing them to do the things that were on my list. Perhaps we should have just stayed home and spent the week at our local pool. Maybe they would have preferred this. I should have waited for them to have a burning desire to go to places like Disneyland before dumping this on them."

It was evident that Emily associated having a good time with doing things for her children, equating "more" and "fancier" with happi-ness. So enmeshed was she in her idea of how a vacation should be that she didn't even stop to ask what her children wanted. Then, when they resisted her, she lashed out. Yet she had set herself up for their rebellion. The lesson is that at the root of every situation in which we are triggered lies an expectation that's entirely ours to own and not our children's to bear.

To have expectations of life, let alone of other people such as our children, is to set ourselves up for failure and resentment. The nature of life is that it doesn't bring us what we expect a lot of the time, and people—with all of their whimsy, fickleness, and confusion—certainly don't. Yet unless we become solidly grounded in our own center, we will continue to expect things of people and be disappointed.

The reality is that trying to micromanage our children and bring them under our control is a foolish endeavor. The more attached we are to our expectations of our children, the more likely it is that they will disappoint us. After all, no one likes to be told they have to meet someone else's expectations in order to gain their approval. It creates resistance within them, born of the desire to design and govern their own life without external influence. While we say that self-governance is exactly what we hope our children will develop as adults, it threatens our sense of dominance when they exhibit this in their relationship with us. We want them to be autonomous thinkers and trailblazers, but not while they live with us. Children see the hypocrisy in this, causing them to resent us and eventually withdraw their trust in us.

Admitting to ourselves that our approval of and affection for our children are highly conditional, dependent on whether they meet our expectations, takes courage on the part of parents. None of us likes to own how manipulative and controlling we can be. But only when we face our dark side with honesty can we become the best parents for our children, setting them free of our expectations and allowing them to create their own.

The Problem with Well-Intentioned Expectations

The expectations we place on our children are things we convince ourselves are for their good. But if we investigate a little more thoroughly, we might find ourselves questioning whose "good" is really at issue.

Jackie, another client of mine, is the dedicated mom of seven-year-old Paula. When she came to see me, she complained that breakfast time was a nightmare for them both. She described her trigger in the following way: "I believe breakfast is the most important meal of the day. I lay out the best spread for Paula. Cereal or an omelet, green juice or a fruit smoothie—I always give her a choice. Yet she resists it all and many days doesn't eat a thing. Can you see why I freak out? I hate sending her off to school on an empty stomach."

Again, like most parents, Jackie began with the right intention—a sincere desire to feed her child well. Yet this quickly escalated into a highly emotional situation in which she lost her temper just about every morning. It's a scene that gets repeated in literally millions of homes on an almost daily basis.

I asked Jackie, "What's your expectation?"

"I want her to start the day off well," she said. "I want her to be healthy. I expect her to understand these things and get on board."

As I listened, I sensed that Jackie's expectations ran deeper. "You want Paula to have the same taste buds and the same hunger level as yourself," I explained. "Just because you believe breakfast is the most important meal of the day, you think Paula should believe this too. Have you ever considered that her metabolism may not allow her to eat all that food so early in the morning? Every child processes food differently.

"Foods also taste different to different people. Because you feel this is the way for you to be a good parent, you believe Paula should blindly follow along. But what if you were to attune yourself to your daughter's eating preferences?"

Jackie initially resisted my challenge. "Breakfast must be eaten," she insisted. "Says who?" I pushed back. "You've bought into the myth that to be a good parent, you need to feed your child breakfast. So rigidly attached are you to this myth that you're dictatorial. But from even a health-focused point of view, let alone the effect on your relationship with your daughter, is it more important that she eat breakfast or that she leave the house in a harmonious frame of mind?"

Jackie was forced to reevaluate. "I guess it's more important that she feels supported and understood," she concluded, realizing now that she needed to let go of her fantasy of feeding her daughter the "perfect breakfast."

Letting go of our fantasies can feel like a death of sorts. Naturally, we believe we are giving up something. To surrender a habit we consider important not only engenders a profound sense of loss, but also flies in the face of the cultural myth that we should be in control. We fear that if we let go of the reins, there will be anarchy and our children will run amuck.

In reality, all we are giving up is an idea of how life ought to be—a mental construct. It turns out that once we actually let go, the "death" we experience takes the form of a lightening of the spirit. A certain freedom accompanies it. We realize for the first time that we have the power to choose whether or not we get triggered—that the triggering happens entirely within us.

When I tell parents they have permission to let go of all triggers around food, they are often simultaneously shocked and relieved. Not having to micromanage their children's every morsel makes their life a whole lot easier. "But then how do I ensure they eat healthy?" they ask. I remind them that they cannot force-feed their children. They can create the conditions for them to eat well, but after that, they cannot turn mealtimes into power struggles. It is important to understand that half our battles around food come from our unmet expectations and our inability to let go of a fantasy of how mealtimes should look.

"What about sleep?" you may be asking. This is another of those emotional issues that generate stress. Half of the problem with getting children to sleep is that we turn it into a battle. When we let go of our need to micromanage our children's bedtimes and sleeping habits, sleep becomes much easier for them. Children will naturally sleep when they are tired, even if not precisely on our schedule.

The same principles apply to issues such as schoolwork, who our children form friendships with, and their weight. In fact, when I take parents through the list of potential triggers and examine them one by one, they realize how easy it is to let go of almost all their triggers. Initially appalled, they soon begin to have hope.

Does this seem like negligent parenting? It's anything but. I show parents that by removing their impositions and, more important, their anxiety from the equation, they pave the way for their children to find their own way. It's a small step with big ramifications for the health of the parent-child relationship.

What's the Unmet Expectation?

Sara, a devoted mother to her two children, Max and Angelique, ages seven and nine, built a wonderful playroom for them. She loaded it with a zillion toys, myriad art supplies, and innumerable mind-stimulating activities. Despite the huge number of items she had purchased, to her credit every single one of them had its specific place on the wall-to-wall shelves she had installed all around the playroom.

Now, how do you suppose the room looked after a day's play? Well, of course, it was a disaster. With so many toys and games to choose from, the children jumped from one to another until the entire contents of the playroom lay in a huge pile on the floor. Since she is a highly organized person by nature, this drove Sara bananas, resulting in war over the playroom every single day. Same trigger each day, same reaction from Sara.

When Sara told me about this in therapy, I asked her to send me pictures. She took fabulous before-and-after shots that she thought would justify her frustration and inspire me to come up with some clever strategy to straighten out her impudent children. Taking one look at the "before" photos, I told Sara to keep the "after" ones to herself. "Why?" she asked. "Don't you want to see the utter chaos my kids create every single day, despite my telling them day in and day out to clean up after themselves?"

I told her that I had seen enough based on the "before" pictures, explaining that her trigger was self-created and self-perpetuated. Given their ages, her children were exempt from all responsibility for the mess.

Sara was shocked, even appalled, by my evaluation of her reactivity. This didn't surprise me. Instead, it prompted me to tell her, "Remove 75 percent of the toys, games, and other activities from the room. Then, instead of labeled shelves for the children to keep their toys organized, get big buckets for them to throw things in. Remove all swords, footballs, and sharp objects that might harm someone or do damage. Cover your fancy wood floor with cheap foam play mats. Let go of your fantasy of giving your children their own Neverland Ranch to play in. Let them play with empty spaces, pieces of construction paper, and their imagination. Give it two weeks and their bad behavior will disappear."

Although Sara had a hard time letting go of her carefully selected mind-stimulating activities, she forced herself to store them all away in the basement. Within days her children were not only squealing in delight at their unencumbered space but were thrilled that "cleanup" just meant picking things up and dumping them into buckets any which way they pleased.

When we unmasked Sara's hidden agenda, it became apparent that the reason her children resisted putting everything back in its place on the shelves was that their agenda involved nothing more than enjoying being chaotic and making a mess. Since Sara's agenda was entirely different, she took her children's refusal to tidy up in the way she thought they should as an insult to her noble intentions as a parent. It was this clash of agendas that unleashed her emotional reactivity.

Instead of enjoying themselves, the children felt ashamed for just wanting to be themselves. In fact, they had become scared of her and hid whenever she came into the playroom. By the time Sara came for counseling, things had escalated to the point that the children didn't want to play in the playroom anymore.

Because of her unmet expectation concerning how successful children are raised, Sara didn't realize that play at this age is supposed to be chaotic. It was only when she was able to see how her own needs fed her triggers that she could let go of her reactivity.

Sara's reactivity was fed by her expectation that her children should be "happy," and that they needed to be ahead of the curve. It was in an attempt to bring this about that she had armed them with all the latest toys, games, and other activities. Her experience with her children is a clear example of how our expectations of the way things "should" be sneak their way into our lives and become a belief, thereby obstructing our ability to connect with our children in an authentic way.

Sara was now able to see how she had created her own monster. Deeply embroiled in her self-made mental movie of what it meant to raise successful children—in this case, Children Exposed to Every Activity at Toys "R" Us—she had superimposed her own beliefs and agenda onto her children. The idea that she should provide a huge selection of things for them to engage in so they might have every opportunity to succeed in life was a delusion she had picked up from the culture in which she herself had been raised.

On a deeper level, as we have seen, the primary cause of our emotional drama is fear. It was out of fear that she wasn't good enough that Sara had tried to control her children so that they could compensate for the feeling of lack she was lugging around from her own childhood. Ultimately, it's always a sense of not being good enough that pushes us to place our expectations on our children. If we feel whole and present in each moment, we have no reason to overcompensate. There's no guilt, no shame, and no lingering fear. We can be authentic, natural, and free, flowing with what our children's spirits need from moment to moment. How different that is from when we come from lack, which causes us to stop paying attention to spirit and instead focus on the needs of the ego—things such as fancy toys, expensive gadgets, and big surprises. The gift of conscious parenting lies in our realization that none of these will help develop our children's sense of worth, and neither will they help heal our own inner wounds. Consciously awakening helps us realize that the experience of self-worth is an inside job.

Out of the Head and into the Heart

Our expectations come from a place of heavy judgment, where without our conscious awareness we create images of how things should play out. When we operate from this place of "should," we inadvertently give off energy communicating that we are right and anyone who opposes us is wrong. Before we know it, we occupy a place of rigidity, superiority, and close-mindedness that immediately pits the other against us. As we all know, once both parties are locked in this dance, it's hard for either to break free.

Suzanne, the mother of an anxious thirteen-year-old named Brad, comes to mind. Brad had developed a habit of constantly complaining about his body, including headaches, stomachaches, itchy ears, and wobbly legs. Without fail, he found something to complain about every single day. This drove his mother mad. Suzanne said to me, "I keep asking him what I can do to help him, but he just keeps on whining. I keep trying to show him that he's fine and there's nothing wrong with his body, but this just sends him into a tailspin of irrationality. I don't know what I'm doing wrong. I know there is nothing wrong with him, and it kills me to see him worry so much."

Suzanne, a lawyer by profession, is a pragmatic, logical person. To witness her son act irrationally was a huge trigger for her. "I grind my teeth every time he approaches me. I brace myself for some sort of complaint. I hate what he's doing to our relationship."

I replied, "Each time he comes to you, you've already decided that he's wrong and you're right. With this assumption, you automatically presume he should change his ways. You expect him to follow your counsel and simply stop feeling what he's feeling. The more you expect him to be different, the more he resists you. The truth is, you are as irrational as he is."

As I expected, Suzanne was baffled by the idea that she was creating her own misery. I explained, "When Brad comes to you, you go into your head. You intellectually deconstruct his complaints, using logic to convince him how he should feel based on your expertise. Brad doesn't need a lawyer for a mom. He just needs his mom. He needs someone who can connect to his feelings and allow them to be. He needs to feel soothed and heard by you. He's using his complaints as a way to reach out and connect to you. The more he reaches out in this way, the more you go into your head. This is why the cycle continues on and on."

It took Suzanne a while to see how her expectation that Brad should be stoic and practical like she was interfered with her ability to connect with him. She was treating him with the same guidelines she treated herself. Not one to give in to her feelings, she was highly uncomfortable with his. The more she tried to change him, the more he compensated.

Suzanne wasn't one to let up easily. "But I know I am right," she argued. "There's nothing wrong with him. How can I empathize with him when I know he's just worrying about rubbish?" Suzanne was adamant that she was right, and this was ruining her ability to connect.

As long as she held on to the desire to be right, her relationship with her son would suffer.

I explained, "You are obsessed with how things should look according to your beliefs. And you probably are right—though this doesn't mean you will be successful in connecting with your son. In fact, our attachment to being 'right' is one of the most mistaken things we can do in a relationship. Your son needs his mother to simply surrender to his feelings and just hear him. He needs you to look into his eyes and say that you understand his pain. His pain doesn't need to be real or justified in your eyes. It's his, not yours. He's looking for you to leave your head and connect with his heart."

Suzanne sighed and said, "I can't remember the last time I looked into his eyes and just connected to him without telling him what was wrong with him. This is going to take a lot of work on my part. I have forgotten how to stay in my heart."

Our expectations of how things should be interfere with how they actually are. In fact, the word "interfere" shoud have been spelled "inter*fear*" as it is our fears that lead us to disconnect from the present moment. Handcuffed by our mental expectations, we paralyze ourselves from responding to life as it unfolds before us, moment after moment.

Living from the heart means we stay open to whatever life brings us. If we expect our children to be happy at Disney World but they end up crying through it all, we surrender to this reality without resistance. If we expect our children to do well on an exam but they fail miserably, we open ourselves to this fact without hesitation. In other words, entering our heart means we allow life to engage with us as much as we engage with it. We stay open to life influencing us as much as we seek to manage it. We embrace the twists and turns as much as we hold the hope of a bump-free road.

Only when we let go of many of our expectations can we enter into the present moment openheartedly, filled with curiosity and a creativity that sees the joy in each new reality. We let go of our perfectionism and aren't troubled by how different reality appears from our expectations. We release control of the outcome of things, instead fully engaging the present moment with surrender and ease.

Every moment is a new one, and the key to navigating any situation is to listen to the messages embedded in each moment. We have goals, yes, and we make plans. But we are always aware that our children will embellish our ideas with their unique stamp, and that this new creation born of their ways and ours is to be treasured as part of the adventure and beauty of life.

The Dance of Nonduality

When we see only one side of an issue, usually our own agenda, it's nearly impossible to make wise decisions. By transcending black-and-white thinking, we mirror the world of nature and indeed the whole of reality. Look around you at the universe in which you live. How much of it is black and how much of it white? And what degree of blackness or whiteness would actually qualify to be labeled "pure" black or "pure" white? Especially now that we know that even the blackest reaches of space are actually full of light our eyes can't see.

Nature is nondual. Instead of presenting us with stark opposites, it offers us a vast palette of colors in countless shades. The universe is a manifestation of a reality that expresses itself in infinite shapes, colors, odors, flavors, sounds, and so forth. Consider, for instance, the vast spectrum of hardness and softness, ranging from a diamond that can cut metal to a soap bubble. Or consider the spectrum of sweetness and bitterness, which plays such a key role in the enjoyment of food. As for hot and cold, what a range of temperatures there is between when ice melts, water boils, and the sun converts hydrogen into helium. All of these degrees of variation, along with innumerable others, exist not as opposites but on a continuum. Indeed, nature has few true polarities, and even the four universal forces that formed the universe may ultimately turn out to be different expressions of a single reality.

Let's apply this to our children's behavior. If you look back on any conflict you may have had with your child, you'll see that you and your child got caught in a negative spiral because you held a polarized view of the situation.

Take an occasion when teens forget their homework folder and we decide this is "bad" behavior deserving of some kind of punishment. When we admonish them and administer the punishment, do our children feel understood? Do they experience our interaction as constructive or affirming? Are they inspired, enthusiastic, and excited to have an opportunity to bring their folders home the next day?

When we don't look at situations in a polarized manner but instead take time to see the broader picture and put things in perspective, the way we address a child shifts dramatically. The focus is no longer on the child's behavior as bad, but on understanding how a situation came about and finding helpful ways to avoid a repeat. Perhaps the child was talking to friends—which is a good thing because we want our children to enjoy friendships—and consequently forgot the folder. Do we focus only on the forgotten folder, or can we celebrate the child's ability to socialize? Or perhaps the child was helping someone and ended up rushing out the door, only then remembering— too late—that they had forgotten their folder.

When my daughter has forgotten something, she always reminds me, "At least I remembered that I forgot it, Mom!" Forgetting something is a call for practical solutions, not moral judgments. Once we realize that forgetfulness has nothing to do with being "good" or "bad," we can help our children manage a tendency to be forgetful. The situation is an opportunity to teach them to make lists and to set reminders and alarms—especially in this era when these tasks are so easy for them to do on the cell phone or iPad.

Why does this method of parenting make a huge difference to our children? Since it relieves them of living with a fear of failure, they feel secure, knowing that their parents will see the many sides of every situation. Consequently they aren't afraid to take risks. They understand that their actions will be viewed as courageous, no matter what the outcome. Children thrive when they are accepted and encouraged, whereas criticism and punishment cause them to wilt inwardly and ultimately make even more mistakes instead of developing good self-management skills.

This liberating approach encourages children to expand their comfort zone and experiment with different ways of being, unafraid that they will be chastised. Such children fearlessly march toward their future, resilient in the knowledge that who they are is worthy of being understood and validated.

The Freedom of Engaging

Does this approach mean we can never have any expectations of our children or those we love? What about intentions? Are these bad too?

I cannot tell you how many times I have said to my clients, "It is clear that your intentions are in place, but your execution is the problem!" If you look closely, you will see that you aren't really setting an intention, but instead you are actually creating an expectation. Intentions—in their purest sense—have nothing to do with expectations of the other person and only to do with the acceptance of a vision for ourselves. Truth be told, there are very few of us who set intentions without huge judgment, conditions, and expectations of ourselves, others, and life itself.

The only real intention we can ever aspire to set without a judgment on our world is when we *intend* to engage with life in the present moment in its as-is form. It is here, and here only, in the active acknowledgment of how it really is versus how we would like it to be, that the portal for change manifests. There is no point in holding intentions for our future if our relationship to our present is completely messed up. Instead, let's *intend* to awaken ourselves in the present moment, fully aware that through this present moment, the future will organically manifest as it is supposed to.

Take the example of Martha, who bought a puppy for her two teenage kids. Answering their insistent wishes for a puppy, she felt she was holding the intention for their well-being. However, truth be told, she bought the puppy hoping that he would keep her children distracted from their social engagements so that they would stay at home more and focus on their academics. After a few months, Martha found herself stuck at home looking after the puppy, with her children nowhere to be found. She found herself cleaning up after him and being his sole caregiver. She felt duped by her children. When she came to see me, she cried, "I had the purest intention with this puppy and has turned into a disaster." I stopped her and clarified, "You didn't have pure intentions. Your actions were laced with expectations. You didn't own your decision to buy a puppy. You pretended as if you were buying it for their joy and fun, but in fact you had an underlying expectation, didn't you?" As Martha awakened to her inner schism, she was able to see how she had backed herself into a tight corner. By confusing intention with expectation, she had set herself, her children, and now this poor puppy up for failure!

Supporting a child as he or she engages life is far grander than a head-driven expectation or even an intention heavily laden with goals. Instead of a vision for the future, which often gets filled with empty promises, engaging life full-on, in the present moment, is a *way of being*, entailing an organic body-mind-soul approach to life. Expectations and goal-laden intentions aim at the future. Engagement, on the other hand, is focused on the present. The only clear path to a future goal is to be able to enter our lives in each present moment with clarity, alignment, and consistency. When we do this, the path to the future unfolds effortlessly. Most of us spend inordinate energy on imagining the future instead of channeling our focus on the present. The present moment is the only matter of relevance. No matter what our grand intention, if the present is murky, the future will be as well.

Had Martha operated out of true engagement, she would have been fully attuned to her children's commitment and realized that they were not going to be able to take care of the puppy and that she would be its sole caregiver. She would have uncovered her true agenda and realized that she couldn't expect a puppy to meet the expectations she had for her children; it would be downright unfair to expect this of the poor creature. This is how staying true to ourselves and our children, by engaging with them as they are—not as we wish them to be—helps us lead clutter-free and aligned lives.

When I began to feel a need to write a new book, I didn't sit down with the intention of producing a bestseller. I sat with the intention to enter the present moment and just write. My intention was limited to present-moment awareness, pure and simple. If I were to hold intentions for how the book would manifest in the future, I would entertain doubt, worry, and stress. This is why I prefer to hold an intention to engage in present-moment action, instead of intentions that take us away from the present moment and are simply dreams and fantasies for the future.

Children learn to take risks when allowed to engage in the process of creativity without obsessing about the outcome. The trick is to embrace its many incarnations moment by moment along the way. If they are fully present in whatever they are doing, it will be what it needs to be at this stage in their development—no more, and no less—and will be accomplished without their feeling pressured and becoming stressed. As parents, we stay close to how our children are expressing themselves in the moment and hold them to this without jumping to a future vision of what it should look like.

I can tell you, it's wonderful to be free of the responsibility of micromanaging the minutiae, trusting that the outcome is less important than engaging in the process. When we hold this perspective regarding grades, for instance, we might say to our children, "It doesn't matter to me if you get an A, a B, or a C. What matters to me is that you stay true to yourself, hold yourself to your own standard, and allow yourself to engage in the study material to the best of your awareness." Children who learn to engage with life in the present moment begin to understand that although their thoughts and fantasies may direct them to believe certain things about themselves, what actually is manifesting in their present-moment reality is what matters. In this way, they shed their obsession with any event in the future, and instead learn to harness their attentions to the present moment. Children who receive this message feel immediate relief that the outcome doesn't determine their worth, but that their efforts and their curiosity matter far more.

When my daughter Maia performed in her first horse show, she experienced a range of emotions. At first she was anxious. This was immediately followed by disappointment when she didn't do well in her first round. Her eyes welled up with tears and she said to me, "I just want to quit."

When I encouraged her to detach from the ribbon she got and helped her go back into the course, she again felt anxious. Her second round was better, which immediately led to her feeling relieved. Within moments she was smiling again.

The third round didn't go as well as expected. In fact, her horse refused a jump. She scolded the horse and began to tear up again. Once more, I assured her that she was a winner in my eyes because of how she was weathering her anxiety and surviving her emotions. I told her, "You can finish the course just because you want to ride. The prize is irrelevant."

She went back to the course. When the final round was a success, she was exhilarated. Because she had done excellently, she was on top of the world. She expected me to change my tune and show pride in the wonderful ribbon she had won. When she saw that I had stayed the same in my approach, she inquired, "Aren't you happy, Mom?"

I told her, "I am neither happy nor sad. The ribbon doesn't change my mood or feelings about your performance." When she looked puzzled, I explained, "The point of entering the competition was that you learn to take a risk and leap into the unknown. You did that the moment you got on your horse. Mission accomplished. Everything else is gravy. Your ribbon doesn't change who you are one iota. You are the same, Maia, whether you came last or first. My pride in you comes from the fact that you were able to feel all your feelings and still march on despite them. You didn't allow your emotions or your anxiety to rule you."

With my daughter, I am interested in these questions:

- *Did she take a risk?*

- *Did she learn?*

- *Did she try?*

- *Did she feel?*

- *Did she express herself clearly?*

- *Did she engage with full-on presence?*

How different this is from a unidimensional expectation that only ts to know, "Did she win?" Placing the emphasis on present-moment engagement of a task frees not only our children but also ourselves from the burden of determining outcomes. Unburdened by how things will turn out, our children learn that engaging is the thing that matters. This simple yet profound shift from expectation to engaging is a portal to true freedom.

Transforming Expectation into Engaging

Our expectations are a disguise for our fears and unmet inner needs. As long as we are unconscious of how these fears drive us, we will continue to push our children in unhealthy me-versus-you dynamics. Unless we awaken to how our issues are projected onto our children, we will keep them stuck as pawns in our own dysfunction.

Engagement is fundamentally different from expectations. Where our expectations come from our heavily ego-based agendas, our engagement with our children comes from a very different place—our hearts. Consider the following examples that illustrate some of the ways in which they differ from the point of view of how a parent relates to their child:

Expectation: I want to be proud of you as my child, and I want you to be successful, so you must get an A grade.

Engagement: I will enjoy the process of seeing you learn, empty myself of my agendas and ideas of how things should be, detach from associating your worth with grades, bathe you in the light of your own limitlessness, support you in your efforts to achieve your heart's desires, help create an environment in which you can focus on your work, be present to guide you through the rough parts, ease you through your anxiety and pick you up when you fall, challenge and comfort you as you walk into the unknown, relieve you of the burden of pleasing me, and awaken you to your own engagement with the material.

Expectation: I require you to show appreciation for me as your parent.

Engagement: I wish for you to stay grounded in your own self-appreciation. I absolve you of the need to please me or meet my needs. I will help you rest more in gratitude than a sense of entitlement, allow you to receive but not be indulged, help you feel connected to the gifts that have been bestowed upon you, and help you practice serving so that you learn to give as you receive.

Expectation: I will make sure my child respects and obeys me.

Engagement: I will detach from my need to control you, let go of my illusions of superiority or grandeur, create a safe space for you to express yourself, give you opportunities to be listened to and to listen, nurture a relationship in which you are honored as much as you honor, foster a connection whereby we naturally enrich both our lives, steer you back on track if you create unsafe choices for yourself, and allow you to test, experiment, and rebel within the container of our connection.

As you can see, expectations are confined to rigid and dichotomous ways of engaging and relating. They are meted out to our children from a hierarchical and superior position. Quite naturally, our children oppose them. Who wouldn't? When we have expectations of our children, we absolve ourselves of any need to change, which naturally causes them to resent us. No one likes to be regarded as the bad guy. No one wants to take the blame all the time. Yet when our children protest and retaliate against this blatant unfairness, they are castigated, reprimanded, and shamed.

When we shift from having expectations to supporting full-on engagement, we move away from holding our children responsible for our happiness. In this way, we hold the space for our children's inner self to flourish in its own unique manner. This approach intuitively understands that all of life's experiences are an odyssey into greater self-awareness, self-development, and self-connection. All else fades into the background, allowing our children's inner authority and expression to flourish.

~ A New Commitment to Shedding Expectations ~

I shed my expectations and agendas,
Knowing they stem from my small mind-space.
Instead, I will enter my expansive heart-space
And release you from meeting my needs,
Expecting only that I do this for myself.

When I see you, I will no longer reflect
My fears, insecurities, longings, and drama.
Instead, I will clear the mental cobwebs
That cloud the shine of your brilliance
So that I can be a mirror of the diamond you are.

As my agendas melt away, so does the hollowness I feel,
Leaving only wholeness in its place.

CHAPTER FIFTEEN

From Mindless Reaction to Mindful Presence

I am often asked, "What exactly is presence?" and I always find myself falling short of an answer that satisfies me. The reason for this is that presence isn't something that can be theoretically described or understood. It can only be experienced. As we all know, to explain an experience is to shortchange it. It's like trying to explain the colors of a sunset to someone who has never seen one, the thrill of riding a Ferris wheel for the first time, or the sensation of floating on a calm ocean. There are some elements of life—maybe all—that can be understood only through the experience.

To me presence connotes the ability to be fully aware of one's present. It requires that we suspend thought, ideas, opinions, and beliefs. We simply *are*. In this "being" state, we are unaware of who, where, or what we are and instead are fully engaged with the process of being alive. As mentioned earlier, if you observe very young children who have been allowed to live unencumbered lives, they will most likely reflect a state of presence, where every moment is treated as a new one, without the imposition of thought.

When we feel fully alert to the present moment, our attachment to our ideas and agendas falls away. Instead we are attuned to whatever arises. We witness, engage, act, let go. In other words, we flow with the tide of life, while also standing vigilant guard on its shores. A part of us is active in the world, while internally we are at rest. We engage life full-on, while never losing touch with the abundance within.

Becoming present allows us to connect with whatever arises around us, all the while maintaining a state of balance and calm. As we aren't operating out of our head and therefore attached to our mental movies, we are able to respond to life's ebb and flow from a state of grounded-ness and openness. Uninterested in getting anyone to follow our ways, we learn to flow with others instead of attacking them. We seek to join with their energy when appropriate, or we move away quite naturally should the moment demand. Either way, we remain agenda-free, eager to enjoy the newness of each unknown moment. The ability to be present helps us create deep and abiding connections with all we encounter, especially our children.

Entering the Present Moment

The only way to create change in our relationship with our children is by learning to enter the present moment. As I discussed earlier, the clash of time zones—the fact that we live much of the time in the past or the future, whereas our children live in the present—is the cause of most of the dysfunction we experience with them.

Entering the present moment means joining with the "as is" of a situation without resistance. Once we move into the present without the "attack" energy of "Why isn't my agenda being met?" we can act without the emotional reactivity that accompanies so many of our interactions with our children.

Recently I noticed how hard it was for me to enter the present moment with my daughter. She was talking to me about fashion, beauty, and how fun it would be "to be a fashion model" (understandably a match to my triggers). She was in a joyful space, rattling off all the wonderful clothes she had seen in a magazine. My instant thought was, "How superficial. How terrible. I am doing a bad job as a mother by allowing her to have these values." Thoughts like these inevitably create a sense of guilt and pressure within us, which in turn causes us to find ways to control these uncomfortable feelings.

I said to her, "Maia, how superficial you are! These are such trivial things in life. I don't want you to grow up to think being a fashion model is the be-all and end-all. I need you to think about more important things, like what your purpose in life is and how you are going to serve others."

Maia's face immediately fell and she became quiet. I took this to mean I could further unleash my agenda on her, and said even more hurtful things. "You are not going to grow up to be a brainless twit, interested in rubbish like beauty and fashion. You are going to grow up to be a citizen of the world, concerned with helping end poverty and doing good things with your life."

At this point, Maia, who isn't one to allow her character to be assassinated by anyone, barked back, "Mom, I was just talking about some clothes. I wasn't talking about my future. I am just twelve, and all twelve-year-old girls talk about this stuff. Why are you acting like I've done something bad?"

Of course, she was right. She hadn't done anything bad at all. The only thing she had done was violate my own sacred image of myself as a conscious parent. My ego's agenda of raising a child who is obsessed with ending poverty or finding the cure for cancer had interfered with connecting to what she was actually experiencing in the moment.

Maia then delivered the sword into the heart of my huge ego, as only very wise children know how to do: "And from now on, I just won't share what's on my mind!" I knew I had messed up big-time. I had made the bed of disconnection that I would later lie in. I had helped teach my daughter that it was unsafe to be twelve, and especially unsafe to share things with her parent without risking criticism and a reprimand.

How on earth was I going to reconnect and realign myself with the present moment? I said, "You are absolutely right and I am out of line. You have every right not to trust me. I was operating out of my fear for the future and forgot you are just twelve and having very age-appropriate thoughts and feelings. I just get scared you will forget what really matters in life."

She said to me, "You need to trust yourself, Mom. You've taught me what matters and what doesn't. But most of all, I am not you, and if I like fashion, then that's what I like."

It's in these kinds of ways that our children put us right back where we belong, aware of our own floundering sense of worth and trust. Had I truly trusted my own parenting, her comments wouldn't have worried me in the slightest. The only reason I felt the need to ensure my daughter wasn't being sucked in by the glamour was that I was unsure of my parenting and at the same time ambivalent about my own relationship with fashion and beauty. My imagined fears had once again hijacked my ability to be attuned to my child in the present moment.

Taking my own advice in the situation with Maia's conversation around fashion, had I been aware, I would have noticed my trigger. Then, instead of allowing it to overwhelm me, I would have set it aside and said to Maia, "Boy, that triggers someone who's old and fashion-phobic like me. But I hear what you are saying about your likes and dislikes. My own fear as a parent that my daughter might not recognize the superficial nature of these things kicks in, but I know and trust that you already know these things." This approach is how we can acknowledge our fear in an authentic way without allowing it to sabotage connection.

You may ask, "Should we never correct our children? Must we always accept them in their present reality? What if they are doing something wrong?" These are valid questions. However, these concerns also emerge from a state of fear associated with lack. They come from a desire to control, fix, and manage.

I say to parents, "Acceptance of the present moment doesn't mean you are passive or resigned to things. It simply means that the sting of the emotional charge is taken out of the situation. Sure, you can correct your child and even assertively create boundaries if these are needed, but the entire exchange is executed without adding in the emotional charge of fear, panic, shame, or guilt."

There is a vast difference between accepting our children on the one hand, and because of this acceptance indulging in their demands on the other. When Maia complained the other day that her pizza slice tasted "off," while I honored her disappointment, I also taught her to, in effect, "deal with it and move on." Were she to have kept whining or complaining, I would not have been deterred in my approach to her. I would still have said, "The pizza slice has been bought. You either eat it or we find you something else at home. I am not going to buy another slice." Instead of getting upset at her not appreciating the pizza or, worse still, forcing her to eat it, I would have laid out her choices and asked her to make the right choice for herself. It is very important that parents do not misunderstand acceptance to mean a passive state of allowance or indulgence. In the same vein, were a child to be rude and unsavory at a dinner party or a restaurant, while it is important to not attack or yell at them, it is also important to lay a boundary around their inappropriate behavior. Sometimes this might mean that you leave the circumstance until they calm down and understand what it means to be appropriate, and sometimes it means that you pull them aside and speak to them in clear and direct ways about the effects of their behavior on others. Whatever the action may be, sitting quietly and avoiding an intervention is not a quality of consciousness by any means.

"But what if my child is engaging in something really detrimental?" a parent may ask. "For example, what if they are playing on their phone but need to be studying for a big exam the next day?"

Present-moment awareness demands that we engage with our children as they show themselves to us in the here and now. Instead of stampeding into their room with our mental stories about how disobedient they are, we need to ask for the phone, explaining that their inability to set it aside is affecting their homework. Without engaging in argument or further explanation, we simply talk to them about the agreement around cell phone use and ask them to place the phone outside their field of attention. Even if they make obnoxious comments or throw a tantrum, our task in this moment is to detach from those distractions without added drama. It must be noted that the greater the drama or resistance, the greater the disconnection between parent and child. I often tell parents, "If your child is unable to see your point of view and cannot abide by your boundaries, it means that there is something else at play here—something that is obstructing your relationship." In these extreme cases, the phone fades as the central issue and the relationship comes into the foreground.

The Power of Impermanence

We forget that everything is impermanent. All things have a beginning, undergo an evolution, and are ultimately transformed into something new. It's happening all the time, both all around us and within us. Nothing stays the same. So much so that even who we were this morning isn't the same as the person we are right now. Not only have our cells undergone transformation, but so has our consciousness, even if we aren't aware of it. Consequently, glomming on to a single moment in time with our children ignores their potential to transform and grow. In fact, when we highlight a certain element of their personality by reacting to it, we further embed it. The more we resist it, the larger it looms in their personality. Going back to the fashion example, had I said, "Oh, I can totally see why you think fashion models have a fun life, but I bet they also get exhausted, having to get dressed up and wear makeup all the time," and let it lie, I would have actually defused my daughter's interest in them. By panicking the way I did, I gave the models way more power than they were demanding. It's in these ways that we perpetuate our own misery!

Every moment in time is a new one that will no longer exist in the next moment. Though this moment was created with assistance from the previous moment, it's also an entirely new moment of its own. It's for this reason that labeling and categorizing a child's behavior at a particular moment is misguided. When we hold on to an image of our child as they were in a moment that's past, we fail to honor who they are in this moment. Preferring to cling to what was, we miss the child's being in the present moment.

Young children don't have this difficulty. They don't cling to what happened yesterday. Unlike the adults in their life, they don't lug around baggage from days, weeks, or even years ago. They are able to forgive and forget their grievances, which frees them to embark on the next experience with gusto. In other words, children intuitively flow with the impermanent nature of reality.

A child's genius in flowing from one state to another infuriates parents. The adult mind can't comprehend how a hug, joke, or kind word can quickly transform a child's mood. We ponder, wonder, diagnose, and rationalize, then feel frustrated when we can't come up with an explanation for their behavior. This is why when parents insist on knowing why their child behaved in an irrational way, I shrug and say, "It is what it is. They are creatures of the moment. You and I will never grasp their power to leap from one mood to another the way they do."

Grounding ourselves in the present means we enter each moment in a state of aliveness and receptivity. In this way we are always ready to see how life constantly offers us fresh experiences with new lessons. When our mind becomes clouded or constricted as a result of emotional reactivity, awareness of the impermanence of everything reminds us to breathe and gives us permission to say, "This is a new moment. I can start afresh."

Children don't like it, and we don't help them, when we catastrophize their mistakes. "Whenever I make a mistake, my parents remind me of all the mistakes I've made since I was two years old," one child complained to me, echoing how a great many children feel. "I don't even remember half of them," the child continued, "but they sure do."

Confided another child, "If I say I'm tired and don't want to do homework one particular evening, my parents lecture me about how I won't get into a good college. They're always talking about the future, whereas I'm only talking about that particular evening."

The present in its "as is" form contains limitless abundance. It's only our fear that doesn't allow us to tap into the abundant nature of each moment that presents itself to us. This is because memories from the past are seared into our consciousness, marring our ability to take a long-arc perspective.

"That was then and this is now" is a chant I often repeat to myself. It reminds me to stop clinging to what I think my reality ought to be like, freeing me to move into the present regardless of what it contains.

For example, if we return from a wonderful outing and my daughter has a meltdown because she's exhausted or worried about something she needs to do, instead of yelling at her for ruining our beautiful day, I say to myself, "We were in a great mood before, but this is now and the mood has changed. Enter the reality of this mood."

One of the most effective ways to build a relationship with our children is to meet them in the present moment. This means that when they return home from school, instead of rushing them to discuss their day or pushing them to get their homework done, we simply greet them where they are. We allow them to meet us in any way they wish. Similarly, when they go to sleep at night, we enter their mood exactly as it is. This meeting of hearts makes it a lot easier to hold to any boundaries we have established.

When we say to our children, "That was then and this is now," we help them shift into the present reality, whether this involves homework or bedtime. Consciously entering a new moment brings clarity to our relationship with them, helping them to detach from the past and enter the new.

The Abundance of the "As Is"

A client asked me, "How do I change my approach to a more conscious one? How do I genuinely stay calm in the face of a C grade when I actually want to scream?"

I said to her, "You cannot fake consciousness. It's better to tell your child that you want to scream instead of pretending you don't. While we should not dump our feelings onto our children, it is important to allow ourselves the space to express them once in a while when the urge to do so is strong. If this became a pattern, it would be worrisome, as we should be able to metabolize and integrate our feelings on our own most of the time. However, if you changed your philosophy, challenging the very idea that a C grade spells failure, you wouldn't have to try to fake it or scream in aggravation. When you genuinely see the wisdom of the C grade, everything changes. When the C grade is no longer about the death of potential, but is about the birth of self-awareness in the child, as well as an opportunity for you both to connect even more deeply, then we see its abundance instead of its lack."

"How do I translate this approach in words?" this client probed.

"Well," I replied, "you can say something like this: 'The grade is not important right now. Let's try to figure out what your strengths are and the areas you need help in. Once we can do this, we will be on our way. Every academic subject is like a muscle that needs to be strengthened. It is more important to have the desire to grow that muscle than to have the complacency that you already know it all.'"

When we focus on self-growth as the only parameter of success, the external trappings of achievement become less important to us. Every moment then serves as an opportunity to become more authentic. Faking it goes out the window. Holding thoughts of abundance, we see the resplendence of every mistake, failure, and risk gone wrong.

This doesn't mean we act carelessly. In fact, just the opposite: It means we stay grounded in what's truly important, the growth of the authentic self. When every decision is made in alignment with who we know ourselves to be in the present moment, then how can anything be a "mistake" or "bad"? Thus when we see our children operating in the best way their present awareness allows, why would we judge them for the failures they will inevitably experience? Shifting our focus, we teach them to value the ways in which they have grown from each and every experience.

I hear many people speak of what they call a "law of attraction." Seduced by its promise of wealth and success, they attempt to make this "law" work for them, only to end up disappointed in most cases. Vision boards that highlight our dreams and desires can be helpful, and I'm all for them. But they aren't helpful if they are a substitute for being fully present in our day-to-day reality because we are fixated on the future.

It's certainly true that our thoughts, albeit neutral, have the power to usher in a host of beliefs, which in turn create emotions within us that function like a magnet, causing us to be drawn to situations that reflect them. If we are steeped in thoughts that spark only debilitating beliefs and emotions, we are likely to find ourselves overwhelmed by anxiety and by negative people and situations. We seem to draw negativity to us. As the old adage says, misery loves company.

Take a situation in which your child is putting on too much weight. You might tell yourself, "My child is overweight." This thought can be neutral, except that it rarely ever is. Instead, it activates your anxiety, sending a signal to your thought bank to release more beliefs of this kind. Your next belief might be, "My child will be unpopular in school." This belief in turn sends a signal seeking other beliefs like it, such as, "I'm a bad parent for not controlling my child's eating." On and on the chain of thought-belief goes. Soon you are so anxious that your child picks up on it, absorbing it. The ramifications can be endless. After all, our thoughts cannot attract reality, but our beliefs can, because they shape who we are from within. The universe responds to the belief systems we harbor within. This is why it is so important to shape the beliefs that can create the greatest freedom within us as opposed to anxiety. In view of how we attract more of the same, it behooves us to respond differently to our children from the negative, fear-driven way we often react.

Instead of panicking when our child puts on weight, we can enter an acceptance of the "as is," without any mental story or judgment of it. We can still respond to the situation, but rather than being activated, we simply act. We may decide to create a new approach to food for the entire family, eliminating all processed foods. Perhaps we take a yoga or fitness class together. We could also create mindfulness around the foods we ingest. Even more important, we can pay attention to the way we ourselves use food as a way of numbing and coping.

Seeing this situation as a call to ourselves to awaken, we release our child from the burden of "fixing" themself. Holding the vision of good health, we are grateful for its call to alter our course. Instead of resenting the situation, we see it as an opportunity for deeper connection and engagement. From this state of presence-filled energy, we may say to our child, "I can see how you may be upset by your weight and the pressure you feel to look different. Can we talk about this?" Or we might suggest, "Let's look at our relationship to food. This goes for me too. Let's talk about ways we can engage with food with greater mindfulness and balance."

With some issues it's much easier to enter into the "as is" of the situation. In other cases it can be difficult. Let's take a common situation that most parents find hard to tolerate and cope with: disrespect.

Maintaining equanimity when our children are disrespectful is hard. Most parents are highly triggered by rudeness and take it very personally. However, instead of setting in motion a chain of angry beliefs about how disrespectful the child is being, all of them based on fear, we could choose not to give the negative behavior extra energy. It then begins to dissipate, since it can grow only if our own negative energy feeds it.

Instead, we enter a different energy by detaching from the exact words and asking ourselves, "Why is my child feeling the urge to engage with me in this manner? Is there something I'm not paying attention to? Am I being too controlling? Or am I being inconsistent with my boundaries? Why is my child lowering her own light by speaking to me in this way?"

If we can't remain calm, we might choose to walk away—but not in a huff! If we can do so gently, we might suggest to our child that they ask themselves whether they are operating out of their highest self right now. If we need to walk away first, we can ask this later when we are once again in full control of our emotions.

I say to my daughter, "Your rude tone earlier suggested to me that you were going through something. Is this true? Can you tell me what it is?" By taking my own feelings out of the equation, I can allow her to have the space to introspect.

Inevitably she says something like, "I am just so angry about what's going on between my friend and me that I got mad at you." Or she may say, "I am so stressed about something at school," or "I was tired."

In therapy, I help parents see how reacting generates a cyclone of negative energy that swallows everyone. I explain that they don't have to abandon how they feel about something, only to let go of the emotional charge around it. Instead of huffing and puffing, prodding and cajoling, or yelling and screaming—all of which simply magnify the behavior we wish to eliminate—we entertain only those thoughts that amplify the change we wish to see. Of course, it goes without saying that this has to be done in a manner that's genuine. This doesn't involve the empty praise of a child's good qualities, since inauthentic praise at a time like this isn't at all helpful.

When we enter a state of honoring, understanding, and being

empathic, we tap into our children's innate desire to succeed and engage in respectful relationships with us. We might say something like, "I know you want to succeed. I know you want to do your best. So let's work on this together." Then, instead of focusing on what the child *isn't* doing, focus on what they *are* doing and want to do more of. This shifts the energy into the right flow.

When our children see that we are able to engage them in a manner that brings out and capitalizes on their strengths, they learn to take their reactive moments in their stride. Not being shamed, blamed, and made to feel guilty frees them to focus on the changes they wish to bring about. As parents, the more we can move away from negative thoughts and statements, the more we open up space for a child's positive energy to flow.

In the case of rudeness and disrespect, we need to tap into the feelings that lie beneath the behavior. We can then expose our children to the ways their rudeness directly impacts their life in a negative way. We might say, "I know you feel frustrated when you're trying to express something, but then I get more frustrated with you. Is there another way you could express yourself so that your needs can be met? Can we take a look at how we set each other off? Let's identify the pattern and see how we can help each other more."

The crucial element in all of this is not to make a child's behavior about *us*—about how insulted, disappointed, or hurt we are. If we make it about us, the child ends up reacting to our energy rather than focusing on their own.

Acceptance takes away the sting of negativity. Acceptance of the "as is" of a situation brings grace, surrender, and most of all gratitude. All of these elements create a positive charge in our mental bank, which has the power to ripple outward in a huge way.

There is nothing passive about acceptance—it is entirely different from resignation. Acceptance is an active process of understanding exactly how the present situation was co-created by us and what it has to teach us. If anything is to change in our life, we need to have zero negativity about our "as is" reality.

An aspect of acceptance that's often overlooked is that because all things exist on a continuum, we can create change by focusing on the opposite pole from where our attention has been drawn. We touched on this in an earlier chapter, but I want to emphasize it now because this is a powerful energy to adopt as a parent. For instance, if in your perception your child is exhibiting the energy of disrespect and defiance, instead of focusing on this behavior as you would normally do—an approach that will serve only to reinforce the behavior—focus instead on the opposite pole on the continuum. This way you accept your child without endorsing ugly behavior.

The way to do this is to notice when your child *isn't* being disrespectful or defiant. Then you amplify this desirable behavior. For instance, when my daughter is calmly eating lunch, I seize the opportunity and say something like, "I love how peaceful you are right now. I feel so connected to you when we simply enjoy each other's company like this." What we mustn't do at such a moment is compare the child's peacefulness with when they are arguing and being difficult—a trap parents easily fall into. Then the compliment turns into a backhanded sermon.

Over time, the more we highlight our children's respect and kindness, the more they will grow to be respectful and kind. By veering away from a focus on their negative behavior, which inevitably increases our own negativity, we simultaneously intensify the respect and kindness we show to our children.

Your Reaction Is Your Child's Trigger

Your child is constantly picking up on your tone, energy, and nonverbal signals. You may have a greater understanding of what your triggers are, but are you aware that your child may be triggered by you? Most important, are you aware that your child may be reacting to you in a particular way because of the way you treat them in subtle or not-so-subtle ways?

We push our children much more than they ever push us. For instance, when does a child ever start each day with lists and schedules as we do? They don't make a zillion plans for us and force us to go places we don't want to go. They don't threaten us when we don't eat the food they like or don't wear the clothes they choose for us. It's we who initiate such dynamics, rigidly forcing on them our standards. Naturally, we couch these things in terms such as giving them opportunities, promoting good health, exposing them to life's possibilities, and showing our support for them. If we were honest with ourselves, we would admit that all of this is just manipulation so we can get our way.

Our energy and ways of being are highly charged with vibes others pick up on. As parents, it's crucial we realize that our very presence, even if we never say a word, has an impact on our children's behavior. This should remind us to always ask, "How am I contributing to this situation? In what way is my energy or my actions encouraging my child to respond in this way?" When we understand our role in co-creating each situation, we no longer blame the other.

Once we acknowledge that all things arise out of an interdependence, we see how simplistic it is to punish our children for their behavior.

No behavior occurs in a vacuum. Something triggers our children, just as something triggers us. The source may be external or it may come from the parents. It may come from a place deep within a child that's beyond their awareness. To hold our children responsible without being both compassionate and curious about the reason for a behavior is both heartless and unproductive.

When we understand that less-than-desirable behavior is a signal of something else, we are reminded to connect with our children in a more meaningful manner. When we view their behavior through the lens of cause and effect, instead of rushing to judgment about their character, we become curious about their feelings and experiences. This approach does wonders in terms of building trust and thereby drawing our children closer to us.

A fifty-seven-year-old father, Conrad, came to see me because he had been suffering from PTSD-like symptoms following a heart attack. The shock of his heart giving out on him was so profound that he was emotionally crippled, to the point of barely being able to leave the house for fear he would have another heart attack and find himself in a situation where he couldn't get help. The only way he knew to manage his anxiety was to stay in his home. Soon he was spending much of his day in bed. His children, who watched as he failed to recover, now began manifesting their own symptoms.

Conrad's eight-year-old daughter, Brenda, not only began doing poorly in school, but also started resisting leaving the house herself. In the meantime, his son, six-year-old Daniel, began acting out at school, becoming increasingly aggressive. At first Conrad and his wife didn't connect their children's issues and their father's inability to cope with his affliction. When they came to see me, it was because they felt they needed to learn better strategies to prevent their children's problems from escalating. It was only when I homed in on Conrad's stress that they realized how this was directly impacting their children.

Conrad had chosen to close up rather than become proactive in response to his heart condition, plunging into a state of anxiety in which he saw no way forward other than to cower. It was this sense of helplessness that his children were absorbing and manifesting in their own lives. Clearly, unless Conrad addressed his anxiety, his children would grow up believing that they too couldn't cope with life.

Conrad's problem was that he couldn't see how benevolent life had been by offering him a wake-up call to change his lifestyle. Because he viewed his heart attack as an extremely negative event, he regarded the entire episode as not only catastrophic but malevolent. I explained that unless he could accept the fact that life had presented him with an opportunity for growth, he would destroy his children's lives. His fear that he was incapable of ever enjoying a full life again now that he'd had a heart attack was the result of his lack of belief in his own resilience. Because he imagined himself to be fragile, he had seduced himself into believing he was safe only if he sat absolutely still.

When I showed him that he was capable of living with the imperfection of a heart condition—and that it didn't need to destroy him, but could act as the catalyst for him to become a more humane, compassionate person—he revealed how he had grown up with extremely controlling parents from whom he inherited the belief that the more you control life, the safer it is. In other words, his heart attack had blown his entire world apart, destroying his very foundation and leaving him curled up like a fetus. He needed a fresh worldview. But how do you develop a new worldview?

Few of us change because we know we need to change. Generally, we tend to change only when we hit rock bottom. Perhaps our marriage is dissolving, our job is at risk, our health is on the brink, or our children are in trouble. In many cases, it seems only a crisis has the ability to shift us.

Sometimes we are so rigid that even a crisis can't pry us free. This was the case with Conrad. It took a long time for him to let go of his belief that he was incapacitated, when in fact he was far from it. It was only when he got in touch with his anxiety, allowing himself to feel his feelings without letting them overwhelm and run him, that he could at last acknowledge that who he was in his essential self had never suffered a heart attack.

Those who truly succeed in life are those who know how to be anxious without letting their anxiety run them. The sacred responsibility we have as parents is to deconstruct the entire idiotic notion that as humans we shouldn't feel anxious. It's akin to saying the sun should shine every day and it should never rain or thunder. Or as Conrad expressed with such righteous indignation, "How dare I be so young and have a heart attack."

We are talking about how change occurs. When our energy shifts internally, the change within us is reflected externally. At first the change may not be noticeable. Just as the Grand Canyon was carved out layer by layer, each change we make builds upon the ones before. As we tap into the abundant energy available to us in the universe, we increasingly empower ourselves to create the change we seek. The more we feel abundant instead of focusing on scarcity, the more our life reflects this.

Instead of attempting to get our children to change, the challenge is to transform our energy from a state of neediness to one of empowerment based on an awareness of the abundance at our disposal. By asking, "Can I become what I need my children to be?" we start to embody the qualities we wish them to absorb.

This doesn't apply only to parenting. It's a principle that has the power to transform every aspect of our life. We can indeed become the change we wish to see in the world. The main ingredient is self-empowerment. The energy lies within us, and we can challenge ourselves to tap into it. The question we need to ask ourselves is, "Do I believe in myself enough to do so?"

When we move away from resisting life's offerings to us, we render not only to what arises but also to how we feel about it. As I said to Conrad, "Of course you feel disappointed, and even downright terrified. This is natural. However, because you are so afraid of feeling your feelings, your desire to feel differently is stopping you from living in the now. Instead, if you just accept that you have moments of collapse, and that this is par for the course, you can teach your children that it's okay for them to feel bad at times without imagining it means they are crumbling from within."

To shift from believing that life happens *to* us, to understanding that life happens *for* us and with our participation, enables us to find the jewel in every experience. We begin to engage life as a true co-creator, fully ready to own our part, and always quick to grow and adapt as the moment requires. Shedding feelings of entitlement to a certain outcome, we realize that part of the reason this outcome didn't manifest comes down to us—and consequently the desired goal can come into fruition only with our willingness to undergo a metamorphosis. Each moment offers us endless paths we could potentially follow, requiring us to become aware of our conscious and unconscious choices so that we can tailor our energy to match the desire we want to see blossom. Once we understand the power we have to choose, we take greater ownership of our life. It's in this way that grit, resilience, courage, and the creativity to live differently are born.

Transforming Reaction to Authentic Expression

Many of us feel as if we have no option other than to react when our children's behaviors enflame us. Our instinct is to lash out. If someone irritates us, we don't think twice but simply react. "Hey, what's wrong with you? Can you stop what you are doing?" It doesn't occur to us to say, "Why am I getting so agitated right now? Can I communicate my needs in a respectful manner knowing that the other is not coming from a place of evil intention? Can I remove myself from this situation if it feels unbearable?"

The state of our external world is in many ways a reflection of that of our inner world. Most of us were brought up by parents who had muddled interior lives. As a result, we mirrored this in our own development and are likely to pass on the same confusion to our children. These fogged-up mirrors of the soul and legacies of unconsciousness get passed down from one generation to the next. Unaware of how this operates, many of us prefer to blame someone for what we encounter in our external world instead of picking up on what's being mirrored back to us about ourselves.

Our children are particularly effective mirrors, because although we can divorce our spouse and abandon our friends, our children are here to stay. It's in our relationship with them more than any other that we are challenged to examine those aspects of ourselves we would ordinarily deny or avoid. When we are able to look into the mirror they provide us with and address our issues, we not only clear the fog from our own vision, but also begin to see our children for who they truly are. In this way, we become a reflection of their authentic self.

Parents are often scared that if they aren't "allowed" to react, they will feel suffocated, inauthentic, or resentful. There are ways to respond that are very different from reactivity. Many of us are simply unaware of how to communicate to each other without getting emotionally charged. We aren't used to being present with our feelings without allowing them to take charge, and neither do we know how to assertively stand up for ourselves without becoming aggressive. Few of us learned how to speak our truth in plain language.

Had we been allowed to speak our truth in its "as is" fashion as children, we would be able to connect to our authentic voice via a direct channel, instead of needing to resort to manipulation, control, and all sorts of emotional turmoil. Speaking one's truth should be the easiest thing in the world, but because it was so threatening to our caregivers, we now find it the hardest thing to do. Returning to authentic expression with our children is one of the most beautiful gifts we can bestow on them, since it opens the gateway for them to be straightforward.

Transforming our reactions into expressions of authentic communication can create a powerful shift in our relationship with our children. Let's see at how this looks with some real-life examples of how to move from triggered reactions to authentic expression:

Reaction:
Stop playing with your phone when I am talking to you! I can't believe you haven't studied for your test. Put your phone away, or I'm going to take it away for good.

Authentic expression:
I know you don't notice that you are being distracted right now. I can see that you are unconsciously avoiding your test. Can I help you make a plan so you can best prepare for it?
   Or:
I'm afraid you don't see the consequences of your choices at this moment, and as your parent it concerns me. I need your help to remind me that you know how your choices are going to affect you. Can we talk about your decision to not study, and how we can shift this energy in you?
   Or:
I see that you are unable to keep yourself from your gadgets. I will give you another five minutes to settle into your responsibilities on your own. However, if after that time you are still allowing yourself to shirk your duties, I am going to need to take away your phone until your work is done. I don't want to be put in this position of taking things away, but I need to see that you are able to regulate yourself.

Reaction:
You are being disobedient and disrespectful. You are not going to speak to me in that tone. You are grounded this weekend.

Authentic expression:
I can see that you feel the need to resort to this negative tone of voice toward me. You are obviously feeling upset, otherwise you wouldn't speak this way. I'm going to take a five-minute

ak from this situation. I suggest you take a few minutes to think about how you want to get your needs met.

Or:

I can see that you are overwhelmed by your emotions right now. I want to hear how you feel, but when you speak to me like that, it's really hard to hear your heart. When you want to share your feelings without tossing insults at me, I am here for you.

Or:

It's really hard for me to listen to you hurling mean words at me. I have feelings too, and it hurts when you speak like that to me. I'm going to leave the room right now and allow myself some space from you. When you feel ready to discuss this in a calm manner, we can try again.

When we express ourselves authentically, we introduce grace, mindfulness, and ownership into the mix. We allow our children to know that they are wise and fully capable, that we are aware of how we are feeling charged at the moment, and that we are willing to make the changes we need to make in order to shift the dynamic between us. When our children see that we are coming from this heart-centered place, and that we aren't invested in making them the bad guy, we enable them to drop their defenses and join us in finding solutions that work for both of us.

It's our sacred responsibility as parents to remember that within every child is a deep desire to be seen, heard, and understood. Indeed, a child's deepest yearning, as I talked about earlier, is to know the answer to the question, "Am I good, am I okay, am I worthy?" They long to be understood for their worldview, their perspective, and their feelings, so that they feel significant in their own right. They want their voice to matter, their opinion to count, and their contributions to be considered valuable.

Our children are highly attuned to their feelings, so that they feel what they feel and aren't afraid to say so. But what do we so often do when we encounter their feelings, especially those that are painful? Instead of tuning in to them, we tune them out. We tell them to "shush." Or we make them feel embarrassed and perhaps even crazy for having such feelings. Consequently they are left believing that something is wrong with them. Of course, this is a direct reflection of our own inability to feel and own our real feelings. When we embrace our light and our shadow, we give our children permission to do so as well. We remind them that true courage lies in being transparent and authentic.

~ A New Commitment to Shedding the Past ~

Even though I want to cling to what ought to be
And all the ways life should have been,
I know that my resistance to what is
Comes from fear,
Which blinds me to the jewels of the present moment.

If I can let go of my need to control
I can enter the unknown with vigor.
Flowing with grit, resilience, and power,
I can become the agent
Of the transformation I wish to witness.

Resisting nothing,
I greet the present moment with awareness and joy.

CHAPTER SIXTEEN

From Chaos to Stillness

From our own breathing to the flow of the seasons, nature follows rhythms. Although on the surface everything changes, the whole is connected to an abiding foundation that lies beneath it. Although effortlessly transforming at every moment, life flows from a bedrock of quiet stillness, needing nothing more than the "what is."

When I was young and took walks on the beach near my home in Mumbai, India, I remember asking my mother, "Where do the waves go?"

She replied, "They go back into the ocean. They came to say hello, and then they say goodbye. One comes and another goes. Turn by turn. So many are leaving, but look how big the ocean stays!" It was a simplistic answer intended for a young girl, but it stayed with me. Without her realizing it, she taught me that everything in life has an ebb and flow to it. Wise are those who aren't seduced by either, but who instead tap into the stillness that underlies all of reality. When we do so, we transcend both the push and the pull of life.

As our children watch us become excited when we get a raise at work or receive praise from a friend, they absorb the way these external events tend to have a hold on us. Similarly, when they see us reduced to despair as we lose our job—or more inconsequentially, put on a pound or two—they absorb the way that our mood can so easily be a slave to external events. In contrast to this, when they see us steady, resolute, and resilient in the face of difficult circumstances, they learn how to flow with life instead of battling it. They learn that there will be days when they are up and others when they are down, but that neither the ups nor the downs affect who we are in our core being. We feel everything, yet none of it defines us. We are defined only by our essential self.

Understanding that life follows rhythms helps us stay grounded in the face of our children's troubles. We understand that their moods aren't permanent, and neither do they define who they are any more than our moods define us. Provided we allow them to ebb and flow, moods come and go. They don't define who we are.

The quality of the ocean doesn't change just because some waves are high or others are low. So it is with our essence. It has a timeless quality, unfazed by our moods, success, or looks. If we are able to surrender our ego and enter our essence as parents, we will be able to let go of much of the chaos and dysfunction. It's all about seeing ourselves and our loved ones not for their surface representations but for their deeper, more timeless essence.

The Power of Silence

One of our greatest untapped allies in life is silence. Most of us are terrified to enter it, believing it to mean nothingness just because it doesn't involve some form of *doing*. Being still in silence is uncomfortable for most of us not only because it runs counter to the diet of constant busyness and achievement we were raised on, but because it puts us painfully in touch with the emptiness within where our true self ought to be.

Our discomfort with confronting ourselves in the naked stillness of absolute quiet leads us to eat too much, drink excessively, socialize mindlessly, and engage in a host of activities out of a desire to simply avoid being still. This constant whirring in our minds creates disharmony and imbalance. The mind cannot function at its optimum level when it's constantly under siege from endless opinions, criticism, and ideas.

Sitting in stillness for a few minutes through the day allows us to begin to be aware of our essence, enabling us to recharge. Taking a few minutes to sit and place our awareness on our breath provides a break from the barrage of information our minds are constantly asked to process. These few minutes of centering allow us to remember what really matters in life—connection to self and others. Despite having all the trappings of external achievement, if we don't have connection, we essentially have nothing.

Just as a quick downpour has the power to clear the air, so it is with ten minutes of breathing and sitting in stillness. Our children can immediately feel the shift in our energy. Checking into ourselves all through the day allows us to pause before we speak, so that we focus on the ways we communicate. This focused attention is essential if we are to parent consciously.

To be still means to be quiet in terms of both verbal and internal chatter. It means to observe our mental chatter but not engage with it. When we practice this on a daily basis, the chatter eventually begins to die down. Chatter can continue interminably only if we are interacting with it. If we stop interacting with it and instead simply allow it to be, it fades.

To practice sitting in stillness, I ask parents to try not saying anything to their children for blocks of time—unless of course their children need them in some way. This doesn't mean the parent ignores the child or leaves them alone. Instead, it's an invitation to enter their children's presence without any desire to mold or change them. I ask the parent to channel the energy they would use for talking to instead observe their children. I suggest they notice how the child sits. Do their shoulders slouch? Then notice their eyes, their smile, their tone of voice. Allowing sufficient time to become quiet has a powerful effect on how we respond to our children.

When a parent asks me a specific and practical question such as, "What should I do if my child left the toothpaste open?" I respond, "Say nothing for five minutes."

"What if they leave the room lights on?"

"Say nothing for five minutes."

"What if they fail a test?"

"Say nothing for five minutes."

"What if they are rude and mean to me or someone else?"

"Say nothing for five minutes."

"What if they hit me or their sibling?"

"Say nothing for five minutes."

About now, I suspect all your alarm bells are sounding. This sounds crazy, doesn't it? It's natural to be fearful when we're told to stop a habit. Perhaps you feel I'm taking away your rights as a parent and thereby endorsing negative behavior? Or I am being too lenient? Or letting your child get away with bad behavior?

Saying nothing for five minutes doesn't mean any of these things. It doesn't mean we don't take action. It simply means we allow space for the wisest action to enter our awareness, since wisdom tends to surface in a situation only if we are able to step away from it for a few moments until we are calm and composed. It means you resist rushing to judgment, even when you think that judgment is obvious. Once you see the power of this approach to transform both you and your children, you'll give yourself the gift of a few minutes of silence to allow the optimum action to make itself known.

My client Olivia described a dinner out with her four-year-old and her parents. Tristan, the young boy, began getting restless. His mother admonished, "Stop that right now. Sit still or we will leave."

He reacted, "I want to leave right now. Let's leave!"

Cornered, Olivia found herself filling with rage. "You better sit still right now," she told the boy, "or else you aren't going to Grandma's house for a sleepover." When Tristan began to scream, Olivia picked him up, took him out of the restaurant, canceled his sleepover, and took him home. She later related, "He was devastated he couldn't go to his grandparents' home. I thought he would have learned his lesson, but the next day he was rude and obnoxious again. I'm at a loss for what to do."

When I showed Olivia that she had reacted way too quickly, she was surprised. "I thought I should say something right there in the moment. Isn't that what you always say we need to do?"

I explained, "There's a difference between mindfully connecting to what a child needs and mindlessly reacting to your own discomfort. Tristan was restless. He obviously needed help to settle down. Instead of finding ways to help him, you rashly reacted to him with threats and punishments. Of course he revolted. The more he protested, the more trouble he got into. What if you hadn't said anything reactive in the first place? What if you had allowed yourself the space to engage with him, maybe sitting him on your lap, or just holding him in silence? Wouldn't that have been better than the outcome you created by yelling at him?"

Olivia saw how she had been stressed from a day at work and consequently was ready to pounce on anyone who didn't conform to her expectations. As she saw how her anger had set her son up for failure, she said, "How do I learn to take that deep pause? I need to learn this."

I responded, "This is a muscle we must all learn to develop. Staying silent doesn't mean acquiescing or being passive. It simply means taking the time to honor what's transpiring and finding the right response for the particular situation."

A period of silence allows us to go within and find another way to communicate our desires. Instead of blindly starting a volley between ourselves and our children, we can use this zone of zero reactivity to move toward our children instead of getting into combat with them. In the quietness of even just a few minutes, our initial opposition on some matter has a chance to die down and we begin to entertain different ways of seeing the situation.

Silence allows us to see not only ourselves but also our children in an entirely new way. Observing them, we tune in to their nonverbal energy and pay attention to their signals. We become sensitive to how they engage with life and with us. The *what* of life gets slowly replaced with the *how*. We ask ourselves questions about a situation that we wouldn't think of when we are either distracted or in the midst of chaos. Questions worth considering at such a moment include:

- *Is this a life-or-death situation?*

- *What's the aerial perspective on this, the larger context?*

- *Is this the best time to bring up this issue with my child?*

- *Is there another way I can frame my wishes so they can be received?*

- *How might I have contributed to the situation before me?*

- *What's the most humane way I can approach this situation?*

In a short but pivotal period of silence, we are able to move beyond small-mindedness and get in touch with our heart's wisdom. The journey to the heart may not always take five or ten minutes; some-times it may take considerably longer. Regardless, it enables us to de-velop clarity, compassion, and courage. For this reason, it's a path that leads directly to our children's hearts.

When Talking Creates Trouble— and the Value of Deep Listening

When things don't go according to our plan for our children, as so often happens, we believe we must talk things through with them. Though there is a place for dialogue and interaction, sometimes our instinct to talk everything through comes more from our own inner anxiety and disconnect than from authentic connection. Talking through something enables us to feel comfortable, since we think we have come to a resolution. Western cultures encourage us to vent, ex-press, and talk about everything that bothers us. Our addiction to discussing things is more a sign of our internal discomfort than gen-uine reaching out to create authentic partnership. Born out of a sense of lack, it often comes from a need to be validated, approved of, and understood. When we operate out of inner lack in this way, it con-fuses our children and actually turns them away from us rather than toward us.

This doesn't mean that emotional stoicism is a more enlightened approach. If either the talking or the stoicism are conducted out of a desire to avoid discomfort and not as an authentic response to some-thing occurring in the present moment, they are equally unconscious. It's this unconscious element that our children most respond to, shield-ing themselves from the imposition of the agendas we don't even know we hold.

So many parents are puzzled when their children seclude them-selves in their room and refuse to leave their sanctuary. They won-der, "Why don't my children want to talk to me when I'm so open and willing to discuss things?" The reason our children turn away from us is that they sense that our desire to talk is all about us—our need to manage our anxiety and exert control.

Paula was having a hard time letting go of her son, Tom, who was fourteen years old and breaking away from the symbiotic relationship they had shared when he was younger. Like many boys his age, Tom was more interested in gaming with his friends than in spending time with his mother. As a result of her insecurity, Paula overcompensated by trying to engage him in conversation each time they were together. If she sensed Tom was either quiet or moody, this would put her on high alert, causing her to say things like, "What's wrong, Tom? Are you feeling angry? I'm here to talk to you, so please tell me what's going on with you. I really want you to be comfortable talking to me, so share what you're going through." When Tom was noncommittal and shrugged his shoulders, saying nothing, Paula took this as a sign of rejection.

At her wits' end when she came to see me, Paula complained, "I feel him slipping away from me. I really wanted us to have a deep bond so we could tell each other anything and everything. I feel as if I'm losing my son." The reason she felt this way was that she believed that talking was the only way to connect with Tom.

Rosalie, mother of nine-year-old Theresa, felt the same way. Each time Theresa was stressed over something such as school or her friends, Rosalie embarked on a litany. Thinking she was being a connector, she said things like, "Oh, honey, I know how bad you must be feeling. I totally understand what you are going through and I'm here for you. Tell me why you are feeling this way so I can help you." On the surface her words appear comforting and even consciously attuned. However, Theresa grew quieter. Frustrated, her mother then became more vociferous. Finally, her daughter screamed, "Stop talking so much, Mom! I hate talking to you because you never listen. I hate that you're always telling me what to do, think, and feel."

Because Rosalie's words weren't being received by her daughter, we need to ask whether what she was saying truly served her daughter's needs or just her own. Like Tom, Theresa was giving her mother a message that she needed someone to listen to her instead of lecture her. Both mothers, despite their best intentions, were coming from a "fix it" energy, which their children were picking up on.

When we talk for the sake of getting our own needs met versus talking to truly connect, our children pick up on our controlling agenda and shut down instead of opening up. I always tell parents that a sure sign their talking is coming from a place of control versus connection is in how their children respond. Do they open up and share, or do they become increasingly more agitated and reticent, eventually clamming up altogether?

Talking for the sake of filling the quiet with sound creates the antithesis of connection. As I said to both Paula and Rosalie, "You give the appearance that you wish to connect to your children, but if you are completely honest with yourselves, you are really trying to get them to either see your point of view or change something about how they are acting. Children pick up on this and immediately create a defensive shield. Unless you are brave enough to examine why you are talking and come clean with your intention, your children will continue to shut themselves off from you."

I encourage parents to talk only when it's essential, especially as children grow into preteens and teens. By the age of ten, our children are very familiar with how we talk and what we say. They don't need our words of advice or admonishment. What they need instead is for us to listen and attune ourselves to them. Create space for them to come to us of their own accord. For this to happen, we need to enter into stillness and become an attractor of connection.

So many of us as parents need to stop making the common mistake of digging, probing, questioning, opining, sermonizing, theorizing, hypothesizing, concluding, criticizing, judging, scolding, and all the other things we do that alienate our children. Instead, we need to keep quiet much of the time, staying open, nonjudgmental, and uncritical, being careful not to insert ourselves where we don't belong.

To talk from the heart instead of the head means to say little. The heart doesn't need words to communicate, only an openness to engage with receptivity and warmth. All of this is energetic. It's a felt sense, more about the wordless depth of mutual respect. As we let go of our obsession with communicating on a verbal level, a touch of hands or a meeting of the eyes becomes powerful. We deeply listen to our children and their many told and untold feelings and desires if they choose to express them. We say nothing until it emerges from this deep listening.

When parents experience frustration in their relationship with their children, I say to them, "This is because you aren't truly listening to them." They take this to mean they are supposed to do whatever their children want. I clarify, "I don't mean that you need to give in to them. Deep listening has nothing to do with indulgence. It's all about communicating our sense of attentiveness, availability, and awareness."

When we commit to listening deeply to our children, we change the frequency of our communication. In place of our anxiety, being distracted, or seeking to control the conversation, we tune in to our child's heart and feelings. I will illustrate from a recent interaction with my daughter. At twelve, she is independent in all her daily tasks such as hygiene and rarely seeks my assistance or advice concerning how to take care of herself. However, one night as she was about to brush her teeth, she called me into the bathroom. "Remember how you used to brush my teeth when I was little? Can you do it again? For old times' sake?"

My initial reaction was, "That's so silly, Maia. You are fully capable of brushing your own teeth." I didn't have to say a word. She picked up on my frequency right away as she saw my shoulders tighten and a frown appear. I noticed her mouth quiver and disappointment cross her face. Her frequency had changed to match mine.

Seeing this, I asked myself, "Why am I resisting her joyous request?" I needed to hear her heart. What was she trying to achieve through her request? The answer was immediately clear. She was taking us back to a period in her childhood that was idyllic in her eyes. She was asking for us to connect in a way she cherished. I melted. "Of course," I retracted. "I would be honored to. I miss those days too." Maia was thrilled, and we had a moment of bonding by pretending she was four again.

Shifting out of our typical control frequencies into a frequency attuned to connection is key to keeping our hearts open toward our children. Our lack of awareness of our own or our children's communication frequencies results in most of the dysfunction we experience in our relationships. We believe that as long as our words are comforting or reassuring, for example, our children won't pick up on our underlying anxiety, when in fact this is the only thing they likely pick up on.

Opening ourselves to deeply listen to our children frees us from constantly fixing and rescuing them. Once again, let me reiterate that listening to our children doesn't mean we indulge them or give in to them. It means that we allow our responses to come from a place of deep attunement into what is optimal for their highest development. Instead of plunging into the mix, we allow ourselves to fulfill a key function of conscious parenting, which is to be the observer. The role of dispassionate observer is key to this work, as it's only through the awakening of these faculties that we can fully tune in to what our children are experiencing or need from us on a moment-by-moment basis.

Discovering the Power of Your Presence

When Peggy, a client of mine, learned how to tap silently into her own powerful presence, she was amazed at how easy it became for her to bring about a transformation in her relationship with her children. Until she learned to be present, she threatened and punished her children regularly, believing that the only way to influence them was to take things away from them or ground them. As a result, even simple interactions quickly escalated into power struggles.

I observed a situation in which Peggy asked her sons to get off their screens while they were in my office for a family session. Since they were unaccustomed to paying attention to her, they carried right on doing what they were doing. Snatching their screens from them, Peggy threatened them with every punishment in the book. In return, they looked at her as if she were stark raving mad. Then, as one of them sulked, the other kicked her shins and left the room.

Peggy turned to me in despair. "This is what always happens," she said. "I only have to tell them to do some small thing, and before you know it our home has become a battlefield."

Peggy couldn't see the irrationality of her approach because, as parents, we are given carte blanche to behave pretty much any way we wish toward our children. When I told her that the way she handled her boys on this occasion was equivalent to her friend pulling her ear because she arrived late or smacking her face for forgetting her birthday, Peggy got the point. We wouldn't dare react to our peers in this way.

We don't realize how negative our fear-based signals are to our children. As I commented to Peggy, "You went from making a request to threatening them in just seconds. There were so many other possibilities. Why didn't you think to use any of them?"

Peggy had no idea what I was talking about. "What kind of possibilities are you referring to?" she inquired.

I explained, "In order for you to react like you did, something had to transpire inside you the moment you made the request and your boys didn't jump to it. Once you identify what this was, we can proceed. What were you feeling when you asked them to put their screens away?"

"That's easy," Peggy said. "I felt mortified. I was so embarrassed by what I thought they might do in front of you. When it was time to get them off their screens, I knew they would resist. I was terrified of their reaction and expected them to blow up."

"Exactly," I agreed. "You expected resistance. So when they didn't put their screens away right away, you interpreted this as resistance. Based on your interpretation, you instantly escalated your request to a threat."

"I did, didn't I?" Peggy admitted, pondering what had transpired.

"What if you expected them to listen?" I prodded. "Would you have handled things differently?"

"I guess I would have been a lot more patient and relaxed about it," Peggy admitted.

I continued, "Had you been in a different state of mind, grounded in your own center, you wouldn't have been fearful of the boys' response. This would have allowed them to feel the power of your presence, which would have been conveyed by your relaxed approach. For instance, you might have stepped in front of your children, lowered their screens, and looked directly in their eyes as you made your request that they follow your lead. Because you would have been coming from an empowered state as their leader, they would have been mesmerized by your clarity and powerful presence, which would have left them no option but to fall in line. Authentic presence is so much more effective than strategies and threats."

Peggy was skeptical of this approach. With its lack of focus on big gestures, it felt inconsequential. She needed to experience firsthand how it actually works. I assured her that when our voice, our gaze, and our very being are grounded in the stillness at our center, we connect deeply with people. We come across as powerless, and therefore need to escalate matters to get a child's attention, when we are disconnected from our own inner power.

Making Time for Time

Although our desire may be strong, things take time to manifest in the physical universe. Nothing happens before its time. For this reason we can't rush life in order to assuage our insecurity and anxiety. In fact, the more insecure and anxious we are, the more we interfere with the positive vibes we send out and the longer things take to manifest themselves.

To simply observe is to understand that things will manifest when it's the right time. The more steadfast we are in this belief, the less manic we will be. In fact, what we require is precisely the opposite of manic energy. We need the energy that flows out of stillness.

So many of us simply can't bear to sit still and wait. Having to observe things take their natural course is painful for us. The bottom line is that we're fearful our desires won't materialize. Because we are afraid, we aren't willing to sow the necessary seeds, then trust that they will sprout in due course. Trust is the key element. How many of us truly trust ourselves, as well as the universe, to deliver what we require?

Where our children are concerned, all the doubt, confusion, and comparing we do is driven by fear instead of trust.

One of the greatest obstacles to trust is the way we are constantly swayed by the "shoulds" of life, which prevent us from tapping into our own internal compass. Because we don't invest in our naturally trusting self, we jump in too soon, interfere where we shouldn't, hover anxiously, and micromanage. All of this anxious activity on our part impedes our children in finding their own way, solving their own problems, and setting their own course.

When we are expecting a child, it doesn't help to be fearful during the nine months of waiting. Instead of being ever anxious that things will proceed on their natural course, it's far preferable that we make the appropriate preparations, such as decorating the room in which the child will sleep and buying the things needed for when they arrive. Well, it's no different once the child is born and we take up the responsibility of parenting. Our task is simply to sow the seeds, then stand back and watch with excitement as our children water those that resonate with them and ignore those that don't. Anxiety comes into the picture only if we are trying to choose the seeds they should water. Who are we to dictate what they should water?

Sowing seeds is about ascribing greater value to the journey than to arriving at a particular goal we fantasize about. We value the process, not our dream of a perfected product whose "perfection" is based on performance. Even if our children don't reach a high level of achievement, we celebrate their being so that they know they are esteemed unconditionally. Paradoxically, this approach has the effect of inspiring them to reach new heights. The better they feel about themselves, the more likely it is they will unabashedly follow their inner calling. They will trust themselves because this is what they observed us doing through their growing years. In times of doubt, they will search their emotional archives and rest on our faith in their development, remembering to go easy on themselves, taking the time to enjoy the journey.

Parenting isn't a mental game of strategic intervention. It's a journey of trust that works only when we truly surrender to the universe and its abundance of energy. The more we are able to trust, the less anxiety we have about our children's future. Fully committed to the right timing of all things, we don't doubt when things don't go our way. We surrender to life's offerings. If we don't need something for our growth, it simply won't show up. We accept that all the beautiful things in nature require time and space to emerge.

In our crazy schedules, we simply don't make time for things we should. We don't put buffers in place so that if we get into a traffic jam, we aren't driven to madness, or if our children dawdle, we aren't jumping down their throats. In today's insane world, creating lag time is an art in itself. Those who are able to organize their life with a sufficient amount of downtime actually give themselves the opportunity to recharge. As opposed to seeing these moments of nothingness as empty and useless, a conscious parent seizes them as valuable opportunities for connection, creativity, and fun. Our children need to know that life isn't all work and neither is it all play. Striking a balance between the two is part of the art of conscious living.

~ A New Commitment to Shedding the Doing ~

Detach from the outer world a bit;
Let the dishes lie, let the anger die;
Let the chores be undone.
It's time to retreat and go within,
To enter silence, quiet the din.
This is the only way to create a shift.

Don't be afraid to enter the self.
Beneath the chatter lies a brilliant jewel,
Assured, present, resolute, still.
The layers need to peel, one by one:
First the shame, then the unworthiness, then the fear.
When you reach the nothingness, you will know you
    are near.

When you reach your true self at the deepest core,
You will finally know authenticity and freedom.
Liberated from fear, you emerge strong and sure,
Ready to meet the spirit of your child,
Unencumbered, unfettered, wild.

CHAPTER SEVENTEEN

From Role to No-Role

W ithout our realizing it, much of who we *think* we are is dictated by *what* we are—our gender, race, social class, sibling order, and how pretty, handsome, or smart we are. Even before a child turns two or three, parents want to know whether the child is athletic, artistic, rambunctious, or introverted. We have a need to identify ourselves and our children with labels and roles, without which we feel unable to relate in the world.

The question, "Who am I without my name, role, religion, or identity?" is an important one to contemplate, especially in the context of parenthood. The reason it's pivotal in the parent-child relationship is that our insistent attachment to roles and other external measures of worth—the "what" as opposed to the "who"—may be convenient in some ways, but it eventually results in passing judgment, rigidity, and a lack of flexibility.

Lara, the mother of eighteen-year-old Lindsey, suddenly stopped coming for her sessions with me. When I inquired about her absence, she told me that she was going through a depression of sorts. Since she was not a person who was prone to depression, I knew she was reacting to something. When she finally escaped the cloud she had been under and returned for a session, she revealed the reason for her depression. Lindsey was preparing to graduate from high school and go to college. The prospect of her daughter leaving home and entering into autonomy as an adult was terrifying for Lara. Instead of feeling celebratory, she was unable to find any joy in her daughter's maturity. It was the prospect of losing her identity as a "mother" to her "child" that brought the depression on. It was her way of saying, "I am not ready for this change. I did not endorse it. I refuse to be happy about it."

Lara began to tear up. "But she is no longer my baby. I cannot believe it. I miss being a mommy to her. I loved that piece of parenting so much. I loved taking care of her and being with her through her experiences. Now she will move on without me."

I understood the feeling of loss Lara was experiencing. It's natural to experience grief at the prospect of our children leaving us and moving out into their own lives. Those of us who are attached to our identity as Mom or Dad have a harder time, of course. Nonetheless, this is an adjustment every parent needs to make. The degree to which we can artfully transform into what our children need from us at this time in their life, the more able we will be to usher them into the next phase of their growth toward maturity.

Lara continued, "Because I have been so sad, I have not been close to both my daughter and my husband these past few months. Instead of being there for them, I've caused them to worry about me."

I gently replied, "Instead of your daughter feeling she could enter her next stage of life unencumbered, she's worried about her mommy. Perhaps this is your way of keeping your connection to her alive. By keeping her close to you, you keep her dependent on you for her happiness. In this way, you continue to feel needed. It's your need to be needed that's trumping your daughter's ability to enjoy this rite of passage. If you aren't careful, you'll rob her of it completely."

Lara gasped, hardly able to believe that she had manufactured her depression as a way of resisting the inevitability of the transition her daughter was undergoing. I reminded her that her deep commitment to her identity as a mom was what had allowed her to raise a stellar daughter. Now it was time for Lindsey to embody all the lessons she had learned from her mother's presence in her life.

At this point I asked, "So now, when it's time to harvest the fruit of all your hard work and see your daughter blossom, do you really want to clip her wings? Wouldn't you prefer to see her become the woman you raised? It's time for you to let go of your need for her to depend on you as a child and enter into the next phase of your journey together as kindred spirits."

The reason Lara was so traumatized was that she hadn't done the necessary work through the years of detaching from the role of mom.

Now that she was being forced to let go, it was extremely hard for her. When we don't see ourselves as our children's spiritual mentor and instead are attached to the role of parent, we limit not only our children's ability to individuate but also our own capacity for engaging in a mutually reciprocal relationship as allies of the deepest kind.

Many parents say to me, "How can I let go of my role when I needed to be a mother 24/7 for all these years? I don't know how to mother halfway."

"A spiritual mentor is one who is able to parent their children and be there for them, but with a keen awareness of enabling them to develop as spiritual beings," I explained. They see their role as transcending just "Mom" or "Dad," focusing instead on what their children's spirits require. They ask themselves, "What aspect of their development requires attention right now? How can I expand and evolve my own consciousness to help my children flow into their most authentic expression of themselves?"

To fulfill the role of a spiritual mentor requires detaching from the parenting Kool-Aid we have been ingesting. Instead of focusing on whether a child got all the problems correct on a test, we focus on how they feel about themself when they don't. Instead of focusing on whether a child fits into a particular social clique, we focus on how they feel about themselves when they are alone. The spotlight shifts from the traditional markers of success to those that are ordinarily ignored by mainstream society. Our interest is in how loud they laugh, how deeply they feel, how fearlessly they love, and how unabashedly they weep.

Tapping Into the Guidance of the Universe

I use the analogy of the universe to help parents move out of their attachment to their roles and guide them to embrace a different way of being with their children. Why the universe? Because it is a reflection of our inner being. If we saw ourselves as mirror images of the universe's abundance, we would tap into this unlimited source of resources within our own being and encourage our children to tap into theirs. We would finally realize that heaven does indeed exist here on earth, and it's only our own unconsciousness that keeps us from enjoying its blissful reality. When we tap into the abundance of the universe, we realize how infinite it is, how resplendent, how plentiful. We can enjoy this abundance not only ourselves but also in our relationship with others, especially our spouse and children, by tapping into the wholeness at our center.

Drawing on the abundant nature of reality begins with accepting ourselves exactly as we are. This is fundamentally different from seeing ourselves primarily in a particular kind of role, such as a mom or dad. Though roles can be helpful at times, they need to be underpinned by the wholeness of pure *being*. Otherwise, roles can easily end up seriously unbalancing our energy as we become locked into a mental image of who we are "supposed" to be as a mom or dad, instead of being who we truly *are*.

Nature can play a powerful part in providing the necessary balance in our lives—a balance that is then passed on to our children. I see this as tremendously important, since it's my experience as a therapist that our modern disconnection from the natural world contributes to much of the malaise, depression, and dysfunction so many children experience. I encourage parents to help their children be in touch with nature and the principles by which it operates. As children of the universe, we want them to grow organically—not in a forced or prescribed manner as is often the case when we impose roles on ourselves and our children.

I see the unfolding of a child's being as a many-petaled flower, with layer upon layer. If we observe just one layer, we won't uncover the full beauty of the blossom. In like manner, our children have many layers, and our task is to support them in exploring their full inner beauty—with the caveat, emphasized earlier in the book, that potential is seen as an everyday experience, not some goal we are pushing our kids toward in the future.

Embracing the energy within nature allows us to step away from our narrow, rigid roles so that we enter the universality of the human experience. This feeling of common humanity allows us to dissolve our ideas of separation and enjoy a newfound freedom to simply be with one another devoid of rules and expectations. It's in this way that we begin to know true connection with another.

Entering the No-Role Zone: Insights from Nature

As we have seen, our attachment to the "shoulds" of parenting that go along with rigid roles keeps us away from our heart, thereby obstructing pathways to deep connection with our children.

As a way to drop out of my egoic role and ground myself in my essence, I find it helpful to turn to what have traditionally been considered the key elements in nature. Although these "elements" are of course far from a modern scientific way of understanding the universe, their timeless quality symbolizes the deep need we all have to learn from some of the key qualities of the natural world that sustains us. Let's take a look at these elements and aspire to mirror their most fundamental qualities.

Earth

The energy of earth is grounded, planted, rooted, and firm. It's the bedrock of our existence. Infinitely generous, it gives rise to and nurtures all forms of life. When we embody this energy in our own family, we are reminded to stay firmly grounded as we contain our children's many moods and emotions, unruffled by their tantrums and times when they are upset. We remain firm, trusting, and confident when we decide on a life-enhancing boundary.

At the same time, we come from a mind-set of abundant caring and compassion when our children experience failure or come up against their limitations. We stay strong when they are fearful or anxious.

What does this look like in practice? To illustrate, if our children are spending an inordinate amount of time on screens, then we don't label them as "bad" and enter into opposition with them. Direct opposition always brings about an equal resistance. Instead, we ask ourselves, "What does my child need to develop into a whole?" If the answer is that they need more time away from their gadgets, then we help them engage in *non*-screen time—not because screens are bad, but because the child's development is becoming lopsided and out of balance.

Similarly, if our children are spending too much time alone, we introduce them to people and experiences. On the other hand, if we have an extremely social child who spends a lot of time with other people, we need to help them balance out their development by encouraging short periods of quiet introspective time, perhaps even taking them to a children's yoga class or choosing to read books side by side for an hour.

I don't mean we orchestrate our children's time and activities, like a conductor who amplifies certain measures while hushing others. This approach encourages us to occupy our role as our children's spiritual guide by keeping an eye on where their development is getting stuck. Helping them become free of rigidity is fundamentally different from forcing them to behave a certain way. Once again, it all depends on the energy with which we engage with our children. If we enter the relationship with the aim of fixing, controlling, and manipulating, we automatically draw the battle lines. Instead, when we enter the dynamic to support them in their own efforts to grow, we receive little if any resistance.

At all times, we are a consistent presence in our children's lives that they can count on to provide them with a foundation from which they can grow and blossom in a balanced way that draws out the fullness of their humanity.

Air

Air is the space around and between everything. Space exudes a lightness and expansiveness, qualities we want our children to embody. Rushed, fatigued, worried, we so often experience the opposite energy, manifested as heaviness, constriction, withholding, and limitation. On the one hand space manifests stillness and silence, which mirror the inner peace of our essence, while on the other hand air is powerful when it takes the form of a mighty wind against which no one can stand.

The symbol of space invites us to consider whether we allow our children their own space, not simply in terms of privacy and the right to possessions, hobbies, preferences, and passions of their own, but also by the way we honor their natural rhythms and pace of life, toning our own energy down when necessary.

By allowing our children to be themselves, we encourage them to have their own private relationship with the universe that doesn't depend on grades, achievement, or "good" behavior. When our children feel this intimate connection with their own space and place in the world, they enter into a sense of ownership of their own dreams and goals.

Fire

I think of fire as burning through the debris in our life. Quick-acting and destructive, it can force change on us that we may have avoided for a long time—an avoidance that can be aided and abetted by hiding behind a role. Thus when challenged on an issue we don't want to deal with, we may be tempted to say, "Because I'm your mother!" or a similar retort.

At the same time, fire is warming, inviting, and lifesaving. Instead of seeing the energy of fire as threatening, I consider it a powerful symbol of letting go of all the negative forces in our life so that our warm, loving heart can shine through.

When we embody fire energy in our home, we are reminded to be warmhearted and inviting of change, while at the same time quick to rise up to counter negative traits such as insecurity, excess, wastefulness, hatred, procrastination, and lethargy. As we allow our obsession with the past or our concerns for the future to burn up, we instead use the energy to invest fully in our own and our children's present.

Fire energy teaches us how something can be both life-enhancing and destructive, depending on the use we make of it. Drawing on this analogy, we understand that our children's shortcomings can become strengths, and vice versa.

The extra-sensitive child can learn that while they may be susceptible to being hurt, this also allows them to be compassionate and kind. The aggressive child can learn that while this might bring them advantages in the world, it can also alienate people. The assertive child can be exposed to situations in which they learn patience and teamwork. In like manner, the shy child can be gently invited to take a certain amount of risk.

The point isn't to oppose a child's natural propensities, but rather to balance them so that the child grows up to be a rounded personality whose life reflects a state of wholeness.

Every parent has the wherewithal to balance their children's energy. If we see that our child is very sensitive, we can balance this with structured rough-and-tumble activities or by helping them develop a slightly tougher skin through compassionate instruction. If our child is thick-skinned and lacks sensitivity, we can help create the antidotal qualities by intentionally exposing them to empathy-building situations.

As I seek to embody this principle of balance in my own life, I try to round out my child's energy by occupying the opposite end of whatever it is she is experiencing. For example, if she is anxious, I become grounded in my sense of trust; if she is angry, I enter stillness; if she is frustrated, I enter peace. By resisting the urge to match her energy and thereby amplify it, I try to take on its antidotal properties. This silent but profound shift in my energy allows her to naturally balance out her energy and find her way back to self.

Thus fire reminds us to be respectful of the power we each have to create life or destroy it. It all depends on which flames we choose to fan.

Water

Water symbolizes the ability to flow with the stream of life. Flow is an important concept in how we approach our everyday activities.

Instead of struggling anxiously, fearfully, being in a state of flow means life becomes something we no longer agonize about.

We encounter this principle in the *Tao Te Ching*, which speaks of it this way: "Act without doing, work without effort." Athletes understand this feeling of flow as "the zone," where excellence becomes effortless as the individual becomes absorbed in the sport. When we are flowing, we accomplish a tremendous amount, and it isn't at all stressful. We are relaxed, yet totally engaged.

Perhaps you've experienced flow at times. It's exhilarating, isn't it? I propose that these peak moments open a window onto the possibility of living the whole of life in a similar way.

Water evokes other images. Just as it is gushing yet sometimes still, gently flowing yet sometimes forceful, we are reminded to be the same with our children. Whereas roles can be restrictive, we are asked to flow with our children's natural state rather than resisting who they are. This involves moving past their obstacles toward expansive seas. It also requires being gentle with them and yet with powerful presence. In other words, water calls upon us to exude both calm and intense energy depending on what a particular situation requires.

So many of us resent how challenging our kids are. However, this negative energy works against us, although we usually aren't aware of just how much it does so. It's only when we commit to embracing our existence with full-on acceptance, instead of insisting on the restriction that tends to accompany tightly defined roles, that we make the shift we need. No matter who our kids are, we all need to start with complete acceptance.

"But how am I supposed to see wholeness in my children when they're pitching a fit?" a parent asks, quite understandably.

If we accept that the individuals in our life are entitled to their own feelings and actions, and that their highest behavior rises from their sense of sovereignty over their life, we will move out of resistance and resentment into acceptance. This doesn't mean we don't honor and validate our own actions and feelings, only that we stop resisting theirs.

The Power of the Antidote

Nature has a way of balancing itself. Hot and cold, light and dark, life and death. Embedded in every reality is its opposite. If we could remember this crucial truth, we might be able to change our relationship with our children drastically.

Let's take the example of a child who doesn't want to have a shower and begins to scream at the very suggestion. It's quite probable that the parent of such a child raises their voice in an effort to reason with the child, then scolds when reasoning fails. The child hears the parent's anger, feels nervous, and starts to kick and scream even more. The parent becomes impatient and now yells full throttle. Throwing themself on the floor, the child begins to hit the parent, who sees red and slaps the child's face.

What we are witnessing is a domino effect, apparently begun by the child's refusal to shower. But it isn't the child who topples the first domino—it's the parent's reaction. This is why children, especially the younger ones, can't effect a change in this situation. It's the parent who must do so. You see, the parent matched the child's energy throughout the encounter. The child raised their voice, and the parent followed suit. The child pitched a fit, and so did the parent, becoming almost hysterical. Instead of bringing calmness to the situation, the parent kept upping the ante, increasing the tension.

This is where we can learn from nature, occupying the energy of the opposite pole instead of feeding the reactivity of the child, decibel for decibel. In the case of the child who resists their shower out of anxiety, our approach should be to create the antidotal energy of playfulness and calm. For instance, one might either playfully transform their screams into a song and ease them into a game of bubbles in the water, or one might gently enter the water with them and soothe them with the soap and bubbles. If the child senses the slightest degree of anxiety within the parent, this will serve only to amplify their own. Instead, the child needs to sense the opposite pole—calm energy— within the parent in order to shift gears.

Our problems with our children arise not from clashing with their energy, which may appear to be the case on the surface, but when both parent and child exhibit *identical* behavior, thus going head-to-head. The way to avoid conflict with someone isn't by insisting on our way because it's "our right as a parent" to lay down the law, but to occupy the opposite energy, the antidotal energy. So if your child is super-anxious, you need to dial down your own anxiety. If your child is particularly aggressive, you can help by reducing your own aggressiveness.

When we talk or try to connect with the same emotional energy that our children are experiencing—something we are prone to do as parents—we inadvertently bolster the energy as opposed to calming it. It's for this reason that talking to an anxious child almost never works. It simply sends them further into their head, which is where all their anxiety lives. Even though we might appear to be showing interest, empathy, or compassion, we most likely have an agenda of ending the discomfort the child is experiencing. Saying to an anxious child, "Look on the bright side," "Let's talk about something else," or "I understand what you are going through, but . . ." are surefire ways to increase the child's anxiety.

We can't expect our children to rein in their behavior. But through effecting a shift in our own energy, we give them the space and permission to change their behavior. As they bounce off our energy, we need to be mindful not only of how we express ourselves on the surface, but, more important, of whether our energy provides the antidote to theirs.

The Power of the Container

A key aspect of knowing what to foster and what to limit in our children is the ability to provide an emotional container for them when their energy is destructive. If your child is tired and says, "I feel cranky because I'm tired," their mood needs to be accepted. But if they start saying, "I hate you," and are rude to you or others in the family because they are tired, their emotion needs to be contained. The container can be a simple pause or something much stronger like a command to "freeze." To be a mirror for our children means to reflect back to them when they are out of sync and return them to awareness.

To be a container for our children's emotions is fundamentally different from overruling them from a position of power, resorting to a role by saying something like, "I'm your father. You will respect me!" Far from becoming domineering, we need to remain a peripheral observer of their emotional reactivity and not get sucked in. To this intent, when my daughter has big emotions, I remind myself she's simply overwhelmed with feeling right now. The still space at her center has become obscured by emotions that are manifestations of her core fear.

The Buddha talked about staying detached from the ups and downs of our emotions. His approach was to observe these states without getting pulled into them. In this way he taught us how to liberate ourselves from the hold transient experiences tend to have over us. This is an invaluable teaching to pass on to our children. When we watch them become lost in the storm of their emotional reactions, we can avoid being drawn into their energy and reacting to it. By remaining grounded in ourselves, we show them that their emotions will pass and they will return to center. But how can they learn this if they have to watch us constantly being pushed and pulled by our own transient moods?

Being a container for our children's emotions isn't easy and requires us to dip into the sacred space within ourselves, a space that's still and calm. Think of this sacred space in terms of the earth's energy, which is thoroughly grounded. The energy of a cathedral, spacious and reverent. The energy of a majestic mountain peak, standing tall and unmovable. The energy of the ocean, limitless and expansive. When we enter this powerful state, we are able to be the safe container our children need when they are losing it.

To access my still center, I find it helpful to take fifteen to twenty minutes a day to sit in a silent space and simply observe my thoughts. If you haven't tried this and wish to do so, you may find it initially unbearable, since few of us are accustomed to stillness except when we are asleep. Or you may find yourself dozing off. However, if you sustain this practice for a period of time, something miraculous starts to happen. You'll find that you begin to stay alert for longer and longer periods. You'll also find that you are able to observe your thoughts with increasing clarity. This is when you realize that you don't need to react to each thought. Most important, you realize that thoughts are just energetic patterns entering and leaving the mind with little hold. The only power they can possess is when we lock onto them and turn them into a story. When we don't do this, the thought just passes.

So too when we provide a container for our children's volatility, it just passes. As our skill in doing this increases, we are able to relate to our children in the way they truly need, sometimes setting boundaries and limits, at other times encouraging them to expand into the spaciousness around them. In due course this dance between pushing back and letting go becomes second nature, with parent and child intuitively following each other's rhythms.

The image of a container is saying to us that when we are non-anxious, we are no longer snared by our own thoughts and emotional reactivity, which allows us to remain neutral in the face of our children's behavior. Instead of blindly reacting, we use humor, storytelling, role-playing, and a host of other relational processes to defuse our children's acting out. In this way the container helps our children to work through their feelings, allowing them to be increasingly true to who they are.

Creating Rooms of Light

When we are filled with inner chaos and mental machinations, so that we are tense and stressed, it shows up as distraction, impatience, and frustration. We feel our tolerance dwindle and are quicker to raise our voice with our children. Parenting stops being fun or meaningful, and we wonder when we will experience relief and a sense of lightness. This is when we may be tempted to fall back on asserting our authority based on our "role." However, if we quiet down and simply observe, instead of jumping in with habitual reactions, our inner quietude creates room for going deeper in our relationship with our children—something relying on a role can't facilitate.

Allow me to outline some of the ways we can begin to create room within ourselves:

Room for Curiosity. Once the verbal assault quiets and we are in an unthreatened state, we find ourselves becoming curious about a child's behavior. Instead of trying to control them, we seek to understand them. We might say something like the following:

> "I'm curious about your thoughts about this. Can you share?"

> "I'm wondering what you feel about that. Can you tell me?"

> "I would love to know how you came to that conclusion. Can you share your thinking?"

> "I'm fascinated by how you think and feel. I would love to know more."

> "You sound like you are really experiencing strong feelings. Would you share them with me?"

Using this noninvasive and open-ended approach, we invite our children to express their deepest feelings, while at the same time encouraging them to shine a mirror on their inner world. We do this without feeling a need to impose our insights on them. We allow them to arrive at their own conclusions. When they are misguided, we can gently offer other options if they are receptive—and I emphasize "offer," so they can consider them, which is quite different from imposing.

To force a child to see things our way if they aren't ready to do so is pointless. At such times, the wise approach is simply to plant seeds by gently suggesting or questioning. Although on the surface doing so may appear inconsequential, our children are always paying attention on some level. In their own time, they will enter into a process of introspection. Being able to do this will serve them well, especially at times when we aren't with them.

Room for Sharing. Once we are in a nonreactive frame of mind, we can dip into our own experiences as a child and ask ourselves whether we relate to our child's situation or feelings in some way. Perhaps we will be inspired to share a story from our own life that may resonate with them. As long as we aren't using it to preach, this can be helpful in the following ways:

Equalizing the playing field.

Sharing our own humanity.

Not demonizing behavior.

Bonding as human to human.

Entrusting our child with a personal aspect of ourselves.

Keeping the lines of communication open.

Implanting some of the lessons we learned—but again, without preaching.

When a child observes that instead of guilt-tripping them, we are opening our heart to them, they feel secure, ready to snuggle in the comfort of our relationship. Opening our heart signals to them that it's also safe for them to do the same. Deep sharing creates a powerful moment of connection, providing them with memories they are likely to hold dear for a long time to come.

Room for Humor. Once our tentacles of control have been withdrawn, we might even see the present situation in a humorous way. This will enable us to take a more lighthearted approach, thereby communicating powerful lessons such as:

Life isn't a tragedy, even if you behaved badly or made a huge mistake.

Life always gives you something to smile and laugh about.

Nothing is so bad that it's the end of the world.

Nothing is gained from catastrophizing a situation.

Taking things lightly allows us to let go and grow.

When we see things from a wider perspective and have a sense of humor about them, children learn to look at life the same way. Instead of putting a dramatic or tragic spin on something, they learn to flow through life with lightness and ease.

Room for Creative Practice. When we are calm, we are more inclined to remember that children are allowed to make mistakes. Indeed, the point of childhood isn't to be perfect, but to learn and grow. Calmness also allows us to implement creative strategies to help our children internalize the lesson we wish them to learn. I use a couple of creative ways to help children absorb some of the values they will need in life:

- **Role reversal**, *in which the child acts as if they were us, and we act as if we were them. This allows a child to see things from our point of view. Just as important, we gain insight into where the child is coming from. The exercise promotes mutual understanding.*

- **Role-play.** *There's no better way for a child to pick up a skill than by practicing it with us over a period of days and sometimes weeks. To help them separate from us in preparation for going to school, falling asleep on their own, or using the potty independently, practicing with them is invaluable. It helps children understand that every skill is like developing a muscle, requiring an investment of time and energy. Using this approach, we teach our children skills versus simply dumping feelings of anger and shame on them.*

We tend to be so caught up in meting out punishments and threats that it doesn't occur to us there may be an entirely different way to handle a situation—an approach that doesn't diminish the child's sense of self but emboldens it. There are many clever ways to teach children appropriate behavior. But to take advantage of these ways, we have to abandon our reactivity.

The payoff for taking time to pause is immediate. Our children's eyes light up, their shoulders relax, and their heart says, "Thank you for treating me like a human being and understanding that I deserve the chance to learn from my mistakes."

~ A New Commitment to Shedding Roles ~

Definitions define but also stifle;
Roles regulate but also control;
Titles tantalize but also demean;
Labels laud but also subvert.

All these external extras
Bolster the false self,
Providing temporary relief
To a deeper, searing problem

Of the emptiness we feel within.

Unless we touch our scars and scabs
All the jewels, crowns, and banquets in the world
Will never be enough
To fill the holes within.

So . . .

Instead of fancy robes
And thick masks,
We need to dare to unmask and disrobe,
Shedding skin,

For it is here
In our naked selves
That we can fully meet each other
And discover who we were all along.

CHAPTER EIGHTEEN

From Emotions to Feelings

People often confuse emotions with feelings, as if the two were the same. I look at them as vastly different. Simply put, we react with an emotion when we are unable to handle our feelings. When we feel uncomfortable, we create a smokescreen of reactivity. For instance, we eat, drink, smoke, blame, guilt, have tantrums, and so on. These feel like feelings but are actually the avoidance of true feeling.

The truth is that feelings can be experienced only from a deep and silent place within us. They need to be cried about, walked with, touched, and even experienced as quivering and shaking. Feelings can be acknowledged only on a visceral, highly personal level. It's because most of us aren't trained to feel our feelings, *really* feel them, that we dump them onto our loved ones in the form of emotional reactions.

When we feel our feelings, we don't have time to engage in reactive emotions. We tune in and allow the feelings to speak to us, wash over us, and transform us. Aware that we are under waves of feeling, we do the opposite of emoting. We hush up, become still, and allow the significance of the feelings to grow us up.

Because we have been conditioned to do exactly the opposite of this, we feel more comfortable in the drama and motion of emotions. Children are ready targets for us to dump our discomfort on. However, they are ill-equipped to handle our emotional projections. It's a burden too heavy to bear, crushing their spirit. For this reason, we owe it to them to process our own internal states. In this way, they won't have to lug them around as baggage for the rest of their life.

The first step is to go *under* the emotion. So, for example, when we notice we are impatient and snapping at our kids, we pause and pay attention right away. "I'm fretting at my child, but what am I really feeling right now?"

If we are yelling at our kids to get in bed, we might ask ourselves, "What's my yelling about?" On the surface it may seem that the yelling is originating from fear that they won't get enough sleep, or that they are disobeying us. If we look deeper we may see that the reality is that we are tired and need some alone time in which to recuperate from a long day. In other words, the emotion is directed toward the child, whereas the feeling is that we need time for self-care. In this case, we might say in a calm voice, "I have had a long day and am tired. I have no energy left and need to rest. This is why I am beginning to sound impatient and can barely hold it together. Can you please help me out here? You need rest too." When we can be honest with our children about our emotional reactions, we move into our heart-space, taking full ownership of what we are experiencing. If we are coming from this space, it's more likely that they will be able to take us in and empathize with what we are feeling.

Let's suppose that our real concern is for the child's need for sleep. Even if we don't express this to our children and simply notice the fear we experience around their lack of sleep, we will find ourselves calming down. We might be aware of this anxiety and detach from it a bit, saying perhaps, "When I act on this anxiety, I create more anxiety in myself and my children. It's far better for my child to be sleep-deprived for a few minutes than it is for us to disconnect." As I always tell clients, "Keep the feeling, lose the reaction."

What's happening in this process of quiet listening and feeling is that the anxiety that's been locked up, and that gets triggered when our children do something that goes against our idea of control, is being integrated. This energy now becomes available for reinvesting in our lives and the lives of our children. No longer knotted up in either defiant resistance or emotional volatility, it becomes a powerful flow of creativity.

Fourteen-year-old Tyler had a huge homework project that he needed to complete by the end of the weekend. A procrastinator, he tended to wait until the last minute before beginning his work. This drove Alan, his anxious father, bananas. Alan is highly strung by nature, and his anxiety went into overdrive when, at dinnertime on Saturday, Tyler confessed that he had played video games in his room all day when he was supposed to be working on his project, and in fact hadn't even opened the book.

At this point Alan lost it. "You are grounded for a month," he yelled. "I cannot believe how lazy you are. You're going to fail the semester."

Tyler objected, "But I'm playing in the final with the soccer team next weekend. I've worked hard all semester to be on the team."

"You should have thought of that," Alan thundered. "Your schoolwork is more important than soccer. You're grounded for a month, and that's final."

Not one to cower, Tyler raised his voice. "I hate projects like this. I don't care about school. I just want to play soccer. I'm good at it. I'll play it professionally someday. You can't make me miss the big game!"

Alan was enraged. "I can't make you? Who do you think you are, talking to me like that? Another word out of you, and you'll be grounded for the rest of the semester."

Tyler stood up and headed for the stairs to go back to his room. "I hate you," he yelled over his shoulder. "You always think I'm going to fail at things. If I fail, it's because you're always on my case. It's all your fault." With that, Alan grounded him for the remainder of the semester.

On Monday at work a colleague commented, "Alan, you must be excited about the game on Saturday. Tyler is so good, you surely know he's going to make a career out of soccer."

Alan was already wishing he hadn't been so extreme. He had encouraged Tyler's interest in soccer and knew he was talented. Having blown things out of proportion in his fit of anger over Tyler's procrastination, he had backed himself into a corner. How could he now rescind the grounding and not lose all credibility?

Alan had begun coming to me for therapy a few weeks before this incident because he was concerned about his son's academic performance. Believing Tyler lacked motivation and wasn't living up to his potential, he wanted me to see his son. As I often do, I had begun by counseling just the parent initially. When Alan arrived in my office later that week and related what had transpired, I helped him understand how he was playing a direct role in perpetuating Tyler's resistance to his academic work.

"I really want Tyler to succeed in soccer," Alan said. "But I also want him to do well in school. What if he doesn't make it to professional soccer? He's going to need a degree to fall back on."

Like most parents, Alan has the best of intentions. Every one of us wants to watch our children soar to great heights. So invested are we in their success that we'll do almost anything to help them, sacrificing for them, as Alan himself assured me in my office that morning.

The problem is that in our great desire to see our children do well, we interact with them through the lens of fear that they might fail—a fear that our children then absorb. But how can we avoid letting our fear take over? Isn't failure a very real possibility?

Fear tends to backfire, accomplishing the exact opposite of what we are hoping for. In Tyler's case, he felt his father's anxiety and resented it. It was too much pressure. Instead of spurring him to want to work on his school project, this pressure caused him to disengage. In other words, he was dissecting the problem accurately when he said that it was his father's fault because he was always on his case.

"Your intention was to help your son, yet everything got muddied by your anxiety," I explained. "When you were afraid you couldn't control him, your emotions took over, hijacking your ability to be objective and eclipsing what you really feel. Rather than working with your son to find creative solutions to the situation, you made yourself into his enemy. Now, instead of his having to deal with his own resistance to the learning process, his focus has shifted to resisting you. In other words, whereas Tyler's relationship with his schoolwork should have been between him and his teachers, you made it about you."

"I really didn't mean to," Alan confessed. "I was just trying to help. I don't know how the whole thing got blown into something so big. I truly don't want him to miss the game this coming weekend. I'm not even that angry with him. I just want to be the best dad."

"The way to make sense of this is to start with what you were initially feeling," I elaborated. "Your feeling was very different from your emotional reaction. Your feeling was concern and a desire to protect Tyler from the consequences of a bad grade. The problem was that you became anxious that his procrastination would get the better of him and he'd be in trouble at school. When you listened to this anxious voice within you, it overwhelmed you, which is why you reacted with rage. Your emotion eclipsed your real feelings."

"I thought they were the same thing," Alan said.

"Your feeling was one of supporting your son, wanting the best for him. But when you became anxious, your fearful emotions took over, leading you down a path that was the opposite of what you intended. Your concern for Tyler naturally raised your anxiety. The point is to tolerate anxiety instead of reacting to it and becoming enraged."

"What do you mean, 'tolerate'?"

"When we are able to notice what we are feeling, whatever that may be, and simply allow it to wash over us without being overwhelmed by it, we learn to tolerate the feeling state without getting caught up in an emotional reaction."

Feelings are organic responses to life's situations. Anxiety as a feeling is natural. However, when we don't know how to simply sit with our anxiety, soothing ourselves, it can take us over. When this happens, emotion floods us and blocks what we are really feeling. Emotions carry a charge of resistance. This is when unproductive emotions such as jealousy, the desire to manipulate or control, the inclination to pout and sulk, the urge to distance ourselves, or the tendency to explode at someone arise. All of this because we are unable to sit with our feelings and soothe ourselves from the inside.

So what should you do when you feel anxious?

The first thing is to recognize what you are actually feeling. Many of us live in a manner that's disconnected from our feelings, which means we are constantly reacting destructively in some way rather than responding constructively. As long as we are tuned in to our feelings and can identify when an emotional reaction is beginning to cloud them, we won't project them onto our children.

When I explained this to Alan, he inquired, "So you are saying that if I were able to sit with my original feeling of anxiety and learned to soothe that feeling, I wouldn't have put myself in a bind by grounding Tyler?"

"Exactly. It's because we have never learned to sit with our anxiety, simply feeling it and observing it, that we flame up and boil over. Had you recognized that Tyler's academic performance is a trigger for you, you could have avoided the reaction you got caught up in. Instead, you would have simply allowed your anxiety to be there, without bringing it center stage. That way it remains a feeling and doesn't have to contaminate your relationship with your son.

"It's kind of like giving myself a time-out," Alan said perceptively. "Allowing myself the space to calm down before making any decision, so that I don't have to regret what I've said."

You could take a time-out to sit with yourself, asking yourself questions such as the following:

- *Why does my son's academic performance trigger my anxiety?*

- *Why am I making this about me?*

- *What does this say about my own self-worth?*

- *Why am I tying how I feel to my son's performance?*

Questions like these can show us that anxiety springs from our ego. It's tied to a sense of entitlement, which causes us to want to control our children. We think that because we brought them into the world, they are a reflection on us. This causes us to believe that we have a right to expect certain things of them. Because we aren't solid in ourselves, when the reflection we receive from them doesn't match our expectations, it unnerves us. This is when we resort to manipulating them, dominating them, being enraged with them.

When we feel grounded in ourselves, we don't need to enter the insecurity of ego, with its correspondent defensiveness. We can simply be who we are without needing to imagine ourselves a particular person in the way the ego does. When we have a solid self, no self-image is required. We don't need to *think about* ourselves *at all* because we are totally engaged in just *being* ourselves.

From this state of the fullness of our center, rather than the inadequacy of the ego, we experience life as benevolent, eager to cast a supportive net whenever we hit a rough spot. We operate from a wellspring of trust that's both peaceful and joyous. This isn't about trying to believe in ourselves, which is still the ego. No trying is needed. We don't have to reassure ourselves, work up faith, or engage in positive thinking about ourselves. We simply enjoy being ourselves, and this spills over into enjoying seeing our children's lives unfold from within them instead of feeling we need to orchestrate the process.

The essential self doesn't need to look for worth—not from our children, and not even within ourselves. We don't even think about our worth because it's incarnate in us. It's our natural state, something we only ever question because family, the educational system, and society cast doubt on it.

Our main discomfort with sitting with our feelings is that we don't believe we will be able to. As we discussed earlier, sitting still is a scary concept to many of us who are engrossed in a whirl of activity. The moment we feel something uncomfortable, our knee-jerk reaction is to look outward. Instead of taking what's arising as an impetus to still ourselves, we do the opposite. We look for ways to escape the discomfort we are experiencing.

"Once I've sat with my emotions, so that I can again feel my connection with Tyler, what do I do then?" Alan asked.

"You support him," I explained. "The best way to do this is to detach yourself from the outcome of his choices. You can invest yourself in fostering his well-being only to the degree that you are detached from the result. When you are profoundly connected, so that he feels your deep love for him and is assured of your interest in his well-being, you open up space for his own motivation to make its appearance. As long as you are pressing him to do things, that won't happen. It's when you take your hands off, and yet remain committed to him, that he'll find it within him to do whatever his soul is directing him to do."

When we've been pressuring a child, whether intentionally or inadvertently, there may follow a period when their motivation lies fallow. This is when we have to soothe ourselves, trusting that after a suitable period of recovery from our pressure, they will find their own way. It's like planting a seed in the fall, then waiting all through the winter months until the warmth and showers of spring cause it to sprout. If, when it lies dormant, we allow our anxiety to cause us to make the mistake of digging up the seed to see what it's doing, we kill it.

A subtle variation on this mistake is to say to a child, "You need to make your own mistakes and deal with your own choices. You are old enough to realize the consequences of a poor grade. It's you who'll have to deal with the consequences of your grade, not me. You're the one who needs to be okay with your effort and your performance." When we give advice of this kind, imagining we are freeing our children to find their own feet, we actually short-circuit what can arise only from within them. We're still trying to create an outcome, though oh so subtly. In this way, we dig up the seed in its essential period of dormancy.

Alan's anxiety again sprang to the fore. "Are you saying that I do nothing to help him besides simply be a loving presence? What if he continues to watch video games when he should be doing school-work? Do I just ignore it?"

"You allow Tyler time to find his feet. Let the appropriate interaction with his teachers take its course if he fails to turn in assignments. In due course, the school will doubtless contact you. At this point, an intervention may be of benefit. Since it's clear the video games have become an escape, you might calmly state something like the following: 'If I saw you doing drugs and did nothing, I would be remiss as a father if I didn't speak up. Or if I saw you getting into your car drunk and didn't take away your keys, I would be failing you. Your school tells me you aren't giving due attention to your studies. You deserve to give yourself the chance to try working on your projects. I will step in if I need to and provide the boundaries I feel you need, but I would rather you create these yourself as you are old enough to do so.'"

Once Tyler sees that Alan is his ally, not his opponent, he's likely to respond positively. He's being offered choices, not compelled. Only as we remain detached from the outcome can we truly be of support—and, as we've been seeing, children instinctively sense the difference between genuine interest in their well-being and when we are moti-vated by our own agenda. But an intervention of this kind needs to come at the right moment, when life itself prompts it, not as a result of our anxiety. Of course, this means we need to be ever vigilant to what's happening. Only through an awakened consciousness that's truly present can we know when the right moment is. To an aware person, the opportune moment presents itself with ample notice, always providing plenty of clues along the way.

Many parents don't realize this, but our children actually long to cooperate with us. However, they have to sense that we are on their time, helping them fulfill their own agenda, not ours. Our children need to know we are coming from a deep trust in their goodness, not from fear of their failure. To emphasize what we saw earlier, the vibes we put out are the key to this, for they will trump our words every time.

"Back to the soccer tournament this coming Saturday," Alan said. "What do I do?"

I responded, "Speak from your heart. Tell Tyler you allowed your own fear to blow things out of proportion. Admit you were anxious and didn't know how to deal with what you were feeling, so you reacted. Explain that you realize that he is trustworthy and wants to excel. Cap it off by telling him how you're looking forward to enjoying seeing him play at the weekend."

As it turned out, Alan followed my suggestions, and Tyler responded favorably by negotiating a plan to get the project completed.

Our feelings are barometers of our soul, whereas our emotional reactions are indicators that our ego has become activated. If we stay with our heartfelt feelings, simply allowing our reactions to rise and fall within us without becoming caught up in them or becoming alarmed by them, we will shift into a calm and more integrated state.

Awareness of what's happening with us is the key to not spewing our unresolved issues onto our children. As long as we remain conscious, our issues won't be projected onto them. As we sit with the stew of emotion inside us, quietly observing it without telling ourselves a story about it, we will settle down, having integrated another piece of our past, for which we will be all the wiser and all the stronger.

As our emotions less and less swallow us up, we discover that we are exponentially more than what our ego has imagined us to be. There are power and resources within us beyond anything we have so far known. It's thanks to the issues that arise with our children, which come as gifts to both them and us, that we at last discover how wonderful it is to be the person we are.

Creating a Direct Path to Feeling

The problem beneath all conflict in our lives and in the world is that we haven't been allowed to feel what we feel. Instead, we've been taught to distort what we feel and turn it against others.

Attachment to how our children feel is actually the antithesis of allowing *them* to feel. We mistake our interest in their feelings for acceptance of their feelings, and we imagine we are giving them space. However, being seduced by our children's feelings in any way, or showing any charge around their feelings, sends them the signal that their feelings are to be feared. Instead of being neutral around their feelings and treating them not only as normal but also as inevitable, our unconscious charge around them causes the feeling to become stuck and sometimes even to spiral out of control.

Our children need to receive the message that feelings are an everyday part of life, like their fears are. There are always going to be feelings and fears, just as there are always going to be thoughts. Allowing them all to exist without meddling with them, controlling them, or avoiding them lets them to come and go in a natural fashion. It's when we intervene and seek to manage them that all goes awry.

When we have a clear and direct pathway to our feelings, so that we are unafraid to simply reflect on them as needed, we won't be swept away by them. We can just say, "I am sad right now," or "I'm feeling frustrated." The simple and clear acknowledgment of our feelings allows us to recognize them without being overwhelmed by their force.

When our children see us reacting to them in self-absorbed, unpredictable, even wild ways, they not only learn to distrust us, they begin to fear us. Unfortunately, when we see a look of fear in a child's eyes, we tend to mistake it for respect. In fact, so seduced are we by the myth that we need to be in control that, on a subtle level, we actually enjoy the submission we engender in our children by giving them cause to fear us. It boosts our ego, making us feel powerful and therefore important.

When we resort to threats, which are emotional blackmail, a child's fear may result in superficial compliance, but it does little to shift behavior in a lasting way. If anything, beneath the surface the child is inundated with emotions such as resentment, anger, and—if our mistreatment of them continues—eventually bitterness. In contrast, when children sense they are in an agenda-free zone with their parents, they rise to the trust we place in them. Developing such trust takes time and commitment, and it occurs only as a direct outgrowth of our own maturing.

If we wish to create a connection with our children, we need to retrain ourselves to stop controlling them. To accomplish this requires us to accept the present moment in its "as is" form. For example, the way to work on our reactivity in the case of a messy room is to ask ourselves, "Why do clothes on the floor affect my inner sense of stability? Why do I feel personally threatened to the point of lashing out at my child?"

Consumed with a mythical standard of "how things should be," we often feel we have no choice but to react. We are compelled. However, by examining each reaction and identifying which myth is driving it (and often it's more than one), we can begin to tame our reactivity. All that's required is to observe what we tell ourselves in such situations. This enables us to recognize which cultural myth or myths we are in the clutches of.

Does this mean we never become upset with our children? Not at all. The issue isn't so much that we get upset, but how we go about responding to the emotion welling up within us. Do we do so in a blindly reactive way, unleashing scary punishments on our children? Or is there a more healthy way to engage in the dance of parenting that will communicate connection and caring?

When we remove the emotional element in any situation and present our honest feelings on a matter, we create a sense of being in a partnership. Sharing our feelings with our children is fundamentally different from emoting reactively. Blame is removed from the equation, as is all volatility. This frees us to discuss an issue in the awareness that both parties have a right to either agree or disagree on a matter. By creating a sense of unity and negotiating in a calm manner, we are eventually able to arrive at a joint decision. The agreement is one all parties take responsibility for. In other words, because our children see that we are truly operating in a manner that isn't controlling, and that we sincerely want their help, they want to support any agreement we make and may even offer suggestions we hadn't thought of.

If you imagined I was advocating hands-off, laissez-faire parenting, perhaps now you are beginning to see how much more involved we need to be in order to parent consciously. It takes considerably more time and energy to share our feelings genuinely and discuss an issue until we reach a commonality than it does to utter the words "Because I said so!" Children don't respond well to being commanded and dictated to. No one does.

What might a dialogue with our children in which we express our feelings free of negative emotions look like? How exactly can we allow them to have a voice, so that they buy into whatever decision our negotiations result in?

The following conversation is an example of how to involve children in decision making even as early as when they are two or three years old:

PARENT: When your room is untidy, it makes me feel uncomfortable because I like things organized and clean. Does your room make you feel uncomfortable in any way?

CHILD: No, I'm just fine with it.

PARENT: What about if Mommy kept the house in the same dirty way as you keep your room? How would that make you feel?

CHILD: I wouldn't like that. I like a clean house. But I like a messy room.

PARENT: So you have different standards for yourself and for me? I try to have the same standard for myself and for you. I like to keep a clean house and would love you to keep a clean room too. Can we create a plan together in which both our needs get met? I prefer your room be clean so that you learn to live in an organized fashion. My life doesn't change if your room is messy, but I want to teach you this valuable skill. It's important to me that you learn to be organized. Just as you like it when I'm organized and neat in the house, I would like you to do this for yourself in your room. What can I do to help you with it?

CHILD: I will clean my room once a week. If it isn't clean, can you come and remind me? Or help me organize?

PARENT: Sure.

Once a child experiences our nonreactive energy, they are more open to our involvement in their life. They lean into our concerns and find ways to work with us rather than against us. It all starts with owning and taming our reactivity so that instead of being frightened by emotional outbursts and closing off to us, our children hear our feelings. No longer do we have to keep demanding, "Are you listening to me?" or "Do you hear me?"

Managing feelings is one of the hardest things to master, especially when we are experiencing fear. What does feeling our fear look like in practice?

Feeling: You feel impatient with your child for being too slow. You feel helpless, frustrated, and incompetent.

Reaction: You want to push them along, perhaps even yell at them.

Entering the fear: Notice that you have been triggered. This is a red light, a warning to halt. Hit your internal freeze button.

Notice your agitation, take a deep breath, then allow yourself to become quiet internally. If necessary leave the room. Examine your fear by asking:

- *What's the nature of the fear I'm experiencing?*

- *What am I afraid will happen?*

- *Is that really such a bad thing?*

- *Will it be the end of the world?*

- *Can I own that my fear stems from my past?*

- *Can I see that it has nothing to do with my child?*

- *Can I allow the feeling to pass through me and tap into a deeper trust?*

As you examine your fear, you simply watch it. As you do so, affirm:

- *My fear comes from my lost inner self.*

- *My fear stems from my idea that I need to be perfect.*

- *My fear is attached to the belief that I'm not good enough.*

- *My fear is connected to the pressure to raise a model child.*

- *My fear is natural and normal.*

- *My fear doesn't define me but is just an aspect of me.*

- *I allow my fear to simply be there as I flow through my day.*

- *The fact that I'm afraid doesn't need to sap my energy.*

- *All I need to do is observe my fear and allow it to be as it is.*

- *I allow my fear to sit silently within. It's mine to process, not someone else's.*

- *My fear will dissolve once I allow it to simply be.*

- *My fear will intensify if I deny it or react to it.*

By allowing your fear to be as it is and recognizing it for what it is, you integrate it. Now you can address your children in a calm and focused manner so that they feel heard and met.

There's no one to protect our children against our reactivity. They have no choice but to either succumb or fight back. Either way, they spend a great deal of their psychic energy battling us—energy they should be investing in daydreaming and spontaneous play. We need to take the protection of our children's spirit seriously. They come to us so we can honor their authentic voice and nurture their true self, not so they can become carbon copies of us.

~ A New Commitment to Shedding Reactivity ~

My relationship with anger, although intimate
And fleetingly empowering,
Has outlived its purpose
And overstayed its welcome.

When it no longer serves to transform
Or inspire courage,
It is defunct and needs to be let go,
Shedding its chaos, noise, and drama,

Leaving behind a quiet
From which truth is born.
The silence may feel deafening at first,
But once embraced, it births the roar of a revolution.

CHAPTER NINETEEN

From Enmeshment to Autonomy

A client by the name of Valerie explained to me, "I constantly badger my son Daniel to do better at school, because it's a jungle out there. I know how young black men like Daniel fare in the real world. I know how ruthless the world is. Because I'm aware of the cruelty of this world, I try to prepare him for it." In Valerie's desire to prepare her son to face the "real world," she constantly imposes on him all her own interpretations of this cruel and unjust world, along with the emotions she experiences. She infuses his worldview with fear and anxiety.

For Valerie, the world is unsafe and unfair. She fears for her son because of his skin color. Her fears are fully justified in her eyes, and it would be foolish to tell her that they are invalid. Many of her past therapists have undermined her feelings by telling her she is living in the past and that racism is a matter of perception, not reality. Valerie has felt demeaned and disappointed that no one seems to understand where she's coming from.

I took a different approach with her. "I fully appreciate where you are coming from. You are right that this world is cruel and unjust, especially to men of color. I fully connect with your feeling that you want to protect your son and prepare him the best you can."

"You do?" said Valerie, surprised and relieved that someone was finally understanding and validating her feelings.

"Your feelings are absolutely valid and very real. The issue isn't whether someone outside yourself understands them or not. The issue is whether you do. They are yours, and because they are yours, you have every right to feel them."

"I have been told that I'm paranoid and that I am going to mani-fest exactly what I fear."

"You are not paranoid. This is a judgment of your feelings. Feelings can never be judged. They just are. Feelings need to be felt in their 'as is' state. What you need to understand is that you haven't been feeling your feelings at all."

"I haven't?" exclaimed Valerie.

"You have been reacting to them, projecting them onto your son. In doing so you are turning him into a nervous wreck."

"How do I feel my feelings without making him nervous? That's the last thing I want to do. I need to make him strong and empow-ered. That's what I thought I was doing."

"You feel your feelings by sitting with them. They are yours, not his. You need to befriend them and allow them to rise and fall as they need to without seeking to fix them. You are looking to fix your feelings. You want your feelings to go away just like your last therapist did. In es-sence, you are doing the same thing she did—you are invalidating them."

"I am?" said an incredulous Valerie.

"You are so uncomfortable feeling anxious about your son that you are doing your best to change him into someone you can stop feeling anxious about. You badger and pester him all day to become someone different, constantly communicating to him that he isn't good enough the way he is. You hate being anxious, and you believe that if you can just badger him enough so that he changes, you won't need to feel anxious anymore. In other words, this is all about you."

"I cannot believe I have been using him to fix me. I thought I was helping him. I see now that all I was doing was controlling him so I could manage my painful feelings."

"Your pain is real. Your fears are real. This is where we get confused. They are real not because they are real for everyone. They are real and valid because they are so for you. But just because it's true for you doesn't mean it's true for your son. Honor them because they are yours to feel, but don't feel that you have the right to make them your son's. They are not your son's reality; they are yours. You are projecting your experiences onto him. Instead, you need to learn to sit with these very painful feelings and process them. This may mean crying from a feeling of helplessness, or it may mean talking about them with others in your position, but it always comes down to your willingness to recognize that they are coming from your past, your perspective, your take on reality. No one is disputing your perspective. The dispute here is what you are doing to your son because of them."

"So how can I ensure he won't be treated unfairly by this cruel world?"

"You can't ensure anything. It's the same as asking how I can ensure my flight won't crash. You are asking for life to give you a certainty that's against its nature. Life is inherently impermanent, possessing both destructive and creative forces. Understanding that this is the basic nature of things will help you stop feeling the need to look for guarantees. Your concern isn't just that life will treat your son unfairly, but it is perhaps in greater measure a question of whether he is too fragile to handle it. Again, this is a projection. We have no way of knowing how much resilience our children have to handle things. However, through the transmission of our fears, we can certainly ensure they don't have much. It's our anxiety that our children of color or our young girls won't be able to stand up against what befalls them that is ultimately going to cripple them, not the reality itself. Instead of shielding our children from painful situations, it's far more helpful to reverse our approach and teach them that undesirable things can certainly happen, but they have the resources within them to cope.

"Some children may in fact fall prey to sexual predators or bullies, so let's teach our young ones to honor their boundaries, trust their inner voice, and feel safe to report any violation of their personhood to us immediately. Some children will be rejected by their peers in the most unfair ways, so let's prepare them for this reality not by making them anxious but by helping them to feel empowered. Let's give them tools to recognize a bully and language to combat them. Instead of teaching our girls to diet in order to fit into society's standards of beauty so that they don't face the pain of rejection, let's teach them that they are fine the way they are, and that if they are called names, they are capable of handling it. By teaching our children that they are whole as they are, we teach them to stand strong."

"So what do I do with his poor grades? Do I just let him be?"

"Your concern can't be with the end results or his performance. Your focus needs to be on yourself. Ask yourself the following questions: 'Am I creating the conditions to allow my son to experience his own relationship with his success or failure? Or am I interfering with this process? How can I coach my son but not take over his academics? What energy am I bringing into this situation? How much negativity am I contributing? Am I teaching him self-confidence or self-deprecation? How are my fears interfering with his success?'"

Valerie was thinking hard. She finally said, "It is all me, isn't it? I have paralyzed him with my fear. He has now completely disengaged. I don't even think he tries. Instead of giving him an abundance of hope and self-confidence, I've created such a distasteful feeling in him. He probably detests studying for a test because he knows I'm going to go into overdrive and make him crazy. I need to stop. I hope I will be able to."

Valerie learned a powerful lesson that day. She saw how a parent's unresolved feelings can turn into damaging emotional reactions that forever disrupt our children's authentic self-expression.

The Pitfall of Emotional Fusion

When parents find it impossible to differentiate between their feelings and their child's, it's because they experience a high level of enmeshment, or what's more technically referred to as "emotional fusion."

As we become more mindful, we begin to sort out the jumble in our mind. It's like taking all the socks out of the laundry basket, then putting them in neat piles. In terms of the family, we stop projecting our feelings onto our children and start putting these feelings back in their right pile—a pile within ourselves, not our youngsters. This process allows us to see our children for who they are, so that we understand them separately from our idea of them.

Separating ourselves emotionally from our children in this way sounds scary to many of us. We take it to mean a separation from our heart's desire, or we think of it as putting physical distance between ourselves and our loved ones. However, I'm describing a completely different kind of separation—a form of separation that makes real connection possible. I'm talking about ending our fusion, so that we separate our emotions from those of our children, our experiences from theirs, our internal stories from theirs.

The reason we don't enjoy closeness to our children much of the time is that instead of encountering them for who they are and appreciating them for their resplendent resilience, we project our own internal state onto them. This internal state is familiar to us because it arises from within us, and projecting it onto a child provides us with a pseudo-feeling of closeness to the child. Little do we realize that we aren't really connecting with the child at all, only with what we project onto them, which is merely our own idea of them. As long as the other person allows us to maintain our idea of them, we feel close to them. However, the moment our idea of the other doesn't work for them, the feeling of closeness ends.

It's for this reason that parents feel so threatened by their teenage children. The teen confronts parental control by declaring, "I'm my own person and I need to find my own way to express my individuality. Since you won't allow this, I need to break free from you." Encouraging someone to be their own person, separate from us, may appear to threaten closeness, whereas it's actually the path to real connection, since only autonomous individuals can form an authentic connection.

The process of increasing our self-awareness leads to healthy emotional separation from our children, because it produces clarity and order in the mind. We take ownership of how we perceive reality and appreciate that others don't have the same perception. It's this ordering of our inner landscape that I refer to as emotional separation. Instead of being enmeshed or fused, we stand on our own two feet emotionally. We can do this because we are connected to our own internal frame of reference. Although this feels threatening, this emotional separation is the only way to connect the beating of two unique hearts.

Developing Emotional Autonomy

As we separate what we feel from how we react, and rein in our ideas and agendas for our children, we begin to change much of our way of being. Where before we operated out of a state of need and lack, now we engage out of self-fulfillment and empowerment. Suddenly our dependency on people for approval, affirmation, and validation is gone.

Emotional autonomy is essential for conscious parenting. The first stage of emotional separation occurs during toddlerhood, followed by all the key transitional stages of childhood: nursery, first grade, middle school, and the ultimate test of high school. When parents find it hard to recognize these key stages as the call to allow their children to have greater freedom to feel, fail, and fall, they create an unhealthy dependency on them. Children begin to feel as if they will fall apart if their parents aren't around to help them process things.

Symbiosis in infancy is exactly what's needed. However, when this symbiosis extends beyond what the child needs and is more about the parent wanting to feel significant, the child suffers. We commonly talk about a teen rebelling, but it's really the parents who are rebelling against their teen's right to an increasing amount of sovereignty. Parents who feel threatened by a teen's quest for autonomy rebel against the teen by attempting to exert greater control. The teen is doing exactly what they are supposed to do. In fact, the more they rebel, the louder the wake-up call for us as parents to back off from our projections. The teen isn't being "bad." Quite the opposite, they are taking it upon themself to initiate a separation from the parent's projections, since the parent didn't initiate this task in the manner the teen needed them to do.

The battles that occur between parents and teens are caused by the parents' war against the natural, healthy, and necessary separation the teen is attempting to achieve. Instead of labeling our teens "difficult," we need to realize that more often than not it's parents who are being difficult. Teens appear difficult only when they have no other way to counter how difficult their parents are being.

Our children are always trying to enter their own empowerment and self-direction. For true connection to occur, we need to see how threatened we feel on an internal level by our children's desire to be their unique self. When we become grounded in our own consciousness, we realize that each of us has a right to our own feelings, separate from one another. The more acute our realization of this, the more capable we become of honoring our children for who they are. No longer injecting our mind-set into them, we respect how they feel, what they value, and the course they choose for their life. We see them as beings distinct from ourselves and realize how privileged we are to help usher them onto their unique path.

Children who are allowed to feel their own feelings and experience their own life in their own way are empowered to take appropriate risks and engage in life as an adventure. Because they are secure in their own being, they are able to trust and love with an open heart. Consequently, they aren't afraid to admit when they need us. In fact, the more independent they are in their emotions and perceptions, the more able they are to engage in a healthy reliance on us when necessary.

As a therapist, I have to be ever-vigilant about my own unconscious need to have my clients depend on me. Elizabeth, one of my clients, was going through a hard time during one of our recent sessions. She cried practically the whole time. I reminded her that she could call on me if she needed to speak between sessions. At our following session she said to me, "I felt hurt when you didn't call or e-mail me to check in on me. I began to feel rejected by you. But then I remembered what you have always taught me about the role of victim and realized that if I needed you, I just had to reach out. You were not being uncaring. In fact, the opposite, you were showing me that I was strong and could handle it."

In the smallest of ways, we communicate to our loved ones that we don't believe in them or don't trust them to be strong enough to figure things out for themselves. Even today, I have to constantly fight my instinct to check in on my daughter with texts that say, "How are you?" or "How are you feeling?" I have to have faith in the closeness of our connection, knowing that if she has something to share, she will. I remind parents that when their child locks themselves in their room, they shouldn't barge in. The child is saying, "I need to be alone right now." Parental respect for their autonomy demonstrates that we feel secure in our connection. Of course, if they need to begin homework or eat a meal, we can certainly enter their space, just not to connect out of our need.

Clients frequently say something like, "I'm so stupid, I can't believe I did that." In response, I don't rush in to change their thinking or push them to tell themselves they're smart and not to worry. Instead, I align with their perception of the situation, saying something like, "I know you feel stupid. This is a valid feeling because it says you want to do better. But remember that your feelings are just a state of mind and nothing to be scared of." We then explore the feeling instead of being hijacked by fear of it.

With our children, the traditional approach is to contradict their negative talk by saying, "No, you're not stupid. You're smart." Does this type of response allay our children's worries and sense of inadequacy? On the contrary, it imposes our thoughts on them. What our children need most at such a moment isn't to suddenly feel smart, but to learn to process the feeling that they are "stupid."

It's here that we tend to get it wrong as parents. In our desire to avoid the discomfort of seeing our children suffer, we rush in, interfering with their relationship with their inner being. Instead, we need to remember that feelings are just that—feelings. They don't define a person. When we are clear about this, we become less anxious about what either we or our children are feeling at any given time, which makes us more able to help them engage the full range of their feelings.

Don't Fear Dissent

When our children understand that dissent isn't necessarily a sign of things going wrong, they develop the confidence to tune in to themselves and voice their feelings. They learn to welcome dissent in their relationships and don't fear the discomfort of negotiating between differing opinions. Instead of seeing dissent as a sign of a problem, they regard it as healthy.

How this works can be seen in the case of Maureen, who came into therapy distressed that she and her seventeen-year-old daughter were fighting all the time. When I inquired what they fought about, Maureen said, "Oh, it could be about anything. I say blue, so she says red. I say Italian, so she says Chinese. Before we know it, we're screaming obscenities at each other. I'm worried I'm going to lose my daughter over these disagreements."

Maureen described with pride how she had always been extremely close to her daughter. "We were like two peas in a pod. We never, ever used to fight. She was like my shadow. She followed me wherever I went. But this year something changed, and now she doesn't want to agree with anything I say. I'm so scared to lose her."

Maureen had controlled her daughter to the point that the girl was unable to develop her real self. She did this to prop up her own weak sense of self. The fact is, this dutiful daughter had been betraying her own feelings and opinions for years in order to provide her mother with a transfusion of selfhood. It was almost as if she intuitively knew she was her mother's lifeline. Maureen was so dependent on her identity as a mother that she felt she would be nothing without this role. This caused her to cling fiercely to her daughter, who had now reached the stage at which she wanted to have her own voice and enjoy some space away from her mother's hovering. This is what had triggered so much dissent.

As the weeks went by, Maureen learned to value dissent as a means of honoring others as separate beings. Instead of feeling threatened by it, she started to integrate it into her life. She discovered that disconnection doesn't occur when there's dissent, but when there's intolerance of each other's differences.

True closeness involves a healthy interdependence in which both parent and child appreciate and help each other without feeling as if they have to compromise themselves to prop up the other. Instead of being weighed down by each other, they are empowered and free to be exactly who they are, while maintaining a close connection. Authentic connection is distinct from enmeshment, because closeness has nothing in common with the need to control. Real connection frees us, whereas fusion paralyzes.

Embracing Pain

If anything causes us to experience enmeshment, it's to see our children in pain. However, when feelings of enmeshment arise in a painful situation, we can use them to grow.

My daughter was barely eight months old. We had been playing on the bed when I became distracted, and she fell off, hitting her head on the hardwood floor. The loud bang still resounds in my memory. She turned pale, rolling her eyes up into her head, and almost passed out. I flew into a panic, unable to believe how remiss I had been. When I contacted the doctor, he said he would conduct some tests the following day if she continued to be listless.

I cradled my daughter in my lap for hours as she alternated between moments of deep slumber and anguished cries because her head was sore. Each time she cried, my heart leapt, leaving me breathless. Try as I might, I was unable to put my emotions aside. There was no one else to blame. With no one to react to, I was forced to feel the full force of the experience. Was this a bad thing? Quite the opposite. Not having an outlet to react to changed my entire outlook on pain.

When I met my clients that week, each of them remarked on how different I seemed. They found me more present, more open, and less in my head. I felt different. Crying for hours and facing every "what if" seemed to have had the effect of dropping me into a place of profound connection to the wonder of being alive. This experience of shifting out of my head and into my heart helped me connect with other parents. I could relate to their distraction, poor judgment, and reactivity in a less judgmental and more human and therapeutic manner.

An aspect of the epiphany I experienced involved seeing how even extremely painful feelings don't destroy us. Quite the opposite: They can teach us empathy. In fact, I have learned that painful experiences have the potential to deepen us in a far more profound way than "happy" experiences often do. By putting us in touch with our limitations and fallibility, they remind us of our common humanity, dispelling all need for one-upmanship.

∼ A New Commitment to Shedding Fear of Pain ∼

I humbly submit to letting each painful experience
    change me.
Although painful to go through, I will trust and
    surrender,
Facing the pain full-on, not seeking to lessen or
    avoid it.
I will do this because I know
To resist it will only make it fester more,
But if I embrace its reality
It will lead to a profound awareness
Of what it is to be human
And thereby
To a more meaningful connection
With those who travel through life with me.

CHAPTER TWENTY

From Judgment to Empathy

The day was perfect, not a cloud in the sky, horses grazing on lush green pastures, children running around. It was a typical day at my daughter's summer equestrian camp on Long Island, New York. Today was the day when the parents had come to watch their children showcase their talents at the annual horse show. The children, each paired with their favorite horse, were joyfully and busily tacking, saddling, and grooming them.

As the horses were about to enter the ring, I heard a loud outburst. "I don't want to ride this horse. I want to ride Rosie. I will only ride Rosie!" The voice was that of ten-year-old Savannah.

"Uh-oh," I thought to myself, thankful it wasn't my daughter. "Here we go. How will her parents handle this one?"

I watched her parents crouched by her, textbook perfect, their voices empathic. "We understand you feel sad you weren't given Rosie. But can we try to find a solution, and—"

Savannah cut them off, her protests louder now. "I will not, I cannot. I want to go home. Take me home now!" By this time she was bawling, and the scene had caused a group of kids to gather around.

Oblivious to the scene she was making, Savannah cried, "You can't make me. I hate you. I'm leaving."

At this point the mother said, "You know, Savannah, if you just ride this new horse today, we'll be so proud of you that we'll take you to the water park on the weekend."

I smiled inwardly: "Here come the carrots." What else was this mother going to start promising in order to bribe her daughter to get on the new horse?

When Savannah appeared unimpressed, the mother cajoled, "And then we can go to your favorite store, Juicy, and buy those cute shorts you've been wanting."

When there was still no response from Savannah, the mother raised the stakes. "If you'll only ride your new horse," she begged, "we can go to the Apple Store and get you the new iPad case you have always wanted. Don't you want that?"

Digging her heels in, Savannah yelled, "I don't care. Leave me alone. I'm going to the car."

Now the father stepped in, grabbing Savannah's arm and yanking her toward him. Holding her roughly by the shoulders, his teeth gritted, he snarled, "You do not speak to us in this fashion. Stop being a brat."

"I'm not a brat! I just don't want to be here anymore. Can we please go?" Savannah pleaded.

The father continued, "We have spent thousands of dollars on this camp. You are the one who begged to come here. So now you either ride the horse you've been given today or I'm never paying for you to ride again."

Shaken up, Savannah whimpered, "I'm sorry, Daddy, but I just cannot do it."

"It's too late for sorry," the mother jumped in. "Sorry doesn't bring a dead man back to life. Look at the scene you've caused. I'm so embarrassed by you, so disappointed in you. We are leaving right now and never coming back."

The mother stormed off, a disoriented Savannah in tow.

Before I could even collect my thoughts, my daughter and a group of her friends came running to me. "Did you see how mean her parents were?" Maia said.

"Poor Savannah, I feel so bad for her," said Allison, tears in her eyes.

"Why couldn't they just let her stay and watch us? What's the big deal?" chimed in Paula, her tone indignant.

I was about to agree with them all and voice my utter disapproval of the way Savannah's parents handled the situation. Had it been just five years earlier, I would have indulged in a self-righteous diatribe of "How could they! I would have handled it so differently. I would never raise my voice in such a situation. In fact, I wouldn't have to because my daughter would never consider throwing such a tantrum." Seeing the situation in the simplistic manner the children saw it, I would have blamed the parents for raising their child to be so narcissistic. Having been in the trenches myself, and witnessed my own reactivity, I have now developed a more humble and compassionate understanding of such situations.

I explained to the children, "It's easy for us to judge Savannah's parents, and you're right that they shouldn't have reacted so fiercely. But you have to understand that they were feeling helpless and didn't have a clue what to do. They weren't purposely being mean but were just caught in what seemed to them to be an impossible situation. When you become parents, you'll understand how they felt."

Although I understood the children's sentiments, it was important they were aware that problems in relationships aren't always one-sided or simple. Children often react to parents by declaring, "You are so mean!" While their underlying sentiment of feeling betrayed may be valid, it ultimately doesn't serve them to feel victimized by anyone, least of all their parents.

In Savannah's case, parents and child had allowed themselves to be hijacked by their anxiety, which led to them shutting out the several options before them. Both sides were paralyzed as a result of what they perceived as the other's wrongdoing. This is how conflict leads to gridlock, leaving us feeling helpless to change the situation. It's so easy for us to judge each other, pitting right against wrong. But I have found that this way of looking at the world doesn't get us far.

When we ask questions such as what was causing the daughter to have a meltdown, we'll no doubt at first make some kind of judgment, such as, "She's just being a brat. She's spoiled. She needs to learn she can't have her way all the time. She ought to be more appreciative." In other words, our initial reaction to negative situations is often something negative itself. It's almost as if we are programmed to respond only negatively to a negative situation—as if to respond positively or even neutrally is to lose face. Once we have made this judgment, we will naturally conclude that the only way to treat a "brat" is to scold them or manipulate them in some way. In our mind we are being rational. Little do we realize that our judgments are faulty and completely biased.

The first step in detangling a reactive situation like Savannah's is to become aware of how we project our biases, opinions, and judgments onto people's behavior, without attempting to understand the deeper significance of what's being communicated. Because they are "our" children, we unilaterally impose our projections onto them depending on our mood at a given moment. When they push back, we take offense and call their right to defend themselves "rude" and "disrespectful." This is because we expect them to be passive recipients of our judgments just because they are children. There's something not only inherently unfair about this but also detrimental to our children's ability to protect themselves against unfair treatment in the future. We then wonder how it is that they allow themselves to be bullied or get into abusive relationships.

What Empathy Really Means

If we are to elevate our consciousness with regard to the common traps of parenting, we must move beyond judgments of right or wrong. So let's examine this in a different way. Let's not focus on the behavior, but instead ask what the individuals were experiencing on an internal level. All our behavior ultimately emerges from what we are feeling. Only by delving into our feelings can we discover what's driving our behavior and discern the action we need to take.

What was Savannah feeling? For a start, she was clearly overwhelmed by the situation. Her emotions had been hijacked by the huge buildup of expectations around her performance. Her anxiety surpassed her capacity to cope with the pressure. The more her parents corralled her, the greater her reaction, until she finally disintegrated. Savannah's parents missed all of this vital information.

Contrary to what her parents believed, none of this was willful or even conscious on Savannah's part. It was all an unexpected and completely unconscious rise of anxious energy. Once anxiety overwhelms the individual, all attempts at rationalization are in vain. The language of logic falls on deaf ears. We need to employ a different language to communicate with anxiety. Parents haven't been taught this language. It's a language that comes from a heart-centered place instead of a mind-controlled one. It's a language of openness and courage versus one of control and manipulation.

Parenting books give us techniques that appear to help us help our children, but in effect they mostly teach us to manipulate them out of feeling what they are feeling. Parenting books aim for "happy-happy" results as opposed to focusing on how we can deeply align with the "as is" of our own and our children's feelings.

Although Savannah's parents first tried the textbook response of attempting to empathize with their daughter, it was clear they were not helping her handle a difficult situation. Although they appeared to be compassionate and to empathize with her, it was clear from the way the situation escalated that they weren't truly empathic. Rather, they had an agenda, and empathy was merely a technique they were using to get Savannah to do what they wanted her to do.

When we truly feel empathy for another, there is no agenda. A genuinely empathic response immediately recognizes that the other is in a state that's vastly different from our own, and that in order to connect with them we will have to forgo completely our own agenda. This swift letting go requires an alive presence that understands how connection with another is an engagement in which energy flows back and forth moment by moment with no guarantee of how things will end up. We understand that it's about the *process* of communicating, rather than where we need to end up or whose agenda needs to be met. It fully recognizes the importance of walking every step of the process together, with both parties engaged and empowered.

A mother tells me she empathizes with her daughter. "I understand what my child is going through," she insists. "I realize she's anxious, and I am trying to help her stop feeling so nervous." Is this really empathy? On the one hand, the mother proclaims that she understands what her daughter is experiencing, so it sounds like empathy. But then she turns around and declares, in effect, "I don't like what you are feeling. I want these feelings to disappear." No, this isn't empathy at all.

Our children pick up on this doublespeak and become confused about how they are supposed to feel. Most of us have made this mistake of thinking we are being empathetic when we really aren't. We think we understand when in fact we don't. This is why many kids yell at their parents, "You just don't understand me!" They are absolutely right. We don't get them.

Empathy is the ability to connect with what the other is feeling. This requires us to accept that it's okay for our child, partner, or friend to feel a certain way. Of course they do, since we are two distinct beings. This is the natural order of things in a healthy relationship. We don't need to change the other, any more than we need to change ourselves. We simply need to recognize the validity of the other's feelings, even as we want our own feelings to be recognized. Initially, holding the space within ourselves for both perspectives is extremely challenging. We can do this only if we aren't under siege from our own emotions. Anxiety constricts our inner space, causing it to quickly morph into control, which soon becomes anger. This is exactly what happened with Savannah's parents.

Children can sense when parents are connecting with them versus when they are being manipulated so they will comply with the parents' wishes. This serves only to make them feel that they are unheard and their wishes are unimportant, which further escalates their anxiety. When we don't connect with them in a genuinely empathic manner, we make things harder for ourselves. When our children feel unheard, they shut down and stop cooperating. If only we knew how to genuinely empathize with our children, we would create wonderful gateways for a close, connected, and cooperative relationship.

In a situation like Savannah's, if she could communicate what was truly going on, she would probably say something like, "It's like there's a storm inside me, swallowing me up, and you're making it worse. I need you to calm down, laugh with me, and show me another way to deal with my fear rather than yelling at me." The reality is that Savannah's parents were interested in her anxiety only insofar as they were trying to find a way to bypass it so she would do what they wanted. Getting her onto the horse was all that mattered. But the more they focused on what Savannah needed to do to make them happy, the more anxious she became.

There's a subtext to all of this. The real issue wasn't whether Savannah rode the new horse. The issue was how to help her ride the waves of her anxiety. None of the parents' strategies—sympathizing, commanding, bribing, or threatening—addressed this issue. The parents themselves now began to unravel, since Savannah's anxiety had triggered their own. In this state, they couldn't possibly help her work through her feelings.

Savannah's parents needed to connect with her feelings. To do this, they would have to leave their own feelings out of the equation. If their own feelings were overwhelming, they needed to walk away and take care of them, as I described in earlier chapters.

The parents needed to turn their attention to Savannah, meeting her where she was. To do this, they needed to set aside their beliefs about what she "should" do and simply accept where she was. They might also say something like, "It's okay that you don't want to ride. There'll be plenty of opportunities. Let's go for a walk." This is how we empathize with another's feelings. We don't shoo their feelings away. Neither do we allow ourselves to become unhinged. Rather, we take our children's feelings in our stride. By so doing, we show them that anxiety is nothing to be afraid of.

Acceptance has to be *real* acceptance. We detach from trying to get a child to do what we had hoped they would do. Riding the horse is no longer on our radar. The only thing that matters is that we are present with our child, alongside them, calm and accepting. We abandon our agenda entirely.

The approach I'm suggesting runs counter to the common approach of telling a child in a situation like this, "Don't be afraid." Instead of urging them to face their anxiety and conquer it, what I'm proposing assures the child, "Anxiety is normal, so don't worry about the fact that you are anxious. Treat it just like you do excitement or happiness. Just allow it to be, neither denying it nor resisting it." When we either deny or resist it, anxiety turns rogue. Better to face it in its raw and natural state. Then, in its own time and way, it will diminish. Not because we have driven it away by force, but because we have grown out of it with grace.

If we could tune in to the parents' anxiety over the fact that their daughter chose not to ride, we would hear thoughts such as:

- *What will the other parents think?*

- *How does my child compare with others?*

- *Will the kids tease her?*

- *What if we've wasted all this money?*

- *What if letting her not ride is teaching her to just give up when something is difficult?*

- *What does this say about her ability to succeed in the world?*

If Savannah's mother were not triggered, she might ask her to take her to the stables and show her all the horses. I wouldn't push her to do this, only request it. If she agrees, she would demonstrate a genuine curiosity in everything she's learned, affirming what she's accomplished rather than focusing on what she still has to achieve. She might also ask her to tell her stories about the horses and her experiences with them. Her entire focus would be on her process of learning, omitting all talk of performance.

Genuinely disconnected from whether she performs or not, she might next ask her if she wants to show her another horse to which she feels a connection. She might suggest that she could even ride that horse instead for a few minutes to see if she feels comfortable—but only if there's a total willingness, without coaxing. Or perhaps she would prefer to walk that horse around the ring. But in no way would she attempt to persuade her to perform, which would need to come from her.

It's crucial that she be entirely comfortable with her choosing to sit out this performance. It's quite possible Savannah would pick up on her energy and detachment to the outcome. Absorbing her relaxed state, she might appreciate that she is indeed competent as a rider and capable of entering the show with any horse instead of just Rosie. However, if she is truly detached, either outcome is acceptable.

Someone may reason, "This approach could be taken to mean it's okay for our children to quit." My response to this is that even more than a love of riding, it's Savannah's desire to explore her interests that's central, which holds true even if she decided to give up riding.

Exploring an interest, perhaps enjoying it for a time, is all we ever do anyway, since nothing can ever be permanent. Sooner or later, no matter how much Savannah might love riding, she may be forced to give it up. This is the nature of our temporal existence.

What really matters is that we are true to ourselves, enjoying whatever we choose to engage in for as long as we choose to engage in it. Fulfillment exists only in this moment now, not in a concept of how long something is supposed to continue. Our inability to value moment-by-moment engagement with the learning process robs us of our ability to appreciate that nothing is ever really in vain, and neither is anything permanent.

We can never make our children guarantee that they will stick with something. Our children are allowed to have feelings and experiences that run counter to our expectations. As they grow, their interests often quite naturally change. This isn't something to oppose, but something to encourage. The essential quality we are seeking to draw out has nothing to do with how long a child sticks with something, but the degree to which they have been able to engage their body, mind, and spirit. This engagement is unquantifiable, and therein lies our discomfort. We have been conditioned to prize tangible results. When we do this, we deprive ourselves of something inestimable, which is the moment-by-moment process of exploring new experiences.

We claim that we want our children to be fearless so they will participate fully in life. However, our obsession with the end result encourages fear in our children, handicapping them with anxiety that prevents them from trying their best. Our children sense when we don't care about their efforts, only their successes. This is why they disengage. Not because they are lazy, but because they are anxious about failing. Savannah wasn't being "difficult" when she wanted only Rosie. She was terrified that she would fail on another horse.

As we confront our own humanity and learn to accept it, we find ourselves experiencing a greater degree of empathy for our children. Empathy is heart-centered rather than mind-based. It's about the other—about their feelings and experiences, not our own.

How to Empathically Address the Realities of Life

You might wonder, "What if my child experiences feelings I don't have a solution for, such as if they don't want to go to school and yet have to? Do I just allow them to sit with what they are feeling? Do I empathize with their desire to stay home? How is this going to solve anything?"

It's important to be clear that we are not talking about raising our children in a bubble of feeling to the exclusion of living in the real world. Rather, the challenge is to help our children understand and negotiate their feelings. Their feelings rule them all the time anyway. They just don't know it, and we don't see it. When we teach our children how to become literate about their feelings, they learn that it's possible to flow with each feeling instead of being overwhelmed by it. To teach this when a child doesn't want to go to school, we start by allowing space for this feeling. Let's be absolutely clear about what this means. Allowing space for their feelings—especially those of anxiety—means that we don't experience any anxiety about the feelings' existence. The moment we have anxiety about our children's anxiety, our children will sense it and will undoubtedly unravel. Instead of convincing them not to be anxious, we need to embrace their feelings for what they are, accepting them as they rise.

Consider how different this is from the way many of us react. We might say something like, "Don't be silly, you have to go to school," "Stop being scared," or "You'll be punished if you don't go to school." Each of these reactions not only doesn't disperse the fear, but it teaches the child to feel ashamed of their feelings and perhaps even afraid of them. Worse still would be to say, as I have heard many parents say, "Okay, I understand you don't want to go to school. You don't have to go." This just teaches a child to capitulate to their fears and avoid reality.

Now let me share with you a more conscious approach. Invite the feelings into the room. Ask the child to draw a picture of the feelings and tell a story about them. Share stories from your own childhood that address your feelings. Then, to assuage your child's anxiety, explain that such feelings are normal and natural. In this way, the child learns neither to be driven by fear nor to run from it, but to accept it for what it is and tolerate it.

Once a child is able to accept their fear, there's a sense in which they make friends with it, which has a soothing effect. This is how we show empathy—not by feeling sorry for the child or trying to rescue them, but by helping them face their fear in a safe setting. Often fear will simply dissipate when we take this approach, not necessarily immediately but in its own time. To rush this process defeats the point of allowing the child to integrate it. To learn to tolerate fear and allow it to take its own course helps a child navigate their internal landscape successfully.

If this process is done with our children from an early age, they will be able to integrate their fear so that the energy invested in it becomes available for finding creative solutions to issues. A child who may initially resist going to school will eventually find a solution for themselves, one that doesn't involve blind surrender but empowers them. As mentioned earlier, techniques such as role-playing and role reversal are great for finding new ways to express the energy that has been invested in fear, since they offer opportunities to be creative, fun, and adventurous.

Because so many of us are addicted to a need to take action, I help parents create a new to-do list for when their children are in pain. I ask them to "do" specific things that will help them align with their children's state of being. Here are some examples:

- *"Do" sit close to your child in complete silence.*

- *"Do" look into their eyes and keep your gaze on them.*

- *"Do" softly echo back their feelings to them.*

- *"Do" show them with your body posture that you are there for them.*

- *"Do" try to understand their experiences without being intrusive.*

- *"Do" keep your opinions, sermons, and lectures to yourself.*

- *"Do" assure them that their feelings are important.*

- *"Do" give them the space to sit quietly and feel what they are feeling until it becomes integrated.*

- *"Do" validate that their feelings are just fine simply because they are theirs and not something to be ashamed of.*

- *"Do" tap into your own anxiety and work through it.*

When feelings are expressed and held sacred in a safe space, our children are able to process them and let them go without having to reincarnate them in indirect ways. This is a powerful gift indeed to offer our children.

Empathy Does Not Mean Collusion

Sometimes we entomb our children in fear of the practicalities of life without realizing it. For instance, when Alice was eight years old, she began expressing a fear of elevators. Outings in the city with her were extremely stressful for her parents. Things got so bad that she refused to take any elevator. So the parents began taking the stairs whenever they entered a high-rise. "I so understand her," Alice's mother said. "I was also a really anxious kid and used to be terrified of many things myself. This is why I don't push my daughter to confront her fears. I feel like I should empathize with her, but I don't know whether I'm helping her or causing her to be more of a nervous wreck."

Unlike Savannah's parents, this mother was trying to fully bond with her daughter's experience. As I remarked earlier, this is a positive move. However, she fails to understand the difference between empathy and overly identifying with her daughter. Because the daughter's anxiety mirrors the mother's own experiences in childhood and reminds her of her own fragility, she has become overprotective, shielding her daughter from the pain of confronting her fear.

The issue isn't the elevator, but instead the daughter's fear that she's too fragile to confront this challenge. This fragility has been directly absorbed from the mother's own early experiences. This is how a state of inadequacy gets passed down from generation to generation.

What should the mother do? The first step is to recognize that empathy is different from collusion. Empathy says, "I understand that elevators can be scary. I will be by your side to help you deal with this struggle. We will face this together." In contrast, collusion says, "I also used to get scared in elevators. Let's take the stairs." The daughter's fear is endorsed as a valid way of life, when it needs to be felt and confronted.

Do you see the fear in this mother's solution of taking the stairs? She's saying that her daughter doesn't have the resilience to overcome a quite normal fear. She believes she's normalizing her daughter's fear by relating it to her own childhood, when in fact she's projecting her experience onto the situation. This overprotective approach doesn't normalize the daughter's fear but instead pathologizes it. Instead of liberating her, it paralyzes her.

To help Alice confront her fear, there are a number of avenues her mother can take. She might create a playful situation in the safety of their home in which the daughter draws her fear, writes stories about it, and the two of them pretend to ride an elevator. In this harmless way, the mother could help her daughter not only to confront her fear in a head-on manner but also to defuse the emotional charge around it.

Role-playing the situation, the mother says to her daughter, "I wonder whether your favorite bear would like an exciting ride in the elevator. How about I take him up one floor and see how he does? You can go up the stairs and meet us off the elevator. If he enjoys his ride, you might like to come back down with us. If he doesn't enjoy his ride, then you can help me teach him how safe it is to ride an elevator. We can teach him which buttons to press to make the elevator go, and we can show him how much fun a ride can be."

Drawing on a spirit of adventure, one could imagine many ways to acclimate Alice to elevators through role-playing. If she has a favorite musical group, the mother could suggest that they take iPods and listen to their favorite tunes as they ride. They could eat Alice's favorite ice cream in the elevator. They could take her best friend with them. The mother's ability to be enthusiastic in the face of this challenge—neither pushing and controlling nor giving up in despair—can make all the difference.

Through this approach, children learn that fears aren't something to be avoided but are instead to be confronted creatively. The mother's determination not to allow the daughter to capitulate to her fear is crucial. But the determination has to stem from a belief that anxiety must be faced. It may also be necessary for the mother to be resilient over a period of time.

Remember, the focus can't be on whether the daughter learns to love elevators, any more than Savannah's issue was with riding a particular horse. A person may actually not like elevators. Nothing says we can't climb stairs instead, and in fact there can be a health benefit. The issue is how we deal with anxiety as it arises. Once the anxiety is no longer a problem, whether we use the elevator or take the stairs is purely a matter of personal choice.

Decluttering Your Inner Landscape

Anxiety drives the majority of our behavior. Learning to deal with our fear as parents is the real challenge, since it's what enables us to equip our children to deal with their own fears.

The way out of fear isn't to try to annihilate it, which will serve only to increase it. Instead, the way forward is to accept and befriend our fear. As I have said before, those who are fearless are those who have learned to tolerate their anxiety. It is not that they don't have anxiety, but instead that they fully expect the anxiety, and once it is experienced, they fully allow it to sit beside them without overwhelming them. I offer clients the visual image of taking fear out of the driver's seat and placing it on the seat beside them. Allowing it to sit beside us while we go about our tasks despite its presence provides an opportunity for it to become integrated.

To make sense of your fear, ask yourself the following kinds of questions:

- *What is this fear I'm experiencing?*

- *What is this moment bringing up for me?*

- *What's the feeling trying to tell me?*

Once we are aware of what our fear is really about, we can figure out how to work with it. Awareness is the key. As long as we are being unconsciously driven by a fear, it will have power over us. This is why investigating what the fear is really about is so important.

Although I am encouraging you to ask yourself key questions about your fear, I'm not advocating that you engage in self-talk, which even when it's positive is entirely unhelpful. Awareness is fundamentally different from having an internal dialogue with yourself. Most of us indulge in a great deal of self-talk, chattering endlessly within ourselves—much of the chatter being in the form of judging, worrying, comparing, and admonishing.

You might think, as some teach, that you can channel your mind's self-talk to a higher good, perhaps overriding your fear, but this is precisely the opposite of mindfulness. When we are mindful, we simply observe our internal dialogue, but we don't get involved in it. Awareness is transformative, whereas self-talk is debilitating, since we can never talk ourselves into a more effective way of living.

Say you feel anxious when you awaken in the morning. The conscious approach would have you pause and notice your anxiety. All that's required is to simply observe what you are feeling. There's nothing you need to do about it. Of course, the mind will tell you otherwise, because it loves to chew on things like this. Simple mindfulness—just noticing what you are feeling—allows you to own and honor your anxiety. By using this approach, you won't attempt to process it by dumping it on your children or partner. It's not something to be acted out or talked about with others, but something to be contained mindfully.

If having a mental discussion with ourselves about our anxiety isn't helpful, neither is overriding it beneficial, as I mentioned a moment ago. When we do either of these, the anxiety simply shows up elsewhere. Being mindful allows us to stay attuned and present, which empowers us to process what's happening. You might say that mindfulness—learning to observe ourselves in an ongoing way, so that we become aware of what's going on inside us—is akin to the daily flossing we do to prevent plaque from building up on our teeth.

As we observe ourselves, we need to ask questions such as:

- *Am I living as I truly wish to—according to who I am and not according to a false idea of who I should be?*

- *Am I integrating all aspects of myself into my life?*

- *Am I setting the boundaries I need in my life to allow me to respect and honor myself?*

Children who are raised by parents who are authentic and transparent learn to have little fear of their inner states. Grounded in who they are, they feel sure of their inherent goodness and are unafraid to engage the world with an open heart that's connected to the goodness of others.

～ A New Commitment to Shedding Judgment ～

My judgment against others
Erupts from a place of lack within,
From an old blueprint
Where I was judged by others in the same way.

Though judgment is far easier than introspection,
I realize that it keeps my heart closed.
It is only when I can enter compassion for others
That I ultimately can forgive myself.

CHAPTER TWENTY-ONE

From Discipline
to Enlightened Boundaries

O nce you have learned to check in and attune to yourself and your children, the next most important task of parenting is almost as sacred as connection. This is the art and discipline of creating boundaries. Notice I said the "discipline of creating boundaries," as opposed to the "art of disciplining." Whereas the latter focuses on changing our children through discipline, the former focuses on disciplining ourselves to change. My book *Out of Control* emphasizes how disciplinary strategies are just a means of control and manipulation. It's our lack of understanding of how to create appropriate boundaries that results in what we call a "disciplinary issue," as if it were the child's fault.

This is the most important lesson in this chapter: *All disciplinary issues with children occur because of a lack of discipline within the parent.* It's really the indiscipline of parents that we need to create interventions for, not the child!

I believe that establishing limits and creating appropriate boundaries are some of the more difficult aspects of parenting. When we attempt them, we tend to be either too rigid or too lax, unaware of how to create just the right conditions for our children to thrive.

Children need structure and predictability in their lives. The basic structure of a day needs to be set by the parent, and it should be tailored both to the particular needs of the child and to what serves the family as a whole. Within this framework, however, there must be a tremendous amount of room for spontaneity, unstructured play, and fun. When our children face unpredictable situations and events, there is likely to be some level of acting out. At these times, the onus lies on the parent to weather the consequent emotional storms that are inevitable during times of change and upheaval.

If we create clear, consistent, compassionate boundaries for our children, the need for disciplinary strategies is unnecessary. Our lack of understanding of what a boundary is and how to establish it is the cause of much chaos and strife in our homes. Whether we like it or not, mastering the art of setting boundaries is essential for there to be harmony. The problem is that while many of us are heavy-handed in establishing limits and boundaries, others of us are downright uncomfortable with doing so. However, getting this piece right is vital. Just like the connection we create with our children helps them feel safe, healthy limits also allow them to feel secure.

You Cannot Set a Boundary You Don't Have

When you hear the word "boundary," you probably assume I'm talking about giving our children boundaries. However, I always start with the parent. I'm less concerned with our children's understanding of boundaries and more concerned with our own internal boundaries. Whenever our children get out of line, it's not so much they who are out of line as ourselves.

If you are wondering what this looks like in practice, it means that our own relationship to our limits is wishy-washy. The line between what we deem appropriate or inappropriate isn't clearly drawn in our mind and heart. Our inability to set a clear limit is the reason our children keep violating our boundaries. As with all aspects of conscious parenting, the misalignment begins with us.

Quite naturally, parents aren't happy when I tell them that their children don't respect their boundaries because they themselves are ambivalent about the boundaries. They think they are being clear, but they don't realize how many mixed messages they send their children. If only our children could articulate how confusing we can seem to them, we would catch a glimpse of the difficulty of living with us. Especially when it comes to boundaries, our lack of clarity and cohesion contributes to the strife within the home, fueling our knee-jerk tendency to blame and react when our children disobey or defy us. Both parties lose as a result of this lack of clarity on our part: Our children feel misunderstood and invalidated, and we feel ignored and helpless. The difference is that the parental Kool-Aid gives us undue power to unleash revenge any which way we deem necessary without regard to how the mess really started.

My client Patricia, a mother of two children aged five and seven, was having a hard time getting her children to sleep at night, often spending a few hours in their bedroom trying to coax them into slumber. Nighttime had turned nightmarish for the entire family. When I asked her to describe the routine to me, she said, "When I put Julia and Steven to bed, I promise to read them two stories and sing two songs from *The Wizard of Oz* because this is their favorite movie. No sooner do I do this than they are pushing the boundary and asking me to sing another song. Then three songs become four, and before you know it I'm screaming at them, they are crying, and the whole experience turns into a nightmare."

I asked, "When you agreed to two stories and two songs, were you making this deal with a clear boundary in mind?"

"Absolutely!" she retorted. "But when they plead with me, I think to myself, 'Why don't I just give in?' They are so adorable, maybe I can do one more. Then I just can't say no to them without them freaking out."

It was clear that Patricia was unclear about the limits of her boundary. As with many parents, her boundary wasn't really a boundary at all. It was entirely fluid, controlled by her children's moods. We can choose to be fluid, but we need to accept that we cannot then turn the switch of fluidity off at any time we like, because naturally our children will react to this sudden turn of events. In Patricia's case, the fluidity didn't come from a choice she made consciously, which is why she got upset when her children didn't toe the line.

I explained, "A boundary is something we need to physically and energetically feel. Either there is a boundary or there isn't. You, not your children, get to decide if the line is drawn in sand or stone. Once you are clear about whether you are drawing a sand line or a stone line, everything else will become clear."

Patricia nodded in agreement. "Yes, I start out with a stone line, then it soon dissolves into sand. I feel as if I'm being a mean mom when I say no to them. But then, when I end up screaming at them, I am indeed a monster mom!"

"Your kids are doing exactly what they should do," I clarified. "They are enjoying themselves and asking for more enjoyment. They are right on track. They aren't being 'bad' by not stopping their enjoyment. It's you who are being ineffective because you aren't abiding by your own boundaries."

Children pick up on our inconsistency, especially when it's rooted in fear, such as fear that we won't be liked or that we are being selfish. The reason we get mad at our children when they push us is that they force us to confront our unwillingness to stand up for ourselves and, more than this, for what we believe is "right" for our children's growth. Once we are clear within ourselves about what needs to happen, we have no difficulty communicating this. I am alluding not to a sense of fundamental righteousness about moral principles, but only to knowing deep within us what the right choices are for ourselves and our children based on how we need to grow into greater consciousness. If our children thrive best with nine hours of sleep, then we need to try our hardest to create the conditions that will provide them this—without making it a war zone, of course. It all depends on the amount of time and energy we invest in thinking through what our children need to grow and how best to go about providing them this.

If our children could articulate their thoughts, they would say something like:

> Hey, parent, can you get your act together and tell me what the deal is? One day it's yes, the next day it's no. What's the real limit here? Don't be swayed by my moods and tantrums. I'm only testing you to see if you know what you're talking about. Once I see that you know, I'll probably back down—though I may not do it without a fight, since I'm really trying to discover my limits. I actually hate fighting, so the clearer you are, the

less I'll fight, I promise. Just don't be a dictator about it. Be kind and loving when setting a limit. Be patient with me as I learn it. Most of all, forgive me when I cross it.

What's the Higher Purpose of Your Boundary?

If we are honest with ourselves, much of the time we aren't even aware of the real reason for the boundaries we create for our children. Most of our boundaries are knee-jerk reactions to the present moment, which means they tend to be based on how tired or anxious we are. They aren't thought out in a purposeful manner.

The way I like to help parents find the purpose of a boundary is by asking them the following two questions:

- *Does the boundary serve both you and your child's higher self (not just your ego)?*

- *Is the boundary negotiable or nonnegotiable?*

When we explore these questions, our hidden agenda in setting boundaries and the unexamined fear that often lies behind these boundaries have a way of emerging.

Every boundary we set with our children needs to have their optimum development as its purpose. A boundary shouldn't be set solely for our comfort or convenience, or because we are anxious. Some boundaries are life-enhancing, whereas others serve our ego. Life-enhancing boundaries help our children cope with life. They strengthen their resilience and help enable them to feel secure. Part of the general order of things, they help our children develop into well-rounded individuals who are capable of functioning in and contributing to society.

What are life-enhancing boundaries? While every family needs to come up with their own, allow me to share with you several that are based on my years of experience as a family therapist and mother:

Life-Enhancing Boundaries

- *Respect for oneself—self-care through hygiene and sleep.*

- *Respect for one's environment—a tidy room and home.*

- *Respect for one's mind—the process of education either formally or informally.*

- *Respect for family and community—connecting and contributing to society.*

In these areas I tell parents, "Set boundaries with clarity, calmness, and compassion. Be attuned to the higher purpose of each boundary and stay focused on that vision. When your children test you and go against you, tap into that higher purpose and hold tight. At this point it isn't about whims of the moment, either yours or your children's, but what serves their higher good. Without yelling, just hold the vision for their higher good and communicate this intent."

Parents ask, "What if my kid refuses to go to school?"

I say to them, "Well, you have to first be clear about where their refusal is coming from. Is it coming from a defiance or a genuine psychological need? If it is the latter, then a quick fix is not in order. However, if it is the former, then, because you are aware that this is a life-enhancing area of growth, you need to hold to the limit that getting an education is an important task in life. While holding to this vision, you may need to be flexible about how exactly this manifests in your particular child's life, as every school isn't a match for every child—just like every career can't be a match for every adult. This may also mean that you take the time to help them prepare for this major life task by easing them into the transition. Maybe you can role-play school for a month before the first day. Or you can help with other skills such as communicating with teachers and peers to make the transition less stressful. Regardless, once you decide that refusing school just for the sake of comfort or convenience is not an option, your children will understand and follow your lead. They might be anxious and scared, but they will know that they must call upon the strength to meet this normative rite of passage ("normative" doesn't mean it is the best one, just that it's what we have set up in society at this moment in time). Sometimes our own fear about our children's fear impairs our ability to maintain clear and consistent boundaries that are beneficial for them.

What if your infant doesn't enjoy bathing and resists bath time? If you are clear about the life-enhancing potential of your boundary, you need to hold firm to this. Your child may take a while to get used to bathing, but they will eventually understand that bathing is a holy act of self-care because you embody the importance of it in your own life. At first you might need to be creative, helping your child discover the joy of bubbles, or you might need to let them shower with you to watch as you enjoy yourself doing so, leading them to eventually internalize the power of cleanliness and self-love. The same principle applies to brushing their teeth. Perhaps initially you will need to give tooth brushing thirty minutes of your time, versus just ten. If you believe brushing is for your child's higher good, you need to be prepared to do what it takes to help your child buy into this practice.

Notice that I didn't put hobbies and extracurricular achievements on the list. While these can certainly be life-enhancing, they aren't mandatory and therefore should be subject to the interests of the child more than to the whims of the parent. Use discretion concerning the lengths you are willing to go to in order to institute boundaries of this kind. It's important to ask yourself, "Is the need to push this activity coming from my own ego, or is it genuinely coming from the needs of my child?" To reflect in this way will help you decide what's really important and what isn't. I often tell parents that if you push a hobby or activity that isn't necessarily life-imperative on your child, be prepared to be flexible about how the child takes this on in their life. For example, if you want them to play an instrument and they are dragging their feet about it, at least offer flexible choices about the number of times a week they practice, and so on. Ultimately, it is only when a human being is offered the chance to buy into their life choices that they will own them and grow with them.

Let's go to the next issue we need to address when creating a boundary. How negotiable is it? Parents need to decide this for themselves. If brushing teeth and bathing daily are negotiable, then parents shouldn't pretend they are nonnegotiable. I had a parent of a fourteen-year-old boy shocked at the fact that he didn't brush his teeth regularly. When I asked if they had invested the time and energy to ensure he understood the absolute life-enhancing imperative of this activity, they said they had no idea they needed to. It is little wonder then that our children don't pick up our ways of living and being; it is because we have not taken the care to communicate these to them in a conscious manner.

Our children take their cues from our behavior. Our actions need to be in sync with our beliefs. We cannot talk the talk but neglect to walk it, or our children will eventually see through our veneer and call our bluff. Once they do, it will be extremely hard to reconstitute that boundary. No matter what its type, in deciding that a boundary is nonnegotiable, beware. I guarantee you'll be called upon to commit to it. I tell parents to be certain before they claim a boundary is nonnegotiable. Few parents are prepared for the kind of full-on commitment required.

To help parents understand how committed they need to be, I ask them to think about how they feel when their children are hurt. "If they are seriously injured, would you feel ambivalent about rushing them to the ER? Would you decide not to go just because they cried endlessly or called you mean?" In the same way, once you decide a boundary is nonnegotiable, you need to follow through on it. All too often we say we commit to a goal. Then when the going gets tough— such as when our children persistently dawdle, protest, or become anxious—we take this as a signal to stop trying.

Where Do Consequences and Punishment Fit In?

A father asked me to help him institute time-outs with his six-year-old son. I told him, "If you are looking for someone to help you with time-outs, I am not the person for you."

He responded, "Are you saying there should be no time-outs under any circumstances?"

I explained that barring a one-off incident when your child is acting extremely badly at the dinner table and you need to ask them to leave the area so the rest of you can eat, I am dead set against children being ostracized to naughty corners, stools, or steps.

Intrigued, the father continued to probe: "But how will a child learn the right way?"

I challenged, "Is the use of force the right way or just the lazy way?" Explaining my position further, I elaborated, "Traditional parenting has long espoused the unbridled use of parental power. Quoting biblical verses, parents equate good parenting with the amount of control they have over their children. Conscious parenting goes against these archaic ways of treating children. Just like America is a country founded on democratic principles that have been the birthing ground for innovation, so too the family—a country in its own right—must veer away from dictatorship. Punishment, time-outs, and using arbitrary threats to shame and silence our children aren't the hallmarks of effective parenting, but instead they are signs of lazy and rote parenting."

When parents see how inflexible I am in my approach toward children, many react. After all, it shines a light on how they were raised. Many protest, "Well, I was beaten with switches and sticks and I didn't die." Those who managed to be successful in life use this as a yardstick. "I turned out okay, so I guess it wasn't such a bad thing, was it?"

The reasons parents wish me to justify the way they were raised are several. For one thing, it enables them to ascribe to their own parents a measure of idealization, which allows them to continue to believe in their parents' goodness. Further, it allows them to rationalize the pain they felt in childhood, enabling them to feel that it was worth something in the end. After all, to suffer all that unimaginable pain for no reason except parental ignorance is pretty hard to swallow. Many parents are unable to call up the courage to admit, "I was yelled at and shamed, and I grew up fearful, insecure, and guilt-ridden," or "The reason I have so many issues with drugs and alcohol is that I was never treated as a sovereign being in my own home and allowed to have my own feelings."

Often the price for owning the pain of our childhood is too high. It's far easier for us to deny our real feelings and put on a façade of happiness. For many, facing the ostracism of their family is an unbearable thought. Sticking with the mainstream ways, no matter how dysfunctional and damaging, is felt to be preferable to having to go it alone. Raised to avoid the truth, these individuals live inauthentic lives, severed from who they truly are and terrified to feel what they actually feel.

The Power of Clear Limits and Boundaries

Since I am against punishment for children, what do I believe is an effective strategy for teaching them the right way to behave? I believe in the power of natural and logical consequences. These aren't imposed. We don't "give" a consequence. They arise directly out of an answer to the question, "What is the need being expressed by my child's behavior?" Once we can determine the underlying need, we can connect the appropriate "effect" with the cause. Beware—it's very tempting for parents to want to *create* the "effect." If consequences are to work, they cannot be tied to us but must arise spontaneously, intimately related to the need being expressed by the behavior.

Before we delve into natural or logical consequences, it's important to focus on the antecedents of our children's behavior. The antecedents involve us and only us. They are directly linked to our ability to create coherent boundaries and maintain clear limits. Once we have decided to create a boundary and commit to it because we have deemed it to be in the best interest of the child, we need to go about setting the limit for this boundary in a compassionate manner that stays firmly rooted in the present reality. If we establish a boundary that allows for no more than thirty minutes of screen time before it's time to do homework, and our child violates this, it's important to hold to the limit consistently, while at the same time showing empathy.

There are a variety of ways to go about doing this. We can come to an agreement with our children where their input is taken into consideration, so that if they break the agreement they know the screens will be removed from the equation until the homework has been completed. Another way is to simply ask them to hand over their screens after thirty minutes, with the reassurance that they will be returned once the homework is done. If a child pitches a fit, the parent stays resolute in their request that the screen be shut down or handed over.

Holding firm on boundaries and limits doesn't mean we use coercion or harshness, which can easily border on abuse. Instead, we help the child engage the issue with a sense of joy and lightness. For instance, the parent can support the child in learning to brush their teeth by being right there with them as they do so, joyfully embodying their own commitment to taking care of themselves, perhaps allowing the child to brush the parent's teeth for them or brush their doll's teeth. It's essential that ego doesn't enter the picture, since coming from ego can quickly create power struggles that run counter to a conscious approach.

"What if my child refuses?" a parent asks. I respond that such a parent needs to understand that their child isn't used to having a parent who holds to a limit. Such a child is likely to require longer to comply with a limit willingly. The parent simply needs to hold their ground by not leaving the space until the screen is either turned off or handed over. When holding a limit, it's important to resist the temptation to create mental stories about what's transpiring and begin lecturing or shaming the child. We simply need to stay rooted in the present moment and keep calmly repeating our request until the child realizes we are not going to move until our request is heard. Once the child begins to see that the parent says what they mean and means what they say, the time it takes for them to comply will be shorter, as they tune in to their responsibilities with respect to screen time.

The key is to teach our children early that there are certain essential elements to the day that need to be followed. These need to be incorporated in the routine in a matter-of-fact way without being made a big deal, so that the child eventually learns to see them as vital principles of being human and staying healthy. The parent has to be committed. Sometimes it's necessary to simply state, "You need to brush right now. Then we can read our books." The key is to hold the limit with clarity and without the charge of ego. It isn't easy for parents to stay Zen in this process, but it's essential to establish consistency.

Following the principle of "if . . . then," the child is exposed to consequences that follow the natural order of things in the home. Once you are clear about a boundary and how you need to hold to it, your children will understand the power of consequences and change their behavior accordingly. Again, let me emphasize that consequences aren't something we "give" a child. Instead, they follow naturally from a child's actions.

With this approach, dependence on external rewards and punishment falls by the wayside. Your relationship with your children will become so solid that it will be the most influential catalyst for growth in their life. You'll find you need to do less and less. Everything begins with how you, the parent, deal with boundaries within yourself. What transpires in your home will be a reflection of this.

The Mechanics of Holding a Limit

We tend not to like saying no to others because we are afraid either of not being loved or of conflict. Not only is it hard to say no in the moment and mean it, but it can be even harder to hold to it. Earlier we considered the fact that when we decide a certain boundary is nonnegotiable, it's important that such a decision come from soul-searching, so that we are sure the boundary fully serves our child in the highest sense and isn't about our own fantasies, unmet needs, or need for control.

Suppose your child is allergic to chocolate, to the point that the allergy is life-threatening. Would you allow them even a tiny piece? Every parent would immediately answer, "Of course not!"

My next question is, "How would you say no to your child's craving for chocolate? Would you be wishy-washy about it?" Because there's a higher purpose for holding to a boundary of this kind, parents don't fear being thought of as bossy or mean. Any fear they may have of being thought badly of simply isn't an issue in a case like this.

Our children may not like that we deny them something. But when a situation is life-threatening, there can be no budging. We tell them something such as, "I know you can't understand my reasons, and you don't have to. One day they'll make sense to you."

An inflexible approach should be used only when something is certain. If there's room for doubt, then any boundary should be established as a result of negotiation between the parent and child. The degree of rigidity we apply concerning a behavior depends on what I refer to as its negotiability quotient. For iPad use, for example, the parent needs to ask whether saying no protects the child's life or health. As the iPad itself doesn't cause harm or death, it's clear that the boundary doesn't revolve around the iPad per se but around the amount of time children spend on it. Since this isn't a clear-cut issue, it needs to be negotiated. Of course, once the limit has been negotiated, it's up to us to hold to this limit using what I like to call the three c's—clarity, consistency, and compassion. We also need to be prepared to renegotiate the issue when appropriate. In addition, the desired behavior needs to be embodied by the parent.

Noah, the father of eleven-year-old Joshua, was struggling to hold a limit around his son's hygiene. "I have held the limit so many times," he reported, "but Joshua doesn't listen at all. I'm fed up with being the bad guy."

Feeling his frustration, I empathized, "If you see your role as being the bad guy, you are inevitably going to be resentful. However, if your boundary involves saving or improving his life in some way, you need to see yourself as the good guy."

Imagining that he was embodying the higher purpose of his boundary, Noah commented, "I have tapped into the higher purpose of this boundary. I feel it's the right thing to do. I embody this in my own life. But Joshua still doesn't listen. Now what do I do?"

I explained that pushback from our children is natural. Our tendency is to believe that our children shouldn't push back against our wishes. But for them to be discouraged from doing so could cause them to become compliant and docile. I often ask parents, "Why shouldn't your child push back? Isn't this a sign of a healthy psyche, intelligence, and courage? Why do you want your child to blindly follow your ways? Shouldn't you try to give them reasons so they buy into what you expect of them? We don't want to raise children who don't think for themselves."

How we respond to pushback is the real issue. "Now comes the even harder part, the long-term commitment," I told Noah. "This is where you are tested to see how far you are willing to go to inculcate this behavior in your family, using the most conscious and loving manner possible. It's a matter of mastering the art of holding to your word. It's no easy thing to do because it means nothing else happens until the required action has been completed. When our children see there's absolutely no wiggle room, they fall in line. This is why they are more able to follow the rules at school than at home, since the conditions are firmly set in place and are applied across the board, with no exceptions. This is how serious you are going to need to be in order for Joshua to pay attention. The older our kids get, the less seriously they take us because they've seen us sidelining our commitment for so long. So yes, you may need to sacrifice him doing well on a test or going to a baseball practice until he realizes you absolutely mean business."

It took practice for Noah to understand what it means to hold to a boundary. Noah presented Joshua with the plan: bathe first and then go to bed. When he first attempted it, his son was rude and disrespectful, refusing to follow his dad's instructions that he bathe himself.

This approach felt a bit extreme to Noah, as it bordered on control. I encouraged him to stay firm. Instead of "not allowing" something, he needed to say straightforwardly, "When you bathe, both you and I can proceed to bed. Until then, neither of us will." When Joshua saw that his father absolutely meant what he was saying, he relented. This allowed Noah to have a heartfelt conversation with him about his health. They made an agreement to help each other follow through. After a week of adjustment, bathing was no longer a problem in their home.

It must be made clear that holding to a boundary doesn't mean we unleash punishment on our children. It simply means they witness us create conditions that are unbreakable. This is why we must carefully think through boundaries and commit only to those we fully believe in. Since it only gets harder to change behavior as time goes on, it behooves us to establish these nonnegotiable habits early in life.

Once again, we see that resolving our own inner conflict leads to fewer conflicts with our children. As we learn to embody our teaching, it becomes easier to align with our children and create an environment in which the way forward is clear to all.

How Do Natural and Logical Consequences *Really* Work?

Once we are clear about the antecedents of our children's behavior and have begun to set clear boundaries and limits in the home, we can move on to the next part of the equation: consequences. Many parents have a hard time discovering the natural or logical consequences of a particular behavior. However, as I alluded to earlier, consequences are always naturally or logically related to the *need* that's being expressed through the behavior. So often we get seduced by the behavior and forget to ask ourselves, "Why is my child acting this way? What are they feeling? Do they need to learn a skill right now? Or do they need something else from me right now?"

Let's take a few examples of typical behavior and attempt to uncover the need, along with an appropriate natural or logical consequence to it.

Behavior: Child doesn't turn TV off on time.
Need: Impulse control, boundaries, and respect for time.
Consequence:

1. Ask the question: What can I do to help my child with their need?
2. Try to teach the child about respect for time. You may wish to give them a stopwatch. You could create a chart together to document the times they watch TV during the day. Or you could have them come up with an agreement about how long they will watch. As a last resort, the TV could be put on a timer so that it automatically turns off.
3. Let the child know that if they are unable to execute step two well, you will have no choice but to take the

television away until they learn to value time and perform their other responsibilities.

Here is another example:

Behavior: Keeps forgetting things at school.
Need: Organization, long-term memory, focus.
Consequence:
1. Ask the question: What can I do to help my child with their need?
2. Try to teach them about cause and effect by not rescuing them and allowing them to suffer the consequences of their choice at school the next day, so that they can feel the natural effect of forgetting an item. Or return to school for the forgotten item, but make them work for it in some way so that they absorb the lesson. Alternatively, they could be encouraged to write a letter to the teacher explaining their error and asking for a way to make up for it.
3. Let the child know that if they are unable to do step two, you will need to teach them this skill yourself. Begin by examining their daily schedule and finding ways to help them organize their time and their desk, as well as to focus their attention. Perhaps teach them mindfulness techniques or get them a professional tutor to help organize their work.

One more example:

Behavior: Consistently fails to get up on time for school.
Need: Greater motivation to attend school, more rest time, help with their anxiety or sadness, support around social issues.
Consequence:
1. Ask the question: What can I do to help my child with their need?
2. If the need is for more sleep, it's up to you as the parent to hold the limit around bedtime the night before. If the

child is defiant and refuses to comply, it's your job to find a way to remove distractions from their room. If they continue to sleep late despite your taking away all their distractions, they will need to learn to suffer the natural consequences of feeling too tired at school.

3. If none of these approaches work, it's most likely your child is suffering from something far deeper like depression, which means they should be evaluated by professionals. There is always a reason when a child doesn't jump out of bed and embrace their day, and being deadened by the pressures of life can cause them to lose the joy of living.

Whereas punishment serves only to create an even wider rift between parent and child, in each of the previous examples an unearthing of the underlying need enables the parent to discover what action is needed. Sleuthing the root of an issue isn't an easy process, requiring not only patience and dedication but commitment to the fact that our children deserve to be treated as sovereign beings with whom we are privileged to connect, not to be shamed or reprimanded.

Rude behavior is a particularly prevalent problem. "What should I do if my child is rude to me?" parents ask. "What's the natural consequence of this?" Sometimes it's hard to know how to respond to your child, especially if you are the one they are being rude to. Rudeness on the part of a child is never what it seems, and the key is to get at the underlying need that's driving the behavior. The child could be feeling stifled, disenfranchised, confused, or entitled. All of these reasons stem from misguided parental energy. When children feel free to be rude and disrespectful, the issue comes down to the parent's inability to connect with them, together with a failure to establish coherent boundaries. This is why helping end rude behavior isn't a simple 1-2-3 process. It requires a multipronged approach that of course begins with the parent.

"But what should I do in the moment that my child is rude to me?" parents insist on asking. I respond in this way: "Your first instinct when a child is rude is to take it personally. This is the first mistake we make. Quite naturally, we react rudely back to them. This sets off a dysfunctional cycle within moments. Instead, it is wise for parents to take a deep breath and step away for a moment. Once you are calm and able to depersonalize the situation, ask, 'What is my child trying to say beneath their rude words and demeanor?' You will be able to find the empathy to connect with them. It might not happen right away, but it will eventually, once the initial tempers of reactivity have calmed down."

I explain to parents that, as in all aspects of conscious parenting, the solution lies in changing ourselves. Once we realize that we have been the cause of our children's disrespect to us—in how we have been either inconsistent in our approach, neglectful, or a complete pushover—we soon realize that we hold the power to change the dynamic between us. We see that once we change, they change.

Once we have taken that pause and refused to enter power struggles, the dynamic begins to shift. When our reactivity has died down, we can engage in heartfelt introspection, asking ourselves, "How have I allowed my child to feel that it's okay to treat me in this way?" and "Why is it that I don't engender respect in my child?"

Turning the spotlight on ourselves can introduce new patterns into the home. Perhaps we realize that we have been enabling our children too much, creating a sense of entitlement by giving in to their demands or setting inconsistent boundaries. Perhaps there is too much control in the home, with too much helicopter parenting, causing the child to feel angry and stifled. Whatever we discover to be the cause of our children's behavior can be modified. We take it upon ourselves to shift our own energy to create the result we desire.

Maura is the perfect example of how this shift changed her relationship with her seventeen-year-old son Jackson. Curfew times were a constant source of conflict. Each time Maura laid down a curfew, Jackson broke it. In trying to be her son's friend, Maura kept reneging on her oath to be consistent, trying to give him chances to make amends. This would be an enlightened approach were it not for all the yelling and screaming that ensued, and for the fact that he was too young to be out until the wee hours of the morning. I told Maura, "It's far more effective for you to establish a boundary than to fight all day long." I showed her that her son was disrespecting her curfew for only one reason—because she allowed it.

Maura was indignant at first. "But I don't want to punish him by not allowing him to leave the house," she reasoned. "I'm trying to stay away from punishment."

I understood Maura's confusion. In trying to be a conscious parent, she felt that she should stay away from anything that looked remotely like a punishment. I explained, "When we take away a privilege from our children out of blind reactivity, then we are punishing them. However, when we take away a privilege from them because they are not capable of living up to its parameters, and are putting their health in jeopardy, we are teaching them that there is a natural boundary to freedom. Your son is not mature enough or old enough to stay out after that curfew hour. For this reason alone, he needs to return home on time. Not teaching him these limits will engender a sense of grandiosity and entitlement. When he understands that he isn't allowed to go out at night because of his own actions, he will learn to respect your need to keep him safe."

Once Maura saw the situation in this light, she changed her ways. She didn't allow Jackson to leave the house at night until he agreed to her new terms. When Jackson saw that his mother was serious, and that she meant business and would indeed not allow him out of the house if he messed up on the curfew, he fell in line.

Maura was shocked by how easy it was to get her son to comply. I explained, "When Jackson saw that you weren't invested in punishing him but were focused on keeping him safe, and that you were going to take this role seriously, he paid attention and respected you for it."

When we parents understand that we hold the power to shift our energy so that our children respond in new ways, we are empowered to create change. Instead of staying stuck in cycles of resentment, discontent, and conflict, we liberate ourselves by taking action in an empowered way. Once we are grounded in our strength and therefore committed to our values, our children naturally follow suit.

What's Your Embodiment Quotient?

When our children don't conform, we expect to be able to teach them life principles through verbal instructions and reprimands. This is no way to teach, because it violates how we optimally incorporate new behavior. We learn best through absorption, which is a process of osmosis. In order for our children to absorb our ways, we need to embody our values in our own life in such a manner that our purpose spills from our being with a radiance that's hard to miss.

Some of us take the model citizen approach, trying hard to say and do all the right things in front of our children. We soon find this difficult, if not impossible, to maintain over time. Since we aren't fully committed to our "good behavior," we tire of it. For example, we may talk about loving life, whereas our actual mode of living sends a different message. Instead of our children seeing us enjoying our days, including relishing our work as an enriching experience, what they see is how we complain about our job, procrastinate with our chores, and resent our commitments. It isn't what we say that registers with them. Instead, they notice our slouching shoulders, the grimace lines around our face, and the stress in our voice. In other words, our nonverbal signals as a result of our own experience of life are what they pick up on, and these tell them whether life is something they should enjoy or resist.

Instead of running our home according to rules, the wise approach is to ensure that the whole family embody a *way of life*. With this approach, there's less conflict because the children know what to expect from their parents and know how the home operates. The decision to participate on the part of our children doesn't come from compliance per se, but from the energy in the home—the natural flow the parents have established.

What does embodiment look like in practice? Let's take one of the areas of self-care we discussed with regard to limits and explore how to embody a boundary we wish to set.

Life-Enhancing Boundary: Self-Care—Bathing, Brushing, Sleep

Questions to Assess Your Embodiment Quotient

- *Do you engage in each of these self-care habits in your daily life?*

- *Do you show how holy these are in your own life?*

- *How do you convey their importance?*

- *Do you embody the higher purpose of these activities?*

- *Do you radiate this purpose, communicating it through your own being?*

- *Do you commit to teaching your children these habits on a daily basis?*

- *Do you stick to this principle at all costs?*

For our children to absorb our energy and pick up on our teaching takes a high level of commitment on our part. Once we are able to commit to this in our own life, it's much easier for our children to understand the way the home functions and to find their place in it. It doesn't mean they won't defy us on occasion. However, they will be in no doubt as to how things are done.

When a parent is fed up with trying to get a child to follow through on a routine like bathing or sleeping, I always suggest they apply this principle of embodiment. Instead of getting frustrated with their child's lack of compliance, I ask them to tap into their own inexhaustible inner resources and live out the reality they wish to see manifested throughout the family.

Scott was having a hard time with his five-year-old son Jeremy's resistance to bathing. "I just can't get him in the tub. At first I wait patiently for him to do his thing, hoping he'll eventually enter the bath on his own. This takes forever, but I try to be patient."

Right away I sensed Scott's inconsistency. "You say you are being patient, but isn't it true that you are seething inside? There's nothing joyful about you in this moment, right?"

Scott was indignant. "But I am *so* patient. I don't lose my cool at all!"

I explained how important it is to actually embody our passion for our values, even those as mundane as bathing. "You want your child to fall in love with bath time, right? You want him to get straight into the tub and enjoy the process of cleansing, correct? Okay, so how are you embodying this energy yourself? You tell me you sit there champing at the bit, frustrated and angry. How does this mirror the enjoyment you wish your child to experience? If you wish for him to embrace bath time, get in there with him and show him through your example how much you love to bathe, as well as how good you feel afterward. Of course, you don't have to do this all the time, only for a few days till he gets the idea. It's the same as when you teach a child to swim. Don't you jump in with them and show them how fun it is?"

Scott began to see how different this approach was from what he had been doing until now. With a focus on his head, he had been communicating his values in a rational way. Only now did he realize that talking about something is very different from enacting it with body, mind, and soul.

Like many parents, Scott needed to understand that whatever we radiate our child will absorb. In this case, by radiating anxiety and anger, he was riling up the child instead of calming him down. Consequently Jeremy picked up the idea that bath time is stressful. This was what lay behind his reticence to take a bath.

The principle of embodiment is especially important with elementary-age children, because they particularly need our guidance in learning how to engage their world. When we tell a child to do something, it doesn't mean they'll perform it like a robot. If we want them to exercise, we must exercise ourselves. If we want our home to be clean and organized, we must keep it that way ourselves. In this way our actions become templates that will serve them well for years to come.

Embodiment has the power to change our dynamic with our children. The change doesn't come about overnight, because it takes time for patterns to embed themselves in the psyche. But the change will follow, and with it our children will develop a compass that will steer them throughout their lifetime.

Entering the Zone of Zero Hypocrisy

I rue the day my daughter learned the meaning of the word "hypocrite," because she now calls me out on my incongruence every chance she gets. She says things like, "Mom, you tell me to get off Instagram, but you're on Facebook all the time. Aren't you being hypocritical?" Or she may comment, "You left your wallet at home the other day and we had to drive all the way back, and now you're scolding me for leaving my folder at school?" Even though I resent her for being so aware of my weaknesses, I'm grateful that she reminds me to be forgiving of her.

As we embody our own teaching, we realize how hypocritical we have indeed been until now. Ask your child about the many ways you are hypocritical and watch how quickly they come up with a list! Naturally, we may not like doing this, since we might feel judged. I believe we should invite the feedback of our children, reminding them to be honest but also kind and thoughtful during such an exchange. I am thrilled when my daughter spots my hypocrisies and brings them to my awareness. I want to know. I want to change. I want to live a more aligned life. Why would I be embarrassed or ashamed about being a human with limitations? When I embrace my imperfections, I not only allow myself the opportunity to grow, but I also teach my daughter not to shrink from growth, no matter how painful it sometimes feels.

If we allow our children to engage with us in open and reciprocal ways, they are more than likely to say things such as:

- *"You tell us to clean up our rooms, but look how messy yours is."*

- *"You tell us we should be active and exercise, but you don't do anything physical."*

- *"You tell us how bad it is to be in front of a screen all day, but you're always on your cell phone or laptop."*

- *"You tell us not to talk badly about people behind their backs, but you're always gossiping with your friends."*

- *"You tell us not to drink, but you drink every day."*

- *"You tell us not to text and drive, but we see you do this."*

- *"You tell us not to yell, but you're always yelling at us."*

- *"You tell us not to use bad language, but we hear you cursing, especially when you think we're not around."*

- *"You tell us not to lose things, but when you lose things, you don't mind."*

When we had a conversation about order and organization, my client Clarice discovered how our children follow our ways. During one particularly emotional session, Clarice declared, "I'm taking Phil to a child psychiatrist to be evaluated for his ADHD. He's all over the place. He can't find things he needs and is always losing things. I'm fed up with rescuing him. You should see his room—it's a disaster."

As I always do when I hear complaints about how children are distracted, I investigated the parent's level of organization, inquiring, "Can you tell me how long it would take me, a guest, to find a pencil and an eraser in your home?"

Taken aback by my question, Clarice stammered, "Well, you know I work full-time, so it's hard to keep the house organized with two boys. Everything's a mess. I've been meaning to clean out all the clutter, but I just don't get the chance. It would take us a while to find the pencils, and especially an eraser, because I have so much stuff everywhere."

I didn't have to explain to Clarice where I was going with this conversation. She understood immediately. Like many parents, she somehow had a fantasy that her child would pick up the skills he needed simply because that was her desire—along with her ramming it down his throat. The actual message he was receiving was the opposite of what she was communicating verbally. What he picked up was that it's okay to be messy and disorganized.

How many parents do you know who nag their children to practice their piano, cello, or violin? The more the instrument and lessons cost, and the more frequently the teacher comes, the more the parent nags.

When I introduced my daughter to the piano, I realized it was because I had played piano as a child and wanted her to love it as much as I did. The only problem? I didn't play anymore. I knew that if I wanted to walk my talk and embody my belief that playing an instrument is good for the soul, I needed to start playing again.

I took piano classes for exactly two months. In that short time, I had several revelations, the most important of them being that I experienced firsthand how hard it can be to practice every day. If I put in twenty minutes a week, I was doing well. Playing an instrument requires us to be in the right frame of mind. We need to feel the desire on a deep level. This is when I made the promise never to force my child to practice anything. Instead of making her practice, I now tell her to engage with the piano on her terms, playing it when the feeling arises within her, not because of external pressure.

As a result of my approach, not only has Maia continued to play the piano for five years, but she also plays the cello. Granted, she hardly practices, but whatever she does is enough, because it has kept her desire to continue learning every week strong. More than anything, she has seen that her engagement with these instruments needs to be based on a love of them, not on some need for perfection or achievement of a future goal.

I sense that most children quit playing an instrument or engaging in a hobby not because they don't like it anymore but because an adult entered the equation and messed things up either by harping on the importance of practice or emphasizing the need for achievement. The child received the message that their relationship with their hobby could no longer be organic and personal, but needed to be based on external criteria for success. This is a surefire way to push a child to lose interest. If the child is left to figure out their relationship with their hobbies, they will most likely continue them long into adulthood without ever having to be cajoled or pushed.

Think about surfing or bodysurfing. Though I'm sure there are exceptions, I don't know of any child who has to be "forced" to take weekly lessons. Those who love the ocean spend hours in cold water as they try to catch the perfect wave, thoroughly enjoying themselves.

Embodiment starts at the feeling level. If we don't feel the way we want our children to feel about things, they will pick up on our ambivalence. If we embody any degree of fear or resistance, they will immediately sense it. On the other hand, when parents embody what they wish to teach, they are exposed to their own internal barriers, which creates understanding and empathy for their child—as I discovered when I managed only twenty minutes of piano practice a week.

Embodiment is the path to empathy. When we understand how we ourselves learn, we engage in a deep fellowship with our children, holding their hand as fellow travelers on the journey of life. Instead of egging them on from behind, we stand together side by side.

Redefining Discipline

We have seen how our knee-jerk reliance on threats and punishments is a relic of the traditional system of bringing up children. As long as we even subtly perpetuate this hierarchical dogmatism in our families, we are tacitly agreeing to enslave our children to autocratic systems. If we wish to raise a generation of children who are empowered to stand up against ignorance, oppression, and violence, we need to allow them to stand up against us when appropriate. We need to face the fear that results from our lack of a solid self.

When we step into an enlightened understanding of what it means to treat our children just as we would like to be treated—as sovereign beings who deserve to be raised with dignity—we will undo all the old patterns around discipline and find new ways to teach our children that are ultimately more educational, more intelligent, more creative, and more effective than any of the old ways of reward and punishment.

∼ A New Commitment to Shedding Discipline ∼

No longer bound by threats, yells, scares, and
 conditions,
I release myself from needing to control you.
Instead of seeking to be your puppeteer and boss,
I now choose to engage with you differently,

Moving from
Wielding power to empowering you to uncover your
 own,
From leading you to awakening your leadership,
From managing you to inspiring you.

When I remember that you are sovereign,
I release my need to dictate and rule.
In these ways, I not only awaken my own humanity,
I give space for yours to flourish as it fully deserves.

CHAPTER TWENTY-TWO

From the Battlefield to the Negotiation Table

O ur fear, emotional conditioning, and difficulty breaking free of the parenting trance have made us afraid of treating our children as our equals. Of course, I don't mean they are our equals in experience, although they can be far more mature than us. I'm referring to them as our equals in their desire to be treated as sovereign individuals with a voice that's clear and, when needed, mighty. This denial of their sovereign rights creates many a battle with our children. Only when we are able to drop our desire to be superior can we enter reciprocal agreements with our children, fully aware that individuals function best when they feel heard, understood, and validated. It's when we understand what is being offered to us that we can move from reluctant participants to vibrant partners in our destiny. As our awareness increases, we begin to see the desire in our children to be treated as sovereign as a sign of their health and appropriate development instead of as an indication of defiance or misbehavior.

As we learn to honor our own internal sovereignty, we inevitably wish to do the same for our children. Our growing consciousness leads us to a natural letting go, so that we allow our children's voice to be heard clearly and articulately. Instead of rushing in to say no in a spirit of resistance, we seek to engage them in an atmosphere of acceptance. Whereas until now we have gotten into power struggles at the drop of a hat, we find ourselves preferring more constructive ways to engage them.

There are several guidelines that can help with this process.

Listening for the Untold Desire

Few things bother us more than when our children appear demanding and act as if they are entitled. As discussed throughout this book, the reason for this is a harkening back to our own upbringing, in which we felt controlled and micromanaged. I'm not suggesting that children don't at times demand things, conveying the idea that they are entitled. There's no doubt they do. But I believe we need to approach their demands in a different way. The path I'm suggesting allows us to highlight the positive aspects of their desire for something, while we simultaneously steer them away from the destructiveness of entitlement and greed.

No matter their age, our children have desires that are important to them, just like we adults do. Granted, their desires are often more on the fantastical side when they are younger, but they are desires nonetheless. Whether they wish to fly to the moon or be a lion, they are in touch with a fundamental sense of limitlessness that's inherent in humanity but that we mostly lose touch with.

Many parents are scared to allow their child to express their desires. They are afraid it will lead to indulging the child. They are also frightened that the child has unrealistic expectations and could end up making a shipwreck of their life.

The idea that our children have a right to create a life for themselves can feel threatening. We don't tend to think of children as having as much right to express themselves and their desires as we ourselves have. I think many of us are afraid that if we give our children too much power, it will go to their head. I understand such reservations. However, their value lies not so much in what they tell us about our children but in how they reveal that we aren't yet firmly planted in the solid ground of our own essence. If we were, we wouldn't feel threatened. On the contrary, we would feel empowered. This sense of our own empowerment is what enables us to support our children as they express themselves and their desires, so that we help them create a gateway to the fulfillment of their dreams.

It may take many years of hard work, but we can often find a way to achieve some or most of our desires. The ability to dream our desires is pivotal to staying in touch with our ability to bring them to fulfillment. In a similar manner, our children also dream and have the ability to bring their truly meaningful desires to fruition. However, if we don't activate our child's belief in their power to create their life, we inevitably chip away at their sense of owning their destiny.

To help your children activate their desires, you might wish to engage them in dialogue around the following questions:

- *What kind of day are you envisioning for yourself tomorrow?*

- *How can I support you in having your plan for tomorrow come true?*

- *What parts of your plan can I help with?*

- *Did you feel that you were able to fulfill a few of your desires today?*

- *What stands in the way of feeling that you are in charge of your life?*

- *What parts of your life would you change, and why?*

- *How can I help you take greater ownership of your life?*

Engaging in dialogue about desire doesn't mean we need to indulge our children in any way. It just means we validate the fact that they have a right to desire. Consider the following examples of how this looks in real life:

CHILD: I really want a new pair of shoes.
PARENT: Those are super-cool shoes. Let's make a plan to help you get them. I can't buy them for you, but I can support you to buy them for yourself if you so desire.

CHILD: I love blue hair. I really want blue hair now.
PARENT: Blue hair rocks! I wish I had the guts to get blue hair myself. But I think I may regret it a few days after. How about you make a list of all the hair colors you like for the

next year, and if you are able to commit to one, we can talk about getting that in the future.

CHILD: I wish I had a bigger house and a newer phone. All my friends do.

PARENT: Totally hear you. What do you like about those things? Tell me so I can see it from your point of view. I would love to gift you with both right now, but I can't. However, you know that you can save for both, don't you? Do you need my help to come up with a plan?

CHILD: I hate you because you won't let me have a dog. I'm dying for a dog.

PARENT: You really love dogs, huh? My gosh, I am so in awe of your love for them. I wish I had your love! I can't get a dog right now because I won't love it like it needs. But trust me when I say that the minute you live on your own, I'm going to gift you with one, because every dog lover should have a dog. You just have to wait a few years. Who can we visit who has a dog you love and perhaps make that something we do every week or once a month?

In these and other ways, we can flow with our children's desires without feeling pressured to give in to their demands. By doing so, we teach them that they can manifest their desires provided that they are willing to put in the time, energy, and effort. It's crucial not to start lecturing about why a particular idea isn't a good one, let alone about how it's "selfish." Instead, the key is to support the desirous nature of our children.

When we probe a little, we're likely to discover that, at a deeper level, many of our children's wishes are actually a desire for a feeling of ownership, happiness, joy, and connection. The approach of supporting our children in their desires instead of talking them out of them allows them to feel safe to express themselves and be honored for their fantasies. We don't have to indulge them, only provide the space for this exploration to take flight.

Honoring our children's desires is a key to resolving conflict and creating solutions. If we allow ourselves to be activated the moment our children mention wanting something, misinterpreting this to mean that they are being greedy or acting as if they are entitled, we're likely to rush headlong into an argument and the disconnection that tends to result.

Moving Away from Blind Indulgence

As we learn to tune in to our children's innate desires, we begin to delineate between those that are coming from a state of ego and those that are an expression of something much deeper in their true self. Just because we enter a state of deep listening doesn't mean we automatically indulge them, whether it's a desire for a particular pair of shoes that emerges solely from the ego or the desire for a pet dog that's coming from a deeper need to bond with a living being.

As with everything in conscious living, we first allow the desire to enter our awareness, then let it rest under the spotlight of conscious insight. We listen, we discern, we validate, and we allow our children to decide how they wish to manifest their wishes, especially if something they wish for comes from a state of ego. For example, instead of rushing to buy them a pair of shoes, we allow them to learn to examine whether they truly need them and why, then help them create a way to earn the shoes, especially if they can be resourceful and responsible.

When we see that their desire represents a need of their true self, we can choose to be more active in helping them manifest it. However, even here, if this manifestation is beyond our financial means, we don't need to twist ourselves into a pretzel to meet it right now. Holding the desire in the light of awareness is sometimes all we need to do.

For example, when my daughter wanted to lease her own horse for the summer and expressed this from a genuine love of horses, I didn't feel the need to jump in and manifest it for her right away. We simply sat with her desire and held it in the light of our awareness. I told her, "It's too early to invest in such a big commitment. Let's keep this wonderful desire in our awareness and see how life moves us toward it or away from it. If, in a few months or after a year, this desire is still burning within you, we can both think of ways to manifest it."

My daughter agreed. It's now almost a year later and we are still holding this desire in our vision. There have been times she has said to me, "I don't know if I can commit to a horse," whereas at other times she has said, "Oh, please get me a horse today!" Since I can see she isn't yet settled in her desire for the horse, I am holding this desire in my awareness for her. I reflect my validation for her desire by saying, "I totally see how you feel. It's natural to go back and forth. You are experiencing an authentic struggle concerning a big commitment. Let's wait until you are consistent in your desire. Once you are at that place, we can talk about actual logistics. I can give you the green light, but only when I see that you are clear about your part of the commitment."

When we teach our children that they don't have to impulsively jump into fulfilling every desire they have, they learn that they can rest in their inner wholeness without these extra accoutrements. They also learn that a desire doesn't necessarily equate to a commitment. That is why so many parents fall into the trap of enrolling their children in ballet or tennis classes, or buying them expensive pets or instruments, only to later realize they acted too soon, mistaking a whim for something deeper. The danger in jumping in and feeding every desire our children have is that we rob them of the delicious process of sitting with their desires and allowing them to percolate. Our refusal to jump in and fulfill their every request allows them to engage with their desire and develop a commitment to it. It allows them to know what it feels like to work toward something and create plans to actualize one's goals. This is far more valuable than simply giving them what they think they want in the moment.

Of course, this requires us to be firmly planted in the awareness that our children are complete and whole just as they are. When we operate out of a sense of life's abundance and trust that our children are fully capable of manifesting their desires when the time is right, we send them the message that their desires are wonderful additions to their life but not the core of who they are. When we are grounded in the awareness that objects of our desire can never satisfy on an internal level, our children slowly learn to tap into their own innate fullness. Objects can never make us feel better about ourselves. Only a deeply attuned sense of ourselves and our worth can do this.

From Winning to Win-Win

We're beginning to see how the power of reinterpretation can alter the dynamic with our children. This is especially the case when there's conflict. As we touched on earlier, conflict is a hot button for most of us. Few of us know how to deal with it in a healthy way. We react to our children's aggressiveness with the same fear we have when they make demands. Feeling pressured, we resort to control. In turn, our children either become more aggressive or shut down.

What we don't realize is that as long as we stay focused on winning, we will eventually lose connection with our children. It's only when we move away from a sense of superiority and fully embrace the commitment to have both parties win that our children feel empowered in our presence, and in turn open their hearts and minds to our influence.

Curiously, what we perceive as aggressiveness on our children's part may actually be a protective, defensive reaction to us. For this reason, when we reinterpret our children's aggressiveness, we make it possible to engage them from a state of mindfulness. Let me share a few insights that we need to integrate into our daily life if we want to shift the energy of conflict into one of partnership:

- *Aggression is actually a form of defensiveness.*

- *Our children resist our attacking energy by attacking back.*

- *Conflict is inevitable when two strong individuals are present.*

- *Conflict is natural when loved ones live together.*

- *Conflict can be healthy—it depends how we process it:*
  - It can open up an opportunity for dialogue.
  - It can allow both sides to express their feelings.
  - It can help realign relationships.

Instead of taking conflict, demands, and aggressiveness so personally, so that we feel threatened, it's important to see these expressions of will in our children as an indication of trust, openness, authenticity, and courage. When we look at conflict in this way, we are better able to harness its energy to further our connection with our children.

We can see how this looks if we compare a common conflict with both a traditional exchange and a redefined one:

Conflict:

Teen wants to stay out late. Parent doesn't agree.

Traditional exchange:

Parent sets a curfew and teen gets angry and sulks. Parent either holds ground or gives in. Feelings of resentment, bitterness, frustration, anger, and disconnection follow.

Redefined exchange:

Parent seizes this opportunity to engage in a heartfelt discussion with teen. Parent says, "Perhaps we aren't going to agree, but we both need to be able to hear each other out respectfully. Then we need to negotiate terms that both of us are okay with. We each need to figure out what's truly important to us and what's not so important. In the end, we will both gain because we will have created a win-win situation that we are both fine with." They go back and forth. Each one lays out their case. Each one sees the other's point of view even if they don't agree. Finally, after much tussling, the teen agrees to come home an hour early, as well as to finish their chores before they leave. The parent agrees to extend the curfew by one hour.

Let's take another example:

Conflict:

Child wants to watch another TV show. Parent doesn't agree.

Traditional exchange:

Parent says it's time to turn off the TV. When the child doesn't act, the parent uses the remote to turn it off. The child stomps and kicks. The parent stomps and kicks. One of them wins the battle.

Redefined exchange:

Parent swiftly sees this as a good opportunity to teach the child the art of negotiation and says, "You want A. I want B. Let's create a plan C so that both of us are happy. Do you have any ideas? We both need to commit to creating a win-win situation that we are okay with. This takes time and effort, but I am willing to do this with you. I think I should agree to ten more minutes and you should agree to this. Or maybe I should agree to the whole show, but then you should agree to no TV tonight. Or maybe I should agree to the whole show, but then you should agree to reading for thirty minutes. What do you think?" The child, who appreciates being involved in the decision making, thinks about it and chooses one of the options or comes up with another solution. Either way, both parties feel satisfied with the outcome.

Instead of getting into battles over control, we need to encourage our children to work with us in a collaborative manner when there's a disagreement. Notice that I said "collaborative" and didn't use the word "compromise." When we compromise, we tend to compromise *ourselves*, selling ourselves out to one degree or another. Although almost everyone thinks people should compromise, to do so is a far cry from the win-win solutions that can be achieved when we move away from a combative or controlling approach and simply collaborate.

Compromise asks us to sacrifice, surrendering something that may be important to us. In contrast, negotiating in a collaborative manner involves seeking a solution that's win-win for everyone. The difference is that instead of trying to beat the other out of as much territory as possible, by collaborating we search for how everyone can get the best deal. There's no capitulation involved, since the point is to satisfy as many wishes of each individual as possible.

Compromise comes from a feeling of lack, whereas collaborative negotiation asks us to embrace the insight that life offers us infinite possibilities. When we collaborate, we don't harbor a feeling of scarcity. Instead, we operate from the assumption that there's enough in the universe to make us all happy and we just have to figure out the way to manifest this. When we start from a feeling of infinite possibility, we quickly realize that there are all kinds of options, plenty of choices.

To negotiate collaboratively isn't about "keeping the peace," which is usually the reason people compromise themselves. To negotiate collaboratively doesn't eliminate conflict, and the sooner we learn to tolerate each other's different viewpoints, the more readily we will be able to brainstorm a way forward that works for all parties. As I said in *Out of Control*, "If we can't tolerate conflict, staying with it to a satisfactory resolution, we'll give up something important to us—and, ultimately, give up an aspect of ourselves."

It's a mistaken idea that conflict needs to be adversarial. At its basic level, it just means that two individuals are in disagreement. How can this be a bad thing? Isn't it the most natural thing in the world to disagree on things? Why do people feel that conflict has to mean disconnection? In fact, it could mean just the opposite if we would only rethink our way of dealing with it. Once we are comfortable with it, we can engage it in a manner that honors everyone's voice and ensures they are heard. This in turn increases the autonomy and empowerment of all parties.

In my counseling practice, I've noticed that both fighting and compromise tend to be routes taken by people who can't stand up for themselves around those who matter to them. Compromise asks us to put up with a solution we aren't happy with and hence is the path of weakness. Arguing and fighting are manifestations of a feeling of inadequacy, which results from a lack of awareness of the abundant resources we all have available to us in our center.

Collaborative negotiation involves approaching a joint decision from a position of strength, which allows us to be calm instead of combative. If we are to resolve a conflict, we need to stand up for ourselves, adults and children alike, and not sell ourselves out. Instead of bringing neediness to the discussion table, the way forward is to tap into the abundance in our center as we collaborate on a solution. It's being in touch with this abundance that allows us to negotiate on a truly level playing field, whereas the ego's method is to pull rank.

When we come from our essence, we are no longer willing to sacrifice our integrity. Consequently, we tackle difficulties constructively. Note that I said tackle "difficulties," whereas the tendency is to tackle the other person! When we focus on the issue, not the person, we begin to get somewhere. We have no need to cling to a fixed position in order to bolster our sense of self. Free of all neediness, we neither sell ourselves out nor make unreasonable demands of our children. We genuinely seek a path that can work for each of us, brainstorming freely and without feeling threatened until a creative solution emerges. It's amazing how when we take this approach, solutions arise where there seemed to be none.

But what if there is no middle way? As I said with regard to limits, when a boundary is nonnegotiable, there's no room for discussion. In this case it's the parent's ability to embody and hold the limit that's the crucial element. However, for all other situations, parents need to learn the art of using conflict as a way to negotiate win-win situations.

When parents embrace this approach, they teach their children the following valuable lessons, the most important of which is that both parties have an equal right to happiness:

- *Life isn't always fair.*
- *We need to tolerate the discomfort of giving up something to get something.*
- *Relationships are partnerships, not dictatorships.*
- *Relationships require constant give-and-take.*
- *Relationships are a safe container in which to express our disagreements.*

- *Disagreements don't have to lead to disconnection; they can result in just the opposite.*

- *Each person's voice—the child's included—is important and will be heard, no matter what the content.*

Teaching children the art of negotiation is one of the most important lessons we can pass on to them. When children learn not to be threatened by conflict, they are able to move in and out of disagreements with ease and don't crumble in fear of them. They learn not to attach personal meaning to differences, but instead to embrace the fact that each person has a different approach to life.

Ending Sibling Wars

Every parent knows that it's common for our children to fight with each other. Yet few things trigger us more than witnessing them unleash their anger and dominance over each other. Inevitably and often unconsciously, we pit one sibling against the other, labeling one as "good" and the other as "bad." Of course, this kind of labeling never really stops the negative behavior, but only perpetuates it.

The first step to ending sibling wars needs to be taken by the parent. It requires us to disengage from the tendency to place blame on one of the children, thereby avoiding any sense of competition. Our response to their fights is a key factor in whether they will grow closer together or further apart. Most important to keep in mind is that they will model their relationship on the relationships they see us fostering with our significant other and our friends.

When children see that parents aren't fazed and don't take sides, the charge around conflict dissipates. For this to happen, it's imperative that parents rein in their desire to control the situation. If one of the siblings continues to exhibit wild and impulsive behavior, the parent needs to deal with this sibling in their own right, separate from the other. The aware parent who is careful not to take sides, and honors the beauty in each child, will raise children who bond and are protective and caring toward each other.

Parents often protest my suggestion of staying out of the fray, saying something like, "But what if my one kid always beats up my other kid? What should I do then?" They paint the situation in black and white terms, where one child is portrayed as the perpetrator and the other the victim. I explain to parents that such situations don't arise in a nanosecond. These are patterns that evolve in the household through the consent of everyone involved, most importantly the parent. I reassure parents, "If you are able to take a step back and witness your role in an unbiased way, you will see how you have been part of the problem between your children. Without your conscious realization, you have played favorites and allowed one child to take on the role of victim. This child is most likely the child you feel most sympathetic toward because they are more like you and don't trigger you as much."

I understand that this is no easy realization for parents to arrive at. No one wants to feel as if they have pitted one child against the other. However, when I reassure parents that this is a common occurrence in countless households, they are more ready to face up to it. I then explain, "Once you are willing to make changes, it's imperative that you declare to yourself and your children that you will no longer be jumping in and rescuing them from each other. You will treat them both as equally responsible no matter what the circumstances. If both are involved, both are responsible."

Once your children begin to understand that there is no payoff in terms of attention from you, negative behavior is more likely to dissipate of its own accord. If one child is truly more of a bully than the other, you will need another intervention to address their aggressive behavior, which will involve teaching them new skills and may even require that the family enter therapy. Regardless, disengaging from the negative interaction is the key to solving sibling wars.

When parents are concerned about the safety of their younger children in the vicinity of older children, I always say to them, "It isn't the job of your older child to babysit your younger child. If you place the onus on your older child to be the good or responsible one, they will revolt. If you feel as if your older child isn't mature enough to be around the younger sibling, it's your responsibility to create a safe separation between them. Instead of expecting your older child to rein in their immature impulses, which they simply may be unable to do, it's your job to create a safe space between them."

It's natural for parents to hold older siblings to higher standards than younger ones. This in itself creates acrimony and resentment between siblings, which then leads to rivalry. In the same vein, it's also common for parents to force their children to love and cooperate with each other. This too creates resistance in children, especially when they aren't ready to do so organically. It's our anxious hope that our children get along and feel close to each other that often pushes them even further apart. Instead of forcing closeness, we need to allow this to develop as a natural facet of their proximity to each other.

At the end of the day, keep in mind that sibling battles are endemic. More than anything, they present us with an opportunity to teach our children about cooperation and conflict resolution. Children need to learn how to get along as part of a pair or in a group, and this requires some instruction and role-playing on our part. Of course, it also requires daily diligence. When we are vigilant in sowing the seeds of compassion between our children at an early age, we encourage each one to glow in the halo of our attention and validation, thereby fostering their desire to grow in closeness and affinity.

Subduing Divorce Drama

Sometimes couples find themselves at a crossroads in their relationship, feeling they have no alternative but to go their separate ways. Though I always advocate that a couple try their hardest to work through their issues, this isn't always the best or most feasible path. Sometimes it's healthier for the entire family if the couple separates. It's important to realize that some "contracts" with our loved ones come with an expiration date, when their purpose in our life stops being, well, purposeful and instead morphs into bitter negativity. At this juncture, wise are those who realize the power of letting go and moving on without resentment or regret.

When this is the case, the first step toward ending a relationship with awakened awareness is for each party to accept their role and responsibility in the events that have played out. Though it's tempting to place blame on each other, such an impulse breeds contempt and cleaves apart the family even more. Instead, if each party accepted that things didn't work out, they would reconcile themselves to the fact that, although some relationships end, this doesn't mean their entire partnership was a failure.

When we assign the adjective "failure" to a marriage, we fail to appreciate all the times that it *was* a success. Instead of seeing separation as a negative, it can be seen as a painful but normal transition that many couples go through. Just as nature is impermanent, so are our friendships and relationships. Instead of clinging to what doesn't work, it's wiser to accept when things end and learn to let go with grace, forgiveness, and gratitude for what was.

Awakened parents who separate or divorce are able to set aside their differences for the greater good of their children. Talking to children about their feelings and allowing them to express the range of their reactions to the separation is important if they are to undergo a healthy adjustment. Ideally, the entire family can go through therapy, demonstrating to the children that, although differences may abound between people, it doesn't mean the desire to stay connected and whole disappears as well.

One of the most common side effects of divorce is guilt on the part of the parent and resentment born of confusion on the part of the child. Often unconsciously, both parties act out from this foundation, unwittingly causing more dysfunction and turmoil than necessary. The cycle often starts when the child, confused about their new living situation, acts out in frustration or even despair. They might say something like, "I hate this and want to live with Grandma." Or they might behave in more aggressive ways such as cutting class, missing curfew, or even failing classes. All of these emotions are fallout from the trauma of the divorce. Unless fully processed with the child, this will escalate.

When a child behaves in these or similar ways, it tends to trigger the parent, who feels guilty already. Feeling as if they caused this trauma in their child's life, the parent may then overcompensate in some way. This often takes the form of coddling the child or denying any misbehavior on the part of the child. Of course, this lack of boundaries and lack of a firm container are the very things that further spiral the child out of control. Before you know it, the household descends into emotional chaos, with everyone's heart broken.

It's imperative that parents take this transition seriously and offer the right kind of support for their family. It's naive for them to believe that they can handle this on their own. Regardless of whether the divorce is ultimately healing for the family, this is a huge trauma for the child, one that will mark and shape their view of the world for years to come. If the parent recognizes this from the outset, they can work with a professional to guide the family through such a turbulent time.

When parents are conscious of their children's needs ahead of their own, they make space and time to build in the coping mechanisms that are needed to help their children through the various steps of this transition. Instead of plunging into a cold war, conscious parents ease their children through the stages, all the while maintaining civility in their dealings with each other. By modeling nonreactivity, parents demonstrate to their children that though not all marriages last, their family certainly will endure this transition and stay firmly grounded as a unit through time.

Red Flag Alert: Getting on a New Highway

While every moment in conscious parenting is about constant course correction, regularly attuning our approach to meet the needs of our children, there are times when we need much more than a mere course correction.

Sometimes, despite our best intentions, our children fall into destructive ways that require us to engage in a major overhaul of our approach. Things may tilt to an extreme place with our kids overnight, leaving us floundering as we seek reasons for why it happened. Sometimes a change of school or a new group of friends can throw our children off course in an extreme way. At such times, our survival instinct kicks in and we do what we know best, which is to react with a high level of emotional charge—the exact opposite of what we ought to do in such situations. Resisting the urge to do what we have always done takes courage.

At such times, we feel as lost as our children do, overwhelmed by the new challenges we find ourselves facing. Perhaps our child has been caught smoking pot for the first time, had sex before they were mature enough, or started having panic attacks because of a new situation at school or with friends. All of these have the potential to plunge us into a state of confusion and fear.

It's during these moments that I urge parents to take a step back and understand that these things aren't necessarily coming out of nowhere, but are occurring because of a buildup of many misalignments along the way. This is why we must stop and shift the energy in the home. Sometimes this requires that the child be pulled out of a particular school, or that the entire family go for therapy. Whatever the trigger, the family needs to understand that things need to change in a big way. They need to meet this challenge with valor instead of feelings of defeat, guilt, shame, or regret.

I urge parents to stay closely connected to their children so that unpredictable situations are more of an anomaly than not. Be aware of who their friends are. Pay attention to their moods, their eating habits, and their hygiene. I caution parents against being passive and complacent, challenging them to be alert and attentive to their children. If a child hasn't eaten dinner for two nights, hasn't done their homework, or is isolating themself in their room too much, these are red flags for a parent. Pay attention to patterns and notice when the pattern deviates. Parents who are attuned to their children are less likely to be caught off guard and more likely to intervene before things become serious. Of course, this requires that parents stay focused, follow through, and be unafraid to ask tough questions or create firm boundaries when the situation demands it.

Entering family therapy is often the only way to start this process. Instead of seeing this as a sign of weakness, I encourage parents to understand that these detours are often essential for the well-being of all. If parents are courageous and heed the call to awaken, they will be able to take charge before the damage is irreparable.

Changing highways is part of life. Finding new highways is part of the creative process of living. Feeling resentful that the old highway became too crowded or stopped taking us where we needed to go is a sign of emotional immaturity. The true winners in life see the end of a highway approaching and willingly turn off, knowing that, though the bridge to the next route may feel perilous, it will ultimately take them to a higher road where the ways of the heart are clear and abundant.

The Courage to Be a Warrior of Peace

We have seen again and again that the true joy and beauty of life can be experienced only when we are able to enter the present moment and fully engage the whole of our existence with awareness of our power to co-create the reality we wish to inhabit. Especially with our children, the power to create joyful and liberated relationships is ours to exercise anytime we move away from the archaic myths the parental Kool-Aid taught us, instead embracing the democratic principles of sovereignty and dignity for all.

Becoming an awakened parent takes courage. Recognizing the power a parent has to affect the future, the conscious parent takes on this responsibility with courage and humility. An awakened family can spark a revolution in their world simply through the day-to-day experiences of life. All it takes is to foster the joy within their children's hearts. It happens in the most ordinary of things—a shared joke over the kitchen table, a loving embrace, and treasured moments at bedtime.

Children whose parents are present and engaged come to rely on a universe of abundant resources. As they witness us embracing challenges, pain, and purpose in an empowered manner, they learn to believe in their own resilience. The more attuned we are to our own unique self-expression, the more this will be the case with our children. The more we live in our heart-space, the more will they.

Consciousness, and the wisdom it brings us, is the path to peace on Earth. It begins in the family, within the awakened hearts of parent and child.

∼ A New Commitment to Shedding Conflict ∼

Where I saw disrespect and defiance before,
I will now see courage and authenticity.
Where I wanted control and superiority before,
I now want partnership and equality.

My fears seduced me to seek dominance,
To desire winning at all costs,
To draw blood just to be right,
To inflict pain on you to hide from my own.

Now I see the fault of my ways,
How misguided were my fears,
How paranoid was my anger,
How insane was my control.

I am ready to shift into a new way,
Where your well-being is sacred,
Where your autonomy is holy,
Where your authenticity is priceless,

Knowing that when I release you to be you,
I set myself free.

Shedding Skin, Shedding Light

As my Band-Aids fall off and I shed my skin,
The work of awareness seems to become harder and
    harder.
As each ruse of distraction and denial gets exposed,
    layer by layer,
My wounds lie more open than ever, sore and fragile.

With fewer places to run and hide,
My fears face me, leaving me breathless,
Imagining I will be crushed beneath their force.
The mirror reflects back a stranger.

Neither the old, but not yet the new,
I hover in a state of disembodiment.
Watching the old patterns gather rust from disuse,
I lie naked waiting for the next disguise.

Like a pendulum, back and forth,
Consciousness plays peek-a-boo.
One day so clear, I am on the top of the mountain,
Only to fall in the viscous gutter the next.

I want to give up, claiming incompetence,
But then something starts to shift.
Silently at first, but then with a roar,
The stillness I have been awaiting arrives.

Suddenly I am implanted on a new path,
The rusty old parts have dissolved into the earth.
Instead of looking forward, I look within,
And witness, for the first time perhaps, my self.

Thirty Daily Reminders to Build Consciousness

Each conscious parenting skill is a muscle that needs to be made stronger over time. Here are thirty helpful reminders to build these muscles. Do one each day over the period of a month, embedding them in your consciousness.

Chant the Welcome Prayer

I welcome all that is involved in the Madness of Parenting,
Aware that I invited this journey to transform me.
I welcome
Its wildness and waste,
Its chaos and confusion,
Its dirt and distractions,
Its sulks and strife,
Its unknowns and unpredictability,
Its helplessness and havoc,
Its anxiety and anger,
Its tedium and tension.
I welcome all that's involved in the Madness of Parenting,
Knowing that when I truly embrace it, in the now,
I am left in awe of its magnificence and bejeweled beauty.

Honor Essence

Focus on *who* your child is today, not what they do.
Let go of emphasis on their performance, tests, achievements, or chores.

Guide your children and yourself to tune in to their own essence and say things like:

"Did you stay in touch with *you* today?"

"Did you feel your heart today?"

"Did you feel your feelings today?"

"Did you listen to your inner guide today?"

"What is your inner voice saying to you today?"

Open the Heart

Allow the image of your child's face when they sleep to enter your heart. Feel your heart opening. Enter this well of warmth. From this place, share yourself with your child.

Remember when your child was sick or in the ER or hospital? Or remember when another child you knew was ill or suffering? How everything that you thought was important suddenly wasn't? All these thoughts make you realize how blessed you are right here, right now. From this place go to your child and let them know what they mean to you.

Savor your child's moods, sulks, and tantrums. They are children for only a short time. Embrace their tears, fears, yells, and falls. Childhood doesn't last forever.

Create Connection

Touch your child's face and tell them what they mean to you today.

Lean into your child's body for a few moments and just allow this connection to wash over you both. If they are too big for snuggles, snuggle them anyway.

Look deeply into your child's face and pay attention to all you see and hear. Immerse yourself in their words and embrace all their energy.

Enter Presence

Detach from the urge to ask your child a single question today. Simply observe and follow their lead.

Allow your child to enter your embrace without any words or judgment, just heart-to-heart connection.

Create the space for your children to "be" today. Watch them as they unfold into themselves. Notice their body language. Try to connect to their feelings beneath the words. Do the same for yourself.

Enter a No-Judgment Zone

Commit to being judgment-free today, no matter what the triggers.

Be curious. Don't make statements out of impatient judgment.

Pause and take a step back. Before you react with judgment, ask, "Does this really matter in the long run?"

Express Feelings Safely

Open conversations with observations, not questions; with comfort, not control.

Invite your children to talk to you by letting them know they don't have to talk at all.

Validate them to feel exactly what they feel at any given moment.

Accept Imperfections

Create humility by reminding them that it's human to have limitations.

Encourage them to embrace their imperfections rather than change them.

Teach acceptance of who they are becoming each day, so they think in terms of progress, not perfection.

Allow Pain

Soothe them so that their tears are a way for the soul to cleanse.

Embolden them so that their pain is a sign not of weakness but of a connected heart.

Normalize their experiences, reminding them that their fears are what create compassion and empathy for others.

Enter Forgiveness

Ask your child to write down five ways you've hurt their feelings this past week. Acknowledge each with ownership, acceptance, and apology.

Invite your child to tell you ways in which you can be a better parent to them.

Build pathways for healing and reconciliation by shedding what has caused conflict until now.

Create a Memory

Seize the moment to create a memory that may last your child their entire life. What simple thing can you do today that will sink deep into their consciousness?

Discover a special activity you could do together with your child. Ask them to pitch their ideas, and create a mission to enable this to come about.

Pledge to spend five minutes today sharing, gathering, smiling, and connecting. Engage in a ritual together at some point every evening.

Activate the Inner Guide

Resist all opinions, advice, and lectures.

Create space for your child to tune in and tap into their inner knowing.

Listen to their leadership and help them explore their own path.

Use Antidotal Energy

Embrace the power of the antidote. If your children are loud, you be soft; if they are anxious, you be grounded; if they are angry, you be still.

Tap into the energy of their feeling vibrations and don't resist it or attack it.

Trust that it's through a shift in your energy that your child will transform.

Practice Conscious Asking and Receiving

Unleash your child's power to ask for what they truly desire.

Allow for moments of appreciation to sink in and create gratitude for blessings.

Indulge the soul's desire to connect, and resist the ego's desire to disconnect.

Take a Spin

Spin everything into the positive today:

> If your child is distracted, say to them, "Wow, you have so much energy, huh?"
>
> If your child is grumpy, say to them, "You must have had a tough day today, so enjoy your space."
>
> If your child is rude, say to them, "Boy, you must be going through something. Let's take a moment to breathe."

Highlight the positive in what your child is doing or saying, no matter what your thoughts about it.

Uncover the abundance in your life today. Find something to be grateful for in your body, your kitchen, your chores, your garden, your home, your family.

Drop the Nagging

End the repetition! Instead of repeating yourself, use your presence, look deep into their eyes, and ask for their cooperation.

Create agreements and buy in on everything you do today. If you don't get this, don't proceed.

Prioritize connection and drop the need to correct.

Let Them Lead

Empower your child to create their own schedule today, and you be their assistant.

Harness your child's inner guide by allowing them to make decisions for the family appropriate to their maturity.

Hand over the reins of your child's unstructured time to them. Let them govern themselves today.

Be the Mirror, Look in the Mirror

Mirror back what your children say, not what you think you hear or want to hear.

Attend to the signs they reflect back to you. If they are shut down, ask yourself, "What's this reflection saying about me right now?"

Raise your own level of presence, attainment, and awareness. Stay focused on how you are reflecting their essence.

Teach Awareness

Track their feelings in the day. Teach them that being aware of their feelings is as important as their academics.

Process their feelings with awareness by shining a mirror on their inner world.

Tune in to your own feelings when communicating so they learn to do the same.

End the Complaints

Channel your complaints into action. Instead of complaining, ask what you can do to change the dynamic.

Shift from blaming your children to taking responsibility for your role in allowing the dynamic to continue.

Believe in yourself and your power to create the change. Transform passive complaining to powerful and assertive action.

Correct Limiting Beliefs

Become aware of your choice to come from lack or abundance.

Attune to which thoughts help you enter courage and power and which cause you to enter discouragement and fear. Teach your children this as well.

Empower them to have choices in what they believe in, and teach them to question belief systems instead of blindly following them.

Be Spontaneous in Play

Drop what you are doing and join your child in whatever they are doing—be it on their iPad, on their computer, or doing homework. Just sit by them and enter their world for a little while.

Invite your child to choose one game or to lead in any one activity—baking a cake, making cookies, gluing pictures, taking a walk, throwing a ball—of their choosing that doesn't involve a screen. Just for fifteen to thirty minutes. Be present through it all.

Be attentive for a moment to laugh with them, be it over a joke, a memory, or a riddle. Create the glue of laughter and good times, knowing that these will last lifetimes.

Make Me Time, We Time, Playtime, Work Time

Help your child structure their time so that they learn to value alone time, family time, fun time, and work time, seeing each as sacred.

Guide your child to embrace the rigors of work as much as they do play, "we time" as much as they embrace "me time," or vice versa.

Show them the value of this sacred balance through your own example.

Practice Daily Self-Care

Prioritize self-care in your own life. Focus on how good self-care makes you feel.

Nourish your body by eating only divine foods and exercising daily.

Cleanse yourself of self-criticism and express the wonder of having a body to take care of and teeth to brush daily. Express gratitude for your own body today.

Own Your Choice

Embolden your children to know that they always have the choice to solve their problems if they wish to.

Empower them by giving them as many choices over their life as possible.

Allow them to learn from the mistakes of their choices, recognizing that failure is a far more effective teacher than success.

Create Sacred Boundaries

Know the reason for a boundary, and once you own it, create it with confidence.

Create buy-in around your boundaries and institute them with care.

Reframe boundaries as ways of living and patiently allow them to percolate into your family.

Find the Zen in the Conflict

Allow the struggles to rise and be expressed, knowing that authenticity often looks like conflict.

Reframe power struggles as power sharing.

Channel the energy behind the conflict to find solutions for empowerment.

Make Peace With the "As Is"

Accept your child and yourself for who you both are in this moment.

Let go of expecting your child and yourself to match your fantasy of who you both should be.

Make peace with your child's strengths and limitations, just as you need to do with yourself.

Embrace Today

Dwell not on the mistakes you made yesterday or things you should have done better in the past. Instead, resolve to create change in this moment, right here, right now.

Embody a new awareness today, committing to make the changes you need to one step at a time.

Let go of coulda, shoulda, and enter what is.

Enter Being

Shed your worries, fears, and need to control it all.

Flow with the rhythm of your child's ways, interfering as little as possible.

Engage in the essential and drop all that's nonessential.

ACKNOWLEDGMENTS

Jennifer Walsh, my outstanding agent at WME—for never losing sight of the power of this message. You are more than an agent, you are a sister of the heart.

Brian Tart, president and publisher of Viking—for your clarity, belief, and vision. Your brilliant stewardship will allow this book to transform parents and heal families around the globe. I am eternally grateful.

My parents—for allowing me to discover, dare, and dream. My courage, creativity, and calling come from your parenting. My gratitude to you is boundless.

My greatest awakeners, my husband, Oz, and daughter, Maia—it is through your indomitable presence in my life that I have been able to unfold, undo, and transform.